Lecture Notes in Computer Science   12330

More information about this series at http://www.springer.com/series/8851

Ngoc Thanh Nguyen · Ryszard Kowalczyk ·
Jacek Mercik · Anna Motylska-Kuźma (Eds.)

Transactions on Computational Collective Intelligence XXXV

 Springer

Editor-in-Chief
Ngoc Thanh Nguyen (iD)
Department of Information Systems
Wroclaw University of Science
and Technology
Wroclaw, Poland

Co-Editor-in-Chief
Ryszard Kowalczyk
Faculty of Information and Communication
Technologies
Swinburne University of Technology
Hawthorn, VIC, Australia

Guest Editors
Jacek Mercik
WSB University in Wroclaw
Wroclaw, Poland

Anna Motylska-Kuźma
WSB University in Wroclaw
Wroclaw, Poland

ISSN 0302-9743   ISSN 1611-3349 (electronic)
Lecture Notes in Computer Science
ISSN 2190-9288   ISSN 2511-6053 (electronic)
Transactions on Computational Collective Intelligence
ISBN 978-3-662-62244-5   ISBN 978-3-662-62245-2 (eBook)
https://doi.org/10.1007/978-3-662-62245-2

This Springer imprint is published by the registered company Springer-Verlag GmbH, DE
part of Springer Nature
The registered company address is: Heidelberger Platz 3, 14197 Berlin, Germany

Preface

It is our pleasure to present to you the 35 volume of LNCS *Transactions on Computational Collective Intelligence*. In Autumn 2019 (November 22) at the WSB University in Wroclaw, Poland, there was the 5th seminar on "Quantitative methods of group decision making." Thanks to WSB University in Wroclaw, we had an excellent opportunity to organize and financially support the seminar. This volume presents post-seminar papers of participants to this seminar. During the seminar, we listened to and discussed over 18 presentations from 16 universities. This volume of TCCI contains 10 high-quality, carefully reviewed papers.

The first paper, "More Security or More Freedom? A Comparative Analysis of the Equilibrium in European Democratic Regimes" by Chiara De Micheli and Vito Fragnelli is devoted[1] to an analysis of the relationship between security and freedom, accounting the choices that governments made and the threats that they recently had to face to maintain these two essential facets of democracy. The authors test, using a broad set of data and empirical tests if, within European democratic political regimes, security and freedom tend to be inversely related. Furthermore, the authors study if it is possible to reach at the same time a high level for both parameters. To test their hypotheses, they measured the variation in the values of the two variables over very large data sets in Germany, Italy, France, Spain, Poland, and the UK—the six largest countries in Europe by population, which are in different stages of democratic consolidation. The start year for their research was 1992 and the end year was 2013.

In the second paper entitled "Trials of Characterizations of Anti-manipulation Method" by Michał Ramsza and Honorata Sosnowska, the authors study the anti-manipulation voting method introduced by K. Kontek and H. Sosnowska. Ramsza and Sosnowska show that the method does not satisfy the consistency condition. The consistency condition characterizes scoring functions. Thus, the method is not a scoring function. Also, the method is not from a family of non-scoring functions, comprising the Copeland method, instant-runoff voting, majority judgment, minimax, ranked pairs, and Schulze method. The paper also shows that the choice of a metric, used by the anti-manipulation method, may imply the winner of the voting.

In the third paper "Pairwise Voting Rules in Restricted Domains: The Disappearance and Persistence of Some Monotonicity Paradoxes" by Hannu Nurmi, one may find that the property of participation is satisfied by a voting rule if under no circumstances it is to the benefit of a voter to abstain rather than vote according to his/her preferences. By Moulin's result of 1988, all voting rules that always elect a Condorcet winner (when one exists) fail on the property of participation. Focusing on preference profiles that are restricted to those having a Condorcet winner, the author asks whether Moulin's result holds under these preference profiles. It turns out that while some types of monotonicity paradoxes vanish in the Condorcet domains, others persist.

---

[1] Hereafter description of the papers are directly taken from summaries prepared by their authors.

The fourth paper, "Group Decision Making Based on Constructing a Short List" by David Ramsey, considers several aspects of a multi-person household making an important consumer decision, e.g. buying a new flat. In such situations, normally several members of the household have input in the decision-making process. Also, when there are a large number of offers, search can be facilitated via the use of the Internet. Basic information about offers, e.g. price, location, number of rooms, and size, can be found on the Internet at very little cost. However, in order to make a final decision, members of the household should physically view a number of offers. The costs involved at this stage of the search process are much higher. In such scenarios, search based on the short list heuristic are efficient. Search via the Internet is used to find a relatively small number of promising offers from a large number of propositions. These promising offers are then more closely inspected, before a final decision is made. Results from simulations indicate that group decision procedures based on each decision maker ranking offers and the short list heuristic can be highly effective and robust.

In the fifth paper entitled "A Note on Equal Treatment and Symmetry of Values," Marcin Malawski investigates under what conditions equal treatment property and symmetry of a value for cooperative games are equivalent. For additive values, null player property or efficiency is sufficient for the equivalence. When additivity is replaced by fairness, both equivalences cease to be true. But the marginal contributions condition ensures the equivalence without any additional assumptions.

In the sixth paper "Decision-Driven Model for Building IoT Architecture in Environmental Engineering," Cezary Orłowski, Tomasz Sitek, Artur Ziółkowski, and Adam Czarnecki present building the model of the Internet of Things (IoT) architecture in environmental engineering. The starting point is the existing four-stage IoT architecture models. The article suggests adding the fifth stage – managing the IoT system construction process, including the creation of three additional layers. The approach proposed in their article was verified in the construction of the air quality assessment system in Gdańsk in which the system architecture integrates the management stage. The developed model is the basis for the ontological model of IoT architecture developed in this article, and is easy to implement in the construction of system architectures in environmental engineering.

In the seventh paper entitled "The Equity Crowdfunding and Family Firms – A Fuzzy Linguistic Approach," Anna Motylska-Kuźma investigates how the equity crowdfunding meets the needs of family firms. For many reasons, the probabilistic approach can be considered inappropriate and too simplistic when explaining the choice of financing source, especially in family businesses which are very heterogeneous. Based on the results of previous research and using the fuzzy linguistic approach, she assessed the factors influencing the financial decisions and compared the equity crowdfunding to the traditional IPO/issuing shares. The main feature shows that crowdfunding fulfils the core need of family businesses well, and using their basic characteristics it minimalizes the weaknesses of social funding.

The eighth paper entitled "Some Propositions of Approaches for Measuring Indirect Control Power of Firms and Mutual Connections in Corporate Shareholding Structures" by Izabella Stach, Jacek Mercik, and Cesarino Bertini, presents some game-theoretical methods that use power indices for measuring the indirect control power of firms and mutual connections in complex corporate shareholding networks. Only a few of the methods considered in the literature so far measure the control power of all firms involved in shareholding networks; meanwhile, none of them regard measuring the importance of linkages. The intention of the article is to firstly propose a modification of the Mercik-Łobos and Mercik-Stach methods using the Banzhaf index to measure the direct and indirect control of investors and stock companies. Secondly, having already estimated the control power of nodes (firms) in a network, they consider the relationship of this power to the power of the linkages that connect the companies in directed networks. Then, they present their own idea of how such link's power can be measured. They regard the power of the link in relation to the firms as well as (more significantly) in relation to the entire corporate network.

In the ninth paper "Some Strategic Decision Problems in Networks," Manfred J. Holler and Florian Rupp demonstrate that network efficiency is a very delicate matter. Neither the restriction to suitable core-subnets, nor intelligent enlargements guarantee efficient results in any case. For instance, the numerical example in Myerson (1977) contains a prisoners' dilemma situation for some agents in the network. Of course, the outcome is inefficient from the perspective of these players – but not for the unrestricted network. Breass' paradox shows that the enlargement of a network can lead to an inefficient outcome in the Nash equilibrium even if all players are taken into consideration. Restricting the network can create a Pareto efficient outcome. A third model discusses the strategic problem of a cyber network attack in the form of an inspection game. From the defender's point of view, the question arises which nodes of the network are essential attack targets and thus need special security attention. In principle two types of nodes are critical: important ones and unimportant ones. Important nodes, as they connect to many other essential nodes and are therefore suitable multipliers for network malware and information capture, and unimportant nodes, from the attacker's point of view, which are, in general, not in the focus of security attention, such that infiltration via them may be undetected for a long time.

The last paper entitled "An IoT Virtual eLearning Space" by Emil Doychev et al., presents the Virtual eLearning Space implemented as an Internet of Things (IoT) ecosystem, which integrates the virtual world with the physical world of the university campus and provides effective support to disabled students. This system is enhanced to be a reference architecture that can be adapted for new applications of IoT.

We would like to thank all authors for their valuable contributions to this issue and all reviewers for their opinions which helped to keep the papers in high quality. Our very special thanks go to Prof. Ngoc-Thanh Nguyen, who encouraged us to prepare this volume and helped us to publish this issue in due time and in good order.

July 2020

Anna Motylska-Kuźma
Jacek Mercik

Contents

More Security or More Freedom? A Comparative Analysis
of the Equilibrium in European Democratic Regimes.   1
   Chiara De Micheli and Vito Fragnelli

Trials of Characterizations of Anti-manipulation Method   21
   Michał Ramsza and Honorata Sosnowska

Pairwise Voting Rules in Restricted Domains: The Disappearance
and Persistence of Some Monotonicity Paradoxes   38
   Hannu Nurmi

Group Decision Making Based on Constructing a Short List   52
   David M. Ramsey

A Note on Equal Treatment and Symmetry of Values   76
   Marcin Malawski

Decision-Driven Model for Building IoT Architecture
in Environmental Engineering.   85
   Cezary Orłowski, Adam Czarnecki, Tomasz Sitek, and Artur Ziółkowski

The Equity Crowdfunding and Family Firms – A Fuzzy
Linguistic Approach   99
   Anna Motylska-Kuźma

Some Propositions of Approaches for Measuring Indirect Control Power
of Firms and Mutual Connections in Corporate Shareholding Structures.   116
   Izabella Stach, Jacek Mercik, and Cesarino Bertini

Some Strategic Decision Problems in Networks   133
   Manfred J. Holler and Florian Rupp

An IoT Virtual eLearning Space   148
   Emil Doychev, Asya Stoyanova-Doycheva, Stanimir Stoyanov,
   Todorka Glushkova, and Vanya Ivanova

Author Index   171

More Security or More Freedom?
A Comparative Analysis of the Equilibrium
in European Democratic Regimes

Chiara De Micheli[1] ⓘ and Vito Fragnelli[2(✉)] ⓘ

[1] University of Sassari, Sassari, Italy
cdemicheli@uniss.it
[2] University of Eastern Piedmont, Alessandria, Italy
vito.fragnelli@uniupo.it

Abstract. In this article we analyze the relationship between security and free-dom, accounting the choices that governments made and the threats that they recently had to face to maintain these two essential facets of democracy. We test, using a broad set of data and empirical tests if, within European democratic political regimes, security and freedom tend to be inversely related. Furthermore, we study if it is possible to reach at the same time a high level for both parameters. To test our hypotheses, we measured the variation in the values of the two variables over very large data sets in Germany, United Kingdom, Italy, France, Spain and Poland, the six largest countries in Europe by population, which are in different stages of democratic consolidation. The start year for our research is 1992 and the end year is 2013.

Keywords: Security · Freedom · Democratic quality

1 Introduction

In recent decades the so called "crime emergency" assumed increasing centrality within the political debate of mature democracies [21]. The "security issue" is one of the dominant themes of the public debate in many democratic countries and is closely connected to the changes in crime rates, and to the responses that public authorities (governmental, administrative, judicial) can give to this social problem, especially in terms of whether these responses increase or reduce the rights to freedom. We agree with the principle reaffirmed by Zagrebelsky, who, commenting on the Paris terrorist violence of November 2015, claims that "even now it is unavoidable to determine an equilibrium point between the restoration of an acceptable level of security and guaranteeing people's right to freedom" [40].

We collect several data on objective parameters that were used to produce suitable indices for both freedom and security. We chose 1992 as the start date for our research because that year is identified as the beginning of a new international course, with the start of a new phase of European integration, through the signing of the Maastricht Treaty

© Springer-Verlag GmbH Germany, part of Springer Nature 2020
N. T. Nguyen et al. (Eds.): TCCI XXXV, LNCS 12330, pp. 1–20, 2020.
https://doi.org/10.1007/978-3-662-62245-2_1

with exception of Poland; the lack of several data for the first years suggested us to omit the years from 1992 to 1997.

The indices were used for testing the classical hypothesis that the two parameters have an opposite behavior, i.e. if one of the two increases then the other one decreases, according to different relationships that depends on the particular history of the country under investigation. Surprisingly, we observed that sometimes the two parameters do not behave according to our prediction, so we introduced the index of democratic quality that enables us to provide good motivation for this behavior.

The paper is organized as follows. In the following section we present the problem of the equilibrium between freedom and security from a political research viewpoint; then, in Sect. 3 we introduce the mathematical elements of the problem; Sect. 4 deals with the concepts of freedom and security and the related indices we used; Sect. 5 is devoted to the approach used for analyzing the data; in Sect. 6, we introduce the index of democratic quality; Sect. 7 concludes.

2 The Research Problem: The Equilibrium Between Freedom and Security in Democratic Regimes

Any organized community faces with the problems of crime and social disorder. Nevertheless, the answer to these problems through deterrence and repression exercised by the rulers becomes a source of questions, particularly when there is the need to balance the power of government with individual freedom, as it happens in democratic regimes. Therefore, in modern democratic regimes, the relationship between security and freedom emphasizes its dichotomous inclination. Any kind of freedom is hardly available unless it is guaranteed by the state, and the democratic state is realized only when the political system effectively (and institutionally) produces security. With the establishment of democracy, the multiple "individual freedoms" must therefore be connected with the "security pact", surpassing the mere ideal of the guarantee of individual freedom by the liberal state.

As Dahl [11] notes, democracy is established when social, economic, war and international pressures make the costs of repression of the opposition greater than the costs of tolerance. In this way, the diffusion and the safeguard of the right to freedom for each citizen become possible. These costs tend to vary due to multiple factors. For example, according to Przeworski [28], there is no causal relation between the level of development and the emergence of democracy; in fact, a democratic regime may survive only in the richest countries, and has few or no chance of survival in poor countries. As Lipset [22] already argued, urbanization, education, economic prosperity, and industrialization constitute important elements that find their counterpart in the political sphere of the polyarchies. Therefore, increasing the level of wealth increases the probability that a democracy develops and persists. So, according to the classical theory of democracy, the economic development makes easier for a democratic regime both to emerge and to survive; on the other hand, for Przeworski the increasing of wealth is a relevant element only for maintaining the democracy, but not for establishing it. For further information, see [9].

However, the costs of tolerance may increase (and those of repression decrease) for other reasons as well. For example, some authors (see [10, 24] and [30]) argued that an excess of demands towards the government tends to provoke a state of crisis in democratic institutions. The institutions of democracy must be able to balance responses both according to the scarcity of available resources and by anticipating the repercussions that acting on each element of the system generates on the others. The case of our two variables - security and freedom - is emblematic, since, as we shall see in more detail in the following sections, they seem to be connected by an inverse relation. It is worth mentioning in this regard that, in modern democracies, some of the most widespread issues still concern the request for a larger degree of freedom. These questions, however, often have to face some more immediate imperatives, concerning the protection of public order and social peace, which arise from the disruptive effect of more or less contingent threats. We refer, for example, to the frequent and pervasive requests for greater security advanced by the citizens of Western democracies in recent decades, which require the state to be more effectively defended from the threats of terrorist violence. In other words, the costs of tolerance and repression are strictly linked to the illegitimate use of violence. In the balance between security and freedom, security has assumed, at least in some of the pluralist democracies, a dominant and increasingly incisive role (especially after the attacks of September 2001).

Under the pressure of the recent migratory waves from the East and the South of the world, the fear of being subjected to criminal behavior began to be conceived as a problem in itself, regardless of the actual rates of crime. The distance between the degree of real crime and the degree of perceived crime (see [4] and [37]) can be explained at least in two ways. On the one hand, the greater attention paid by the media to the phenomenon, and a lower density of formal and informal social resources; on the other hand, the middle class is more frequently a victim of habitual crimes, the distance from criminality.

For democratic governments, crime has now become a strategic issue of great importance, so that, frequently, anyone who mobilizes - both in the institutional sphere and in the social sphere - to prevent crimes or similar behaviors, obtains approval and legitimacy. With a hyperbole, one can allude to "ruling through criminality", when the creation and direction of the problem become means for acquiring greater support [8].

In recent decades, the desire to limit the risks to the population, including events due to chance, found throughout modern democratic systems, seems to have induced governments, to resort more and more frequently to repressive methods. This need substantially resulted in a pervasive control of individual and collective action and its environment: space control, social control, personal control, self-checks; ever more areas seem to be subject to increasingly more severe forms of regulation, inspection and supervision. In comparative terms, after a long process of democratic strengthening that led to a widening of individual freedom, it is possible to find an increase in supervision in almost all the social sub-systems (in general, the economic sub-system is an exception) [17].

Repression cannot, however, compress personal freedom beyond the limit that qualifies the respect for the fundamental principles on which a polyarchy is constituted. Even if, in a hypothetical emergency situation, a democratic government can nevertheless intervene by adopting ad hoc measures aimed at restoring normality, it is still necessary to avoid the possibility that state institutions would take advantage of the extraordinary nature of the moment to extend their prerogatives beyond what is guaranteed by the constitutional norms.

While crises can affect all political regimes, democracies are probably the most vulnerable ones. In this regard, it is significant the conceptualization of the "state of exception" elaborated by Schmitt [35], according to which it is justifiable, in legal and *de facto* terms, to suspend the law and every constitutional guarantee, in the light of a superior right of the state's self-preservation. Following this thesis, the request for protection could justify a possible excess of power and its prerogatives [1]. A protective power, however often urged by citizens, presents the risk - as already indicated by Hobbes [19] - that "For he that hath strength enough to protect all, wants not sufficiency to oppress all". On the other hand - as underlined by Zagrebelski [40] - we must not forget that the first reason that makes it possible to allow extraordinary restrictions on constitutional freedom is their effectiveness.

Therefore, the practical reasons emerge strongly, as well as the ideological and intellectual controversies, which lead to deepening, in modern democracies, the determination of the point of equilibrium between an acceptable level of security (or its restoration) and an equally acceptable system of guarantees of freedom. It is within this framework that the theoretical and empirical examination of the trade-off between freedom and security is inserted.

3   The Freedom-Security Trade-Off: A Theoretical Analysis

For our purposes it's particularly important to see *how* and *to what extent* security and freedom, two essential dimensions of democracy, are mutually balanced.

We have already noted that one of the critical points of this relationship is its tendency to be dichotomous. On the one hand, security is a prerequisite for enjoying all other individual and collective goods. On the other hand, it often results in an antagonism with freedom. This happens when, to obtain greater security, the efficiency of the repressive and investigative action is considered dependent on the restriction of personal liberties. For example, when the physical integrity of citizens is threatened by terrorist attacks, the relationship between security and freedom highlights its antagonistic features, since the reduction of freedom is one of the main operating conditions of the repressive apparatus of the state to control the terrorist threat and to obtain an increase in security. The analysis of these two dimensions in democratic regimes therefore means first and foremost answering the question: how much freedom can we renounce to for greater security if we want to maintain a high quality of the democracy? Or, as Dye [14] puts it: "How far can individual freedom be carried without undermining the stability of society and threatening the safety of the others?".

In this regard, we can propose the following hypothesis: where democratic freedoms are guaranteed and respected to the highest degree, the limited and temporary suspension of some guarantees, when the security threats are very high, does not give rise, in itself, to an involution of democracy. On the other hand, when the patrimony of freedom and democratic guarantees is low, and there are high threats to security, the danger of a deterioration of democracy is high, since the limitation or temporary suspension of scarce guarantees of freedom can threaten the persistence of the democratic regime itself.

Usually, we may consider a relation among freedom (F, independent variable) and security (S, dependent variable) that can be represented as $S = f(F)$, where a decreasing of freedom increases security. The challenge is to balance these two variables in such a way to obtain an acceptable level for both, in order to maintain the democratic system. In fact, according to Beetham [6], to guarantee security is one of the aims of a democratic regime; on the other hand, when the guarantees of the democratic freedom are respected and applied at a maximum level, a reduction of security does not imply to move towards an inefficient regime. The equilibrium is a consequence of different aspects rooted in the current situation from the historical, social and economic point of view. For sake of simplicity, we suppose these to be constant in the period under investigation. In general, a very high level of freedom may be reduced by a small amount with a very high increase in security and, symmetrically, when the freedom is strongly limited it is possible to raise its level with a very small reduction of security; consequently, the equilibrium is at an intermediate level.

The mathematical relation between freedom and security has to satisfy the hypothesis that if one of the two issues increases, then the other one decreases. We chose a weighted sum like $S^\alpha = K - a F^\beta$, with $K, a, \alpha, \beta > 0$, where the coefficient a represents the relative weight of freedom with respect to security and the exponents α and β allow further differentiating the relevance of the two elements. The constant K represents a suitable value binding the two factors. Assigning different values to the parameters K, a, α, β it is possible to obtain the curves in Fig. 1.

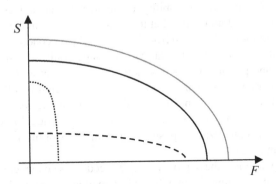

Fig. 1. The trade-off between Freedom (F) and Security (S).

After fixing the values of the parameters, the resulting curve represents the relation between security and freedom. This relation allows to select of the level of security (freedom) for the situation at hand, and consequently, determining which is the level of freedom (security) that allows reaching it, in the light of what we said above. It should be clear that even if we considered freedom as the independent variable in certain situations it could still be a better choice to reverse the problem and look for the level of freedom that produces a fixed level of security.

Referring to the function f among freedom and security, looking at Fig. 1, we may remark that comparing the continuous grey line and the continuous black line, the former offers a higher level of security whatever the level of freedom. This remark suggests that this may be interpreted as an index of the quality of democracy or of the functioning of the institutions that control social welfare. We may add that the dotted line represents a totalitarian regime characterized by a high level of security and a strong limitation of freedom; analogously, the dashed line may be viewed as a representation of a social anarchy situation in which freedom is still very broad but security is very low and it cannot be increased even with a dramatic limitation of freedom.

4 Research Design

4.1 Operational Concepts of Freedom and Security

The issue of freedom (understood as political freedom) is differently declined in different times and under different political systems. During the Italian Renaissance, freedom was considered a necessary condition for the prosperity of a community, i.e. an essential requirement for safe living. In fact, pre-liberal freedom coincides with security, which must be guaranteed by laws, that is, by the State that qualifies as the best guarantor of freedom itself.

With the emergence of the liberal state, the state itself and, consequently, the law becomes the target of criticisms, the greatest threats to freedom come precisely from the state (as shown for example in France by the events of the revolution and the subsequent terror period). More precisely, we distinguish between a positive freedom ("freedom of") that is expressed in the effective ability to pursue different choices and actions, and a negative freedom ("freedom from") that translates into freedom from a pervasive and limitless political authority. "Freedom from" is seen as the precondition of any "freedom of". It follows that these social rights can be guaranteed only after that the respect of fundamental civil and political rights is guaranteed. In this sense, political freedom is simply the area where a person can act without being hindered by others, not because of incapacity, but because such behavior would represent undue coercion. The wider is the area of non-interference, the greater is the degree of individual freedom. We recall that, based on this conceptualization, positive freedom does not survive without negative freedom (see [7] and [33]).

Going from the liberal to the democratic state, freedom is no longer a privilege of few citizens, but becomes a common right which all individuals living in the state can enjoy. Consequently, in operational terms, we may define and measure the degree of freedom of a country as the extension of certain rights to all those living within its borders, whether citizens or foreigners.

Therefore, we measure the "freedom of" by looking at the degree of freedom of communication, of the press and expression, of worship, and the absence of any kind of discrimination (gender/racial/ethnic). Finally, we pay attention to freedom in the economic sphere. Instead, to evaluate "freedom from" we consider the use of coercion by the state in the criminal and judicial fields and the guarantee of protection for every individual and every minority group. We may remark that the concept of freedom refers to guarantee the objective rights and, perhaps more, the subjective rights, of both the individuals and the collectivity. Relatively to the freedom from, we consider also the recent topic of privacy rights[1].

After the development of suitable indices for each type of freedom, they are aggregated in order to provide a synthetic (annual and total) value for each democracy we analyzed. The measurement of freedom (as well as of security) took place through the collection, measurement and processing of an extensive and complex data set.

Referring to the issue of security, considering its different enucleated facets, we mainly use the concept of criminality as *explicans* to evaluate the level of security in the democracies under investigation. Crime is a complex phenomenon and includes a large set of events, some very different from each other. Just to give some examples, it can be analyzed on the basis of the object of criminal activity, thus distinguishing between "economic crime" and "political crime", or concerning the ways in which such activity is perpetrated - hence "violent crime" differs from "predatory crime"- or even from the perspective of those who commit it, hence the distinction between "organized crime" and "widespread crime". Furthermore, the criminal action can be studied by observing the reactions that it induces in the victims, both at the individual level, where emerges in terms of "personal fear of crime" (fear of crime), and at the collective level of institutions and social groups, where instead it is viewed as "social concern for the spread of criminal events and behavior" (concern about crime) [34].

In fact, it is assumed that there is an inverse correlation between crime and security. Here, we consider security in "objective" terms, i.e. as something that can be observed using statistical methods and that is the product of specific criminal actions and of the social outcomes which they give rise to. More specifically, our hypothesis is that a decrease in the (weighted[2]) amount of crimes indicates a decrease of the probability of being the victim of illegal behavior and increases the safety of the community or of individuals and vice versa (see [18, 29] and [39]).

We analytically distinguish among widespread criminality, organized crime and political crime that we represent through specific indices with the aim of "weighting" the different types of crime. This operation is necessary in order to avoid both overestimating and underestimating the importance of certain criminal activities compared to others and to make the comparison among different situations more reliable.

In addition, we also use an index of "maximum criminal violence", produced by the number of (weighted[3]) homicides detected annually, since, in a nutshell, what makes a society most insecure is the fear for one's own life and of considering murder a dramatic but possible eventuality in relation to the normal operation of the political and social system. Ultimately, this index is useful for integrating our security measurement system.

Somehow, the so-called "widespread crime" or "petty crime" is a novel question [36]. It is defined as a phenomenon or as a situation that persists over time and is located

---

[1] Our research is based on the analysis of data the International Privacy Index that accounts for 14 criteria, both formal and substantial (see http://chartsbin.com7view/by8 and www.privacyin ternational.org/reports).

[2] Given the wide disparity in the number of inhabitants in the analysed countries, the number of crimes is reported per 100,000 inhabitants to make the comparison possible.

[3] A similar operation is carried out for the killings (see footnote 1).

in a given territory, causing a state of tension due to the high frequency of crimes and of illicit behavior occurring.

This prolonged condition of insecurity can be subjective, when individuals or social categories perceive the threat, or objective, if there is a strong probability that a crime will occur [15]. We decided to consider as indicators of the risk on the national territory the following crimes, committed as acts of widespread violence and/or produced by gangs: thefts, burglaries, robberies, personal assaults, and rapes.

Political crime takes the form of the use of violence with specific and explicit political aims and "exposes (...) the contradictions of the political and social system, since the existence of deep political conflicts in social relations can be considered as a sort of alarm for the society. Political extremism, in all its forms, indicates that pressure is building upon the structure of social relations and that the weaker links are at risk of being broken" [27, page 257]. For the purpose of our work, we analyze this type of crime by measuring the threats and acts of terrorism that affect a country and the number of people involved. Limiting and defining analytically the concept of terrorism - compared to other riots - is not simple; to this end, we use the definition of terrorist attack formulated by the Global Terrorism Database (GTD) which defines it as: threatened or effective use of force and illegal violence by a non-state actor to achieve a political, economic, religious or social objective through fear, coercion or intimidation. From this, it follows that in order to consider a violent action as a terrorist act, according to the GTD, all the following characteristics must be present:

– the action must be intentional (the result of a conscious calculation by an author);
– the action must involve a certain level of violence or immediate threat of violence (including violence against property, as well as violence against people);
– the authors of these acts must be non-state actors, i.e. acts of state terrorism are not included.

Furthermore, two of the following three criteria must be met for a terrorist action:

• criterion 1: the act must be aimed at achieving a political, economic, religious or social objective. In terms of economic objectives, the exclusive search for profit does not satisfy this criterion, but must involve the pursuit of a deeper systemic economic change;
• criterion 2: There must be evidence of a willingness of forcing, intimidating, or transmitting some other kind of message to an audience wider than the immediate victims;
• criterion 3: the action must not fall within the context of legitimate war activities. The act must therefore be considered outside the parameters permitted by international humanitarian law.

To identify a practical concept of organized crime is a complex task, although its field of investigation is well established (see [3] and [25]), since it includes the so-called "mafias", whose definition has highly problematic features. In 1876 Franchetti [16], defined the mafia as a total social fact, but the difficulty in defining it is, as can be seen from the reflections by Dino [13], in its capacity to present itself as an entity in continuous transformation, able to camouflage itself and to disappear. This characteristic is further underlined by Santoro [32] when he asks "how can we know a reality that is hidden and that pretends (...) not to exist? How can we know a reality that seems to exist more in its effects than in its structures, and that changes its nature depending on who is talking about it and the context in which it is discussed?".

Because of similar difficulties in defining it and because of the ambivalences and uncertainties of the sources (mostly judicial, sometimes autobiographical, often journalistic, rarely the result of a direct empirical analysis) an interpretative pluralism based on different analysis paradigms (see [5] and [31]) emerged. On the other hand, the need to isolate this dimension of criminality is based on the fact that it challenges, in a temporally continuous and territorially diffused fashion, the monopoly of legitimate violence exerted by the state.

Therefore, the study of the phenomenon of the so-called mafias is particularly difficult. Hence, we identify which events are commonly attributed to organized crime, to determine their existence and importance and to use them as indicators, measuring, weighting and indexing them. We included in our category the following "typical" acts of organized crime (and we are aware that we are introducing a subjective choice here): drug trafficking, crimes related to the aiding and exploitation of prostitution, money laundering. Furthermore, other types of crimes such as attacks, massacres and kidnappings that had clearly been committed by the *mafia* were included in the data set.

4.2 Cases, Indicators and Indices

After establishing the operational definitions, we isolated the indicators for each variable. In order to correctly formulate the indicators we analyzed, in addition to sectorial reports and specific literature, multiple statistics and survey data, seeking with this diversification of sources to obviate the limits of each single method of investigation[4]. The indicators have been processed, indexed and measured for the six European most populous countries (Italy, United Kingdom, France, Germany, Spain and Poland)[5]. Then, the various indicators were aggregated into indices. In accomplishing this methodological step, we proceeded as follows:

a) for each indicator, a cardinal scale from 0 to 5 was created. The minimum value 0 corresponds to the absence of the measured case while the maximum value is identified through benchmarking technique. The upper limit has been fixed inductively on the maximum value found among all those measured (this is done for each country and for the whole time period analyzed) and from there to any value it exceeds it, theoretically up to infinity, in order to allow for a diachronic and synchronic comparison among the six selected European democracies;

b) the scale was subsequently divided into intervals, not necessarily equal, each of them marked by one (zero point) or more landmarks that identify the limits within which the values are placed in the different intervals (i.e. the various units of the rating scale);

---

[4] For a review of the statistical methods applied to crime analysis, see [38].

[5] A similar procedure was used, on a larger sample (30 countries) by the authors of the so-called "democracy barometer" (www.democracybarometer.org).

c) as far the distribution of *scores* is concerned, the values assigned from 0 to 5 have been established in relation to the positioning of values in the corresponding unit of the cardinal scale. Indicators with values expressed in non-numerical terms have also been transformed into scores from 0 to 5 to make them compatible with the calculation of the global index;

d) the unidirectional orientation of the scale has therefore been established, i.e. the fact that two or more indicators of the same variable have no opposite polarity. In short, the minimum score (0) must correspond for all the indicators to the occurrence of the less desirable situation and the maximum score (5), to the most desirable situation;

e) once the scores for each indicator have been established, they were combined in a single index.

The final result of this aggregation is the average of the scores in a series of summary indices for each variable we identified.

Indices of Freedom

- Index of "freedom of": the higher the value of this index, the greater the freedom of information, of the press, expression, worship; protection for minorities (gender, ethnic, racial); the rights guaranteed in the economic sphere. More specifically, we included 8 parameters: freedom of belief, freedom of information, effectiveness of freedom of expression, women rights, lesbian, gay and other gender rights, minorities rights, juvenile convict rights, economic rights. Each of these parameters has a weight of 1/16, so that the total weight of the index of "freedom of" is 1/2.

- Index of "freedom from": the lower the value of the index, the greater the degree of coercion exercised by the state on the citizen, both in the criminal sphere (the guarantees offered by the judicial system are lower), and in the civil sphere, in terms of control and interference (protection of privacy). More specifically, we included 16 parameters: no death penalty, no torture, quality of life in prison, deaths in prison, inhuman treatment in prison, density in prison, ratification of the statute of the International Criminal Court, ratification of the Convention against torture, ratification of the International Convention for the Protection of All Persons from Enforced Disappearance, violation of the European Convention on Human Rights, maximal pre-trial detention, theoretical average pre-trial detention, practical average pre-trial detention, effectiveness of long-term pre-trial detention, maximal detention of immigrants, privacy rights. Each of these parameters has a weight of 1/32, so that the total weight of the index of "freedom from" is 1/2.

Indices of Security

- Common Crime Index: the lower the value of the index, the greater the number of crimes perpetrated and therefore the greater the probability for individuals/citizens to be subject to violence generated by different reasons (economic, social, political and non-specific); to risk personal safety for unmotivated acts; to be subject to predatory risk with the regard to material assets and property. More specifically, we included 6 parameters: robberies, thefts, personal assaults, sexual violence acts, juvenile crimes, frauds. Each of these parameters has a weight of 1/24, so that the total weight of the index of common crime is 1/4.

- Index of specific and organized crime: the lower the value of the index, the more the society, the institutions and the territory of the state are subject to violent acts by organizations strategically oriented to the acquisition of economic, and/or political resources through illegal methods and actions. More specifically, we included 5 parameters: persons under trial for organized crimes[6], prostitution crimes, kidnapping, drug crimes, money laundering. Each of these parameters has a weight of 1/20, so that the total weight of the index of specific and organized crime is 1/4.
- Index of political and terrorist crime: the lower the value of the index, the greater the number of terrorist acts and of people involved in them, strategically aimed at the change of one or more components of the national and/or international regime. More specifically, we included 2 parameters: terrorist attacks, number of defendants for terrorism. Each of these parameters has a weight of 1/8, so that the total weight of the index of political and terrorist crime is 1/4.
- Index of maximum criminal violence: the greater the value of the index, the greater the degree of protection of human life from homicidal criminal violence. More specifically, we considered the number of voluntary homicides per 100.000 inhabitants, with weight 1/4.

5   The Data Set

As already mentioned in the previous paragraph, in order to compare different data, some of which represent statistical incidences on very different bases of reference and other values of type YES/NO, we proceeded to grade the first on 6 levels, from 0 to 5. The value 5 represents the situation with a maximum of freedom or security. For the YES/NO values, a value between 1 and 5 has been attributed on the basis of the importance of the data, in the YES case, and 0 in the NO case. Then, we calculated a weighted average of the individual data of freedom and security, assigning the same weight to each of the indices developed in the previous section. Furthermore, we also assign the weight to the individual data that compose the individual indices, so that the sum of the weights is 1.

Then, we cleaned our data, eliminating the pairs (freedom, security) obtained with the weighted average for those years when a limited number of data was available, in particular 16 or less for security and 11 or less for freedom. In this way, we obtained Table 1. In Fig. 2, we report the pairs (freedom, security) in order to simplify how the situation evolved in each country.

From some observations emerging from Table 1, we find some interesting and not completely predictable scenarios. Germany, France, Italy and United Kingdom are characterized by an initial period, from 1998 to 2001, in which the pair of variables (freedom, security) assume values that are approximately similar, or in any case linked by the classic relationship, so that an increase of one corresponds to a decrease of the other (the average values of the pairs (freedom, security) for this period are (2.38, 2.87) for Germany, (2.42, 3.29) for France, (2.51, 3.39) for Italy and (3.23, 2.57) for United Kingdom).

---

[6] Our motivation is that the higher the number of persons under trial, the higher is the effectiveness in prosecuting the crimes.

Table 1. Freedom and security in the six European democracies (weighted average)

	1998	1999	2000	2001	2002	2003	2004	2005	2006	2007	2008	2009	2010	2011	2012	2013
Freedom																
Germany	2.28	2.38	2.45	2.42	3.05	2.80	3.14	3.17	3.17	3.22	3.22	3.39	3.83	3.36		
Spain					3.05	2.80	3.14	3.17	3.17	3.22	3.22	3.39	3.83	3.36	3.42	
France	2.40	2.37	2.48	2.44	2.91	2.91	3.29	3.29	3.23	3.30	3.41	3.41	3.85	3.32	3.44	2.91
Italy	2.40	2.54	2.54	2.57	2.75	2.79	3.19	3.16	3.19	3.24	3.24	3.18	3.58	3.02		
Poland					2.85	2.98	3.29	3.26	3.20	3.23	3.32	3.32	3.64			
United Kingdom	3.19	3.25	3.22	3.27	3.74	3.74	4.08	4.08	4.02	4.02	4.08	4.08	4.61	4.02	4.33	
Security																
Germany	2.73	2.68	2.93	3.13	3.03	3.25	3.30	3.68	3.93	3.88	3.84	3.84	3.89	3.83		
Spain					3.41	3.39	3.13	3.81	3.81	3.53	3.65	3.63	3.55	3.47	3.47	
France	3.35	3.35	3.30	3.17	3.21	3.08	3.17	3.54	3.54	3.76	3.58	3.87	3.95	3.66	3.74	2.93
Italy	3.39	3.34	3.39	3.43	3.64	3.34	3.35	4.23	4.27	4.24	4.37	4.41	4.45	4.45		
Poland					3.33	3.53	3.53	3.58	3.57	3.41	3.20	3.16	3.16			
United Kingdom	2.58	2.49	2.63	2.59	2.63	2.65	2.69	3.30	3.30	3.44	3.36	3.58	3.15	3.20	3.37	

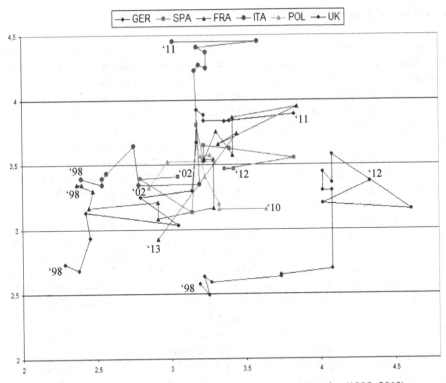

Fig. 2. Freedom and security in the six European democracies (1998–2013)

Subsequently a transition occurs, in which the values of the pairs (freedom, security) do not change following the aforementioned relation. Then, we arrive to a new situation in which the pairs (freedom, security) again assume values that are approximately similar, or in any case correlated. Two clear examples arise from the Italian situation in the years 1998–1999 and 2008–2009 and the British situation in the years 2000–2001 and 2009–2010. More wide periods correspond to 2006–2011 (with the exception of 2010) for Germany (average (3.27, 3.87)), to 2005–2009 for France (average (3.33, 3.66)), to 2005–2011 (with the exception of 2010) for Italy (average (3.17, 4.33)), to 2005–2012 for United Kingdom (average (4.16, 3.34)). It should be noted that Italy and United Kingdom in both periods of stability have values of freedom and security slightly higher than those of France and decidedly higher than those of Germany.

In Italy there is stronger focus on security, whereas in United Kingdom the focus is more on freedom. Finally, it is worth noting what happens in France after 2010, when after a growth in freedom (from 3.41 to 3.85) there is a reduction of both the values of freedom and security, going from (3.85, 3.95) in 2010 to (2.91, 2.93) in 2013.

Spain and Poland have a relatively constant level of security, while there is an increase in freedom, for Spain in the period 2003–2010 and for Poland in the whole range examined.

6   Index of Democratic Quality

To further deepen our analysis, we decided to use the available data to define a (partial and relative) index of democratic quality, i.e. a numerical value that would allow to evaluate the "quality of democracy" of a nation on the basis of the freedom and security measures obtained and described in the previous pages. The index shows the reciprocal positioning of the six polyarchies with respect to the two dimensions studied, referring to the fluctuation in a given range represented by the extremes possible values of the variables; consequently, the value of the index depends on the reference data.

For computing the index of democratic quality, we started from the formula $S^\alpha = K - a\,F^\beta$ (see Sect. 2); rewriting it as $K = S^\alpha + a\,F^\beta$ we may observe that the value of K is unchanged when the values of the two parameters suitably change, while the value of K grows when the values of the two parameters increase.

Then, we grouped for each country the years in which the values of freedom and security are constant or have minimal variations in order to determine the values for a, α and β. More precisely, we identified the following eight groups of years, two for each country: Germany {1998, 1999, 2000, 2001} and {2006, 2007, 2008, 2009, 2011}; France {1998, 1999, 2000, 2001} and {2005, 2006, 2007, 2008, 2009}; Italy {1998, 1999, 2000, 2001} and {2005, 2006, 2007, 2008, 2009, 2011}; United Kingdom {1998, 1999, 2000, 2001} and {2005, 2006, 2007, 2008, 2009, 2010, 2011, 2012}. For each of these eight groups, a least square approximation was carried out in order to obtain values of K corresponding to the available information on the level of democracy. The resulting values for the parameters are $a = 1.5$, $\alpha = 2$ and $\beta = 1.5$. This analysis has a further result. Looking at Table 1, it is easy to notice that fixing a couple of values of freedom and security, the previous values of a, α and β, produce different values of K. For instance, using the values of the couples for United Kingdom in the years 1999, 2009 and 2010, (3.25, 2.49), (4.08, 3.58) and (4.61, 3.15) respectively, the corresponding values of $K = S^2 + 1.5\,L^{1.5}$ are 15.0, 25.1 and 24.8; In other words, different values of freedom and security for 2009 and 2010 produce similar values for K and very different from the value for 1999. This result may be interpreted as a growth of the British democracy from 1999 to 2009. This interpretation of the parameter K as index of the quality of the democracy, allows a different reading of the values in Table 2.

This index enables us to notice that for Poland the index increases from 2002 reaching the maximum in 2005, then it decreases up to 2009, and grows again in 2010. For Spain, the index decreases from 2002 to 2004, then grows reaching the maximum in 2010 and again decreases up to 2012. These two countries have a similar level of quality of the democracy, with a small advantage for Spain that has a more consolidated democracy. Italy and Germany have high values for the index, with a growing trend. Italy has an average value 17.46 for the period 1998–2001, 27.21 for the period 2005–2009 and in 2011 and 29.97 in 2010. The German average values are 13.74 for the period 1998–2001, 23.85 for the period 2006–2009 and in 2011 and 26.38 in 2010. It is easy to see that the Italian averages are larger. Also, for United Kingdom the index has a growing trend, from an average value 15.31 for the period 1998–2001 to an average value 23.88 for the period 2005–2011. The global evaluation of the two dimensions confirms that France has worsening performances: the index grows from the period 1998–2001, reaching

Table 2. Index of democratic quality

	1998	1999	2000	2001	2002	2003	2004	2005	2006	2007	2008	2009	2010	2011	2012	2013
Germany	12,64	12,69	14,37	15,47	17,18	17,58	19,24	21,98	23,88	23,75	23,42	24,13	**26,38**	23,93		
Spain					19,60	18,52	18,17	22,98	22,98	21,09	21,99	22,51	**23,84**	21,26	21,52	
France	16,79	16,68	16,73	15,76	17,75	16,97	18,97	21,49	21,23	23,13	22,24	24,41	**26,94**	22,46	23,59	16,02
Italy	17,06	17,22	17,56	17,96	20,12	18,14	19,78	26,28	26,76	26,74	27,81	27,92	**29,97**	27,68		
Poland					18,29	20,14	21,39	21,61	21,30	20,32	19,33	19,06	20,38			
United Kingdom	15,18	15,01	15,61	15,58	17,77	17,86	19,61	23,26	22,97	23,93	23,64	**25,15**	24,78	22,32	24,85	

Note: the minimum value is underlined; the maximum value is in **bold**.

the maximum in 2010 and decreases till 2013, when the value is similar to the period 1998–2001.

7 Conclusions

7.1 The Results of an Empirical Test

The overall examination of the results confirms, first of all, that the two variables of security and freedom are closely linked and that their variation, upwards or downwards, is characterized by an inverse correlation. The six democracies (with the exception of France in recent years), during the period of time considered, simultaneously increase the degree of freedom and security while maintaining an inverse correlation. Returning to the starting hypotheses, these variations in the value of the two dimensions can be graphically represented - for each country - by their position on different democratic curves characterized by a different value of the two variables. For example, a polyarchy moves its location from the curve closest to zero (continuous black curve) to the furthest curve (continuous grey curve) of Fig. 1. A democratic regime, therefore, over the years, can guarantee greater freedom and greater security, while maintaining a similar proportion between them.

With reference to the empirical analysis carried out, we observe that in the six major liberal-democracies of the EU (in terms of population) it is possible to extend the rights and guarantee personal security, frequently maintaining the two variables linked by the same inverse relation. This is the case - as we have seen - of Germany, France (until 2011), Italy and United Kingdom, which are characterized by an initial period, from 1998 to 2001, in which the pairs (freedom, security) assume approximately similar values and translate into the upper curve for the period 2003–2011 (with some exceptions; see details in Table 1). Each of these democracies seems to maintain its peculiarities substantially unaltered. In United Kingdom (see Fig. 2) freedom is configured as the privileged dimension of its democratic development, while maintaining security at an acceptable level (as shown by values in line with other comparative countries). Vice versa, in Italy and, even more so, in Germany (see Fig. 2) the political system produced a more accentuated development of security, compared to freedom. In the transition from one curve to another some consolidated democracies (United Kingdom, Italy, Germany) tend to maintain the same kind of balance between freedom and security, being characterized by the maintenance over time of the broader protection of one than the other. Indeed, the UK democratic regime, while increasing security, recently in a decisive and unusual manner - perhaps due to the greater attention to the terrorism problem - continues to extend the already high level of rights. It follows the persistence of a very similar relationship between the two variables. In Italy, as in Germany, however, security is more widely and continuously protected, although this does not prevent the extension of the rights of freedom in the same period, especially in recent years (for example, the new rules to obtain citizenship and granting wider rights to gender minorities).

The two democratically younger states, Poland and Spain, exhibit a high level of security (which we can hypothesize to be partly related to the legacy of previous authoritarian regimes) while the progressive consolidation of democracy characterizes them for a constant increase in the value of the indicators of freedom, an almost missing dimension in the former non-democratic systems of these countries. From our empirical elaborations, we could say that democracy presents itself as a regime capable of reconciling the needs of maintaining peaceful coexistence with the growing institutional guarantees of individual freedom. For the Polish case, however, particular caution must be used in evaluating these statements. The precautions are due to the limited availability of data that can be used for our comparative survey, which is limited to the period 2002–2010. In particular, the end date (2010) does not allow to include the effects of the recent reforms (for example, on the appointment of judges of the Constitutional Court and on radio and television broadcastings) implemented by the government, after the electoral victory of the nationalist right party (PiS) in October 2015[7]. The fact that, as a result of these policies, there is the fear of a strong regression of the guarantees of freedom is evidenced by the decision taken on 13 January 2016 by the EU Commission to apply to the Polish government the "Rule of Law Framework", a new mechanism (approved in March 2014) to protect the rule of law within the EU, and which was never used before.

On the other hand, the French case stands out because it is the only one that regresses the value of the two variables after 2011; indeed, security and freedom not only decrease, but reach the lowest value ever (for the period considered) in 2013 (see Fig. 2). In recent years, France moved from a higher curve down to a lower one, revealing itself as the only country that worsens the performance of these two crucial aspects of democratic quality. The other nations examined, comparatively to France prove to be more secure, even freer. In France, there was a probable and widespread increase in the perception of insecurity, not necessarily connected to the increase in criminal events, and despite the frequency of protests for the lack of recognition of important rights both to minorities of citizens, and above all to those who, while residing in the territory of a state, are not considered part of it. Accounting also the subjective evaluation of security, other possibilities appear. The feeling of insecurity does not derive, in fact, only from factors attributable to criminal behavior, but can take root in the perception of "foreign" elements affecting daily life, such as the spread of drugs, prostitution and more recently, especially migratory phenomena. Another factor that fuels the sense of insecurity can be the reduction of institutional trust, hence the perception of the lack of attention by the institutions to the problems of citizens [39]. In general, insecurity stems from the threat posed by everything that appears unpredictable and uncontrollable and for this reason compromises the stability of everyday life [15]. Therefore, on the one hand we can consider security in "objective" terms, represented by the "danger" that expresses, statistically, the probability that one or more subjects may be victims of a criminal attack on their person or property in certain spatial conditions. On the other hand, security in "subjective" terms is distinguished, and it is found in the various types of behavior by which each individual expresses the personal perception of the phenomenon, such as the fear of immigration, the increasing of diffusion of alarm systems or the recent Italian law on self-defense.

---

[7] The Polish elections of 2019, that are out of the period under our investigation, confirmed the PiS as the first party, even if it lost the absolute majority in the upper chamber and reduced the number of votes in the lower chamber.

7.2 Further Developments

What emerges from our analysis supports the idea of the capacity of democratic regimes to adapt their behavior to new social needs, preserving the qualitative features and increasing these characteristics, even during a crisis.

Normatively, these are good news for those who believe in democratic values and hope that democracy may continuously increase, overcoming the challenges and threats that it has to face. Also, from an explicative point of view, the results are promising, as they suggest at least three directions in which to move forward the theoretical and empirical analysis of democracy.

The first direction is the explanation of the relation between security and freedom that we conceptualized according to two hypotheses. The first hypothesis follows the classical idea by Hobbes [20, chap. XVII, XVIII, XXI] that there exists an inverse relation, i.e. when one increases the other one decreases, with the risk that, without a careful balancing, the system collapses. The second hypothesis requires that this relation has to be contextualized accounting for all of the factors related to the quality of democracy, in the sense that a reduction of one of the two parameters may have no effect if it is counterbalanced by high values of all the other factors.

Our empirical analysis confirms the first hypothesis; more precisely, we observed that for many countries the values of freedom and security move in an inverse relation but the values are not constant, varying the quality of democracy.

The second direction refers to the theory by Morlino on the morphology and dynamics of a model of good democracy. Morlino [23] says: "There exist democracies with different features depending on the level of realization of one or of the other one dimension, and on the different combination of choices and real opportunities. The existing connections among the different dimensions do not make them alternative to each other; more precisely, they can be joint together." This thesis seems to be contradicted by those that consider freedom and security as antinomian aspects of the quality of the democracy. The relevance of this choice in order to pursue the quality of the democracy is pointed out by Pennock [26] and confirmed by Almond and Powell [2]. The latter note that: "Pennock admits the existing tensions among these political goods: security and freedom, welfare and justice may be conflicting; the increasing of one of them may imply the decreasing of the other one. Moreover, the level of development and capacity of a political system, its ability of producing these goods and the environmental threats and problems may limit the kind and volume of political goods that may be produced." Referring to this discussion, our analysis allows us to validate and integrate both theses, as it is clear from what we showed that it is possible to increase both security and freedom, and consequently the democratic quality of the regime with respect to these two variables, even if they maintain their inverse relation.

The third direction concerns the hypothesis that the history of a regime, in particular the authoritative ones, influences the process of building democratic quality. We may notice that the polyarchies with more recent authoritarian regimes, as Spain and Poland, are those that less protect the guarantees for freedom. The countries in which the fear of social disorders and anarchy led in the past to a totalitarian regime, as Italy and Germany, are those that try to better preserve the rights of citizens, thanks to a high level of democracy.

On the other hand, United Kingdom still maintains its historical and institutional characteristics of libertarian state, which guarantees large freedom rights, preserving security. France has a different evolution, because it follows the growth of the quality of democracy until 2011, when the level of both parameters decreases until 2013, when they reach their minimal values. Even if it would be necessary to collect data for a further period of time in order to check if this situation is a temporary one or if the increase in the crime rate and a contemporary restriction of the individual freedom are a consequence of a deeper crisis of the political system, we may say that our data clearly show a regression of the level of democracy in the last years in France.

Finally, it is important to remark that the performances of the democracies, from the viewpoint of protection from the crimes and guarantee of social rights, show unexpected trends, according to which a relatively young democracy like Italy, suffering for a long time of a high degree of fragmentation and a low degree of governability [12] is able to offer a high level of security and freedom to the citizens.

Acknowledgment. The authors gratefully acknowledge two anonymous reviewers for their comments and suggestions that improved the quality of the paper.

References

1. Agamben, G.: Stato di eccezione. Bollati Boringhieri, Torino (2003)
2. Almond, G.A., Powell Jr., G.B.: Comparative Politics: System, Process, Policy. Little Brown, Boston (1978)
3. Arlacchi, P.: La mafia imprenditrice. L'etica mafiosa e lo spirito del capitalismo. Il Mulino, Bologna (1983)
4. Balkin, S.: Victimization rates, safety and fear of crime. Soc. Prob. **26**, 343–358 (1978)
5. Becchi, A.: Criminalità organizzata: paradigmi e scenari delle organizzazioni mafiose in Italia. Donzelli, Roma (2000)
6. Beetham, D.: Democracy and Human Rights. Polity Press, Cambridge (1999)
7. Berlin, I.: Four Essays on Liberty. Oxford University Press, Oxford (1969)
8. Calaresu, M., Tebaldi, M.: Local security policies and the protection of territory: an analysis of the Italian experience (2007–2009) city. Territory Archit. **2**, 1–18 (2015)
9. Clark, W.R., Golder, M., Golder, S.: Principles of Comparative Politics. SAGE, Washintgton (2009)
10. Crozier, M., Huntington, S.P., Watanuki, J.: The Crisis of Democracy: Report on Governability of Democracy to the Trilateral Commission. New York University Press, New York (1975)
11. Dahl, R.A.: Poliarchy. Participation and Opposition. Yale University Press, New Haven and London (1971)
12. De Micheli, C., Fragnelli, V.: Robustness of legislative procedures of the Italian parliament. In: Nguyen, N.T., Kowalczyk, R., Mercik, J. (eds.) Transactions on Computational Collective Intelligence XXIII. LNCS, vol. 9760, pp. 1–16. Springer, Heidelberg (2016). https://doi.org/10.1007/978-3-662-52886-0_1
13. Dino, A.: Sul metodo mafioso. Rassegna Italiana di Sociologia **50**, 309–316 (2009)
14. Dye, T.R.: Understanding Public Policy. Prentice Hall, Englewood Cliffs (1992)
15. Fiasco, M.: La sicurezza urbana. Il sole 24 ore, Milano (2001)
16. Franchetti, L.: La Sicilia nel 1876. Condizioni politiche e amministrative della Sicilia. Libro primo. Vallecchi, Firenze (1925)

17. Garland, D.: The Culture of Control: Crime and Social Order in Contemporary Society. Oxford University, Oxford, New York (2001)
18. Hebberecht, P., Sack, F.: La prévention de la délinquance en Europe. Nouvelles strategies. L'Harmattan, Paris (1997)
19. Hobbes, T.: De Cive. Marietti, Torino (1972)
20. Hobbes, T.: Leviathan. The Project Gutenberg E-book of Leviathan (1651). www.gutenberg.org/files/3207/3207-h/3207-h.htm
21. Hughes, G., McLaughlin, E., Muncie, J.: Crime Prevention and Community Safety: New Directions. Sage, London (2002)
22. Lipset, S.M.: Political Man: The Social Bases of Politics. The Johns Hopkins University Press, Baltimore (1960)
23. Morlino, L.: Democrazie e democratizzazioni. Il Mulino Bologna (2003)
24. Olson, M.: The Rise and Decline of Nations: Economic Growth, Stagflation, and Social Rigidities. Yale University Press, New Haven (1982)
25. Paoli, L.: The paradoxes of organized crime. Crime Law Soc. Change Int. J. 27, 51–97 (2002)
26. Pennock, R.J.: Political development, political systems, and political goods. World Polit. 18, 415–434 (1966)
27. Pisapia, G.D.: Terrorismo: delitto politico o delitto comune. La Giustizia Penale 3, 257–271 (1975)
28. Przeworski, A.: Democracy as an equilibrium. Public Choice 123, 253–273 (2005)
29. Roché, S.: L'insécurité: entre crime et citoyenneté. Déviance et Société 15, 301–313 (1991)
30. Rose, R.: Risorse dei governi e sovraccarico di domande. Rivista Italiana di Scienza Politica 5, 235–276 (1975)
31. Santino, U.: Dalla mafia alle mafie: scienze sociali e crimine organizzato. Rubbettino, Soveria Mannelli (2006)
32. Santoro, M.: Introduzione. In: Santoro, M. (ed.) Riconoscere le mafie. Cosa sono, come funzionano, come si muovono, pp. 7–34. Il Mulino, Bologna (2015)
33. Sartori, G.: Democrazia e definizioni. Il Mulino, Bologna (1957)
34. Sartori, L.: Lavavetri, punkabbestia e rom, spritz, furti e graffiti: cos'è l'insicurezza in Italia? In: Donovan, M., Onofri, P. (eds.) Politica in Italia, pp. 283–302. Il Mulino, Bologna (2008)
35. Schmitt, C.: Le categorie del politico. Il Mulino, Bologna (1972)
36. Schneider, J., Tilley, N.: Gangs. Ashgate, Aldershot (2004)
37. Stafford, M.C., Galle, O.R.: Victimization rates, exposure to risk and fear of crime. Criminology 22, 173–185 (1984)
38. Vettori, B.: Le statistiche sulla criminalità in ambito internazionale, europeo e nazionale. Edizioni Universitarie di Lettere, Economia, Diritto, Milano (2010)
39. Walklate, S.: Crime and community: fear or trust? Br. J. Sociol. 49, 550–569 (1998)
40. Zagrebelski, V.: L'equilibrio tra libertà e sicurezza. http://www.lastampa.it/2015/11/17. Accessed 11 Nov 2016

Trials of Characterizations
of Anti-manipulation Method

Michał Ramsza$^{(\boxtimes)}$ and Honorata Sosnowska

Warsaw School of Economics, Warsaw, Poland
{michal.ramsza,honorata}@sgh.waw.pl

Abstract. This paper studies the anti-manipulation voting method introduced in [8]. We show that the method does not satisfy the consistency condition. The consistency condition characterizes scoring functions. Thus, the method is not a scoring function. Also, the method is not any from a family of not scoring functions comprising Copeland method, instant-runoff voting, majority judgment, minimax, ranked pairs, Schulze method. The paper also shows that the choice of a metric, used by the anti-manipulation method, may imply the winner of the voting.

Keywords: Anti-manipulation method · Voting

1 Introduction

Voting is a method of communication. It allows solutions for some social dilemmas. In this paper, we present some properties of the anti-manipulation voting method, [8], which may be used to aggregate opinions of experts, for example, jurors of classical music competitions.

In 2016, the XV International Violin Henryk Wieniawski Competition took place. There were 11 jurors and 7 contestants in the final of the competition. In the final, the Borda Count was used in the inverse version, that is with 1 for the best. In what follows, we shall use the version with 7 for the best and 1 for the worst. Both versions yield the same results.

The Borda Count is a particular scoring method. In this scoring method, jurors assign a score, which is a real number, to each contestant. Ties are possible. In the Borda Count, each juror orders contestants from the best to the worst without ties. The best contestant gets a number of points equal to the number of contestants. The contestant next in order gets the same number of points decreased by one. This procedure is repeated. Thus, the last contestant in order gets one point. Then, for every contestant, the sum of points from all jurors is computed. The contestant with the highest total score wins.

This research was supported by the National Science Centre, Poland, grant number 2016/21/B/HS4/03016 and SGHS19/07/19.

The Borda Count is a method of voting very sensitive to manipulation. There was some news about the "war of jurors" in the Wieniawski Competition in Polish daily "Gazeta Wyborcza" (https://www.gazeta.pl) and in the most influential Polish music journal "Ruch Muzyczny", [6].

Table 1 presents voting results of jurors $J1, \ldots, J11$ over contestants $A, \ldots, G$. Jurors $J4, J5, J8$ gave the highest scores to contestant A and low scores to contestant B. Conversely, jurors $J2, J3, J7$ gave the highest scores to contestant B and low scores to contestant A. Contestant A won the competition. One can think that jurors especially diminished scores for the competitor of their best contestant.

Table 1. Votings of jurors in the final of the XV Wieniawski competitions. Source: own calculations based on results of the competition obtained from the Organization Committee.

	$J1$	$J2$	$J3$	$J4$	$J5$	$J6$	$J7$	$J8$	$J9$	$J10$	$J11$
A	7	3	2	7	7	4	3	7	7	7	7
B	4	7	7	2	2	7	7	2	5	6	5
C	5	5	5	3	6	6	5	5	6	1	6
D	3	6	4	5	1	5	4	4	3	5	1
E	1	4	6	1	3	3	6	3	4	3	4
F	6	2	1	6	4	2	1	6	1	2	2
G	2	1	3	4	5	1	2	1	2	4	3

The situation, described above, caused investigations of a method that would be less sensitive to manipulations. Kontek and Sosnowska [8] proposed such a method. The method, called the anti-manipulation method, is constructed as follows. There are k jurors. Each juror assigns scores to the candidates as in the Borda Count method. Then, the following procedure is used.

1. For each contestant, a mean of scores is computed. This results in a vector of the Borda Count means $M = (M_1, \ldots, M_m)$.
2. For every juror, a distance between the vector of means and juror's vector of scores is computed.
3. 20% jurors with the highest distance of their vector of scores from the mean are removed[1].
4. The arithmetic mean M of the remaining jurors is computed as in the first step.
5. The contestant i with the highest mean M_i is a winner.

---

[1] In fact, as defined later, the jurors are assigned weights with the most distant jurors given zero weight.

Let us note that the distance and the method of removing jurors may be chosen in any way. Kontek and Sosnowska [8] used Manhattan distance. With this distance, $R = \lfloor k/5 \rfloor$ jurors with largest distances from the mean M are removed. When this procedure is applied to the scores in Table 1, a different contestant wins voting as opposed to voting without this procedure. These two contestants were subjects of the "jurors' war" mentioned above. Contestant A won the competition, while contestant B would have won had the anti-manipulation method been used.

First, let us note that A is the Condorcet winner. So, the anti-manipulation method is not a Condorcet method. There are many not Condorcet methods, some very popular, for example the Borda Count, the Litvak method [2,10,15]. Second, the anti-manipulation method uses the procedure of removing jurors. An experiment, described in [8], shows that removing jurors results in a lower manipulation level than the elimination of opinions deviating significantly from the mean. Also, 20% threshold is obtained as a compromise between the Borda Count and Majority Criterion, [8].

There are a lot of voting methods, [5,14]. There is, to the best of our knowledge, none that removes voters in a non-random way. This raises the question of possible properties that may characterize the anti-manipulation method. We use the concept of equivalence of voting methods as a tool.

Two voting methods are equivalent when for the same profile of voters' preferences and the same set of alternatives, both methods lead to the same results, that is, give the same winners. We compared the properties of the anti-manipulation method with the properties of the Borda Count and scoring methods. We got that the anti-manipulation method is not equivalent to the Borda Count or any scoring method. We used the consistency condition as the primary tool of the analysis.

Consistency condition guarantees that the result of voting in subgroups, should it be the same, is the result of voting in a whole group composed of these subgroups. The anti-manipulation method does not satisfy the consistency condition, which is one of the axioms for the Borda count and scoring method. Thus, this method cannot be equivalent to the Borda Count or any scoring method. Also, using the consistency condition, we showed that the anti-manipulation method is not equivalent to any method from a group on non-scoring methods. The analyzed group comprised the Copeland method, instant-runoff voting, the Kemeny-Young method, majority judgment [1], minimax, ranked pairs, and the Schulze method. Additionally, we showed a dependence of the anti-manipulation method on the particular choice of a metric.

The paper contains five sections. Section 2 presents the axiomatizations of Borda Count and scoring methods. In Sect. 3, we show an example of voting where the anti-manipulation method does not fulfill the consistency condition and give different winners according to chosen metrics, namely, the Manhattan and the Euclidian metrics. In Sect. 4, we present examples of voting where the consistency condition is not fulfilled for the Copeland method, instant-runoff voting, majority judgment, minimax, ranked pairs, and the Schulze method. Section 5 offers conclusions.

2   Axiomatization of the Borda Count and Scoring Functions

Young, [22,23], provided axiomatizations of the Borda Count and scoring functions. In this section, we recall these results.

Let $A = \{a_1, \ldots, a_m\}$ be a set of alternatives (in our examples contestants) where m is a number of alternatives, N set of voters (in our examples jurors). Voter's preferences are linear orders on A. A function from a finite subset V of N into linear orders on A is called a profile. A social choice function f assigns to each profile w a nonempty subset of A, called a choice set.

A scoring method may be defined in the following way [23]. There is a sequence $s = (s_1, \ldots, s_m)$ of scores, which are real numbers. A vector s is called a scoring vector. Every voter ranks alternatives from best to worst and assigns scores to them. Score s_i is assigned to alternative on i-th position. For each alternative, the sum of scores is computed. The alternative with the highest sum of scores wins. The Borda Count is a special scoring function. The best alternative gets the score of m, the second-best alternative receives the score of $m - 1$, and each consecutive alternative gets the score diminished by one. The worst alternative receives the score of 1.

Formally, let Λ be a set of all linear orders over A, $p \in \Lambda$. E_p is $m \times m$ permutation matrix with 1 at the (i,j)-th position if and only if a_i is the j-th most preferred in the preference order p. For every $x \in R^{m!}$ we define the matrix $D(x) = \sum_{p \in \Lambda} x_p \cdot E_p$. Let $D_i(x)$ be i-th row of $D(x)$. A simple scoring function f_s is defined as follows

$$a_i \in f_s(x) \quad \text{if and only if} \quad \langle D_i(x)|s \rangle \geq \langle D_j(x)|s \rangle \quad \text{for all } j,$$

where $\langle \cdot | \cdot \rangle$ is scalar product. For anonymous social choice function g and scoring vector s, the composition $f_s \circ g$ of f_s with g is defined as follows

$$a_i \in f_s \circ g(x) \quad \text{if and only if} \quad a_i \in g(x) \quad \text{and} \quad \langle D_i(x)|s \rangle \geq \langle D_j(x)|s \rangle$$

for all j such that $a_j \in g(x)$. The composite scoring function is a social choice function that is a composition of k simple scoring functions, $k > 1$, defined on score vectors $x \in R^{m!}$. The Borda Count, scoring method and anti-manipulation method are social choice functions.

Social choice function is anonymous if it depends only on the numbers of voters having each preference order. Social choice function is neutral if $f(\sigma(w)) = \sigma(f(w))$ for any permutation σ.

Social choice function f is consistent, [22], if for any disjoint sets of voters V', V'' and profiles of preferences w', w'' of voters from V', V'' respectively, the following consistency condition holds

$$\text{if} \quad f(w') \cap f(w'') \neq \emptyset \quad \text{then} \quad f(w') \cap f(w'') = f(w', w''), \tag{1}$$

where (w', w'') denotes a joint profile of w' and w''.

The following social choice functions are consistent: Condorcet in its domain, that is where the Condorcet winner exists, plurality, Borda, and any scoring function. Non-consistent functions will be presented in Sect. 3 and 4. Other names for consistency include "separability" [19], "convexity" [21], "elimination" [3,4] and "reinforcement" [12,13]. The failure of this property can be seen as an example of the Simpson paradox when there are the same trends over two disjoint sets, which are different from the trend over the sum of these sets. Merlin, [11], formulates the consistency condition in a slightly different way. However, we will not discuss it in this paper.

A social choice function is faithful when the socially most preferred alternative is the same as the individually most preferred alternative when society consists of one individual.

A social choice function has the cancellation property if the following condition holds. If for any pair of alternatives a, b, the number of voters preferring a to b is equal to the number of voters preferring b to a, then there is a tie between all alternatives.

Lemma 1 (Young, [22]). *Borda Count is neutral, consistent, faithful and has the cancellation property.*

Theorem 1 (Young, [22]). *For a finite set of alternatives, the only social choice function which is neutral, consistent, faithful and has the cancellation property is the Borda Count.*

Theorem 2 (Young, [23]). *Social choice function is anonymous, neutral and consistent if and only if it is a scoring function.*

Two social choice functions are equivalent if they give the same results for any profile of preferences and set of alternatives.

3 Properties of Anti-manipulation Method

In the definition of the anti-manipulation method, the used distance and way of computing 20% of jurors are not precisely defined. In this paper, we use two types of distance: the Manhattan distance and the Euclidean distance. They are the most popular types of distance in the relevant literature. Moreover, the Manhattan distance is easy to compute. We present two types of removing procedure using some examples.

Example 1. There are 10 jurors. They are ordered according to distances of their vectors of scores from the mean. Table 2 presents the distances between jurors' score vectors and the mean score vector. In this situation, 20% of a number of jurors equals 2. Thus, we need to remove 2 jurors having the largest distances from the mean score. For the data presented in the Table 2 these are jurors $J1$ and $J2$. This procedure is equivalent to multiplying scores of jurors by components of a weight vector, also presented in the Table 2.   □

Table 2. Distance of jurors' score vectors from the mean.

Jurors	J1	J2	J3	J4	J5	J6	J7	J8	J9	J10
Distance from the mean	10	9	8	7	6	5	4	3	3	1
Weights for scores	0	0	1	1	1	1	1	1	1	1

Computing the number of jurors to remove is more complicated when 20% of a number of jurors is not an integer, or some values of distance are repeated. Two methods of removing jurors are proposed for these situations.

Example 2. In the following example, there are 17 jurors. Table 3 presents distances between jurors' score vectors and the mean together with two weighting vectors. In the presented situation, 20% of a number of jurors equals 3.4, and there are some ties between distance. We consider two weighting methods.

Table 3. Distance of jurors' score vector from the mean.

Jurors	J1	J2	J3	J4	J5	J6	J7	J8	J9	J10	J11	J12	J13	J14	J15	J16	J17
Distance from the mean	10	9	8	8	8	7	7	6	6	5	5	4	4	3	3	3	3
Weights for scores (i)	0	0	2/3	2/3	2/3	1	1	1	1	1	1	1	1	1	1	1	1
Weights for scores (ii)	0	0	2/3	2/3	2/3	4/5	4/5	1	1	1	1	1	1	1	1	1	1

i) *Integer part method.* As mentioned above, 20% of a number of jurors is 3.4 and the integer part is $\lfloor 3.4 \rfloor = 3$. Thus, we need to remove 3 jurors. Firstly, we remove jurors J1 and J2. The problem is that the next three jurors have the same distance from the mean. Thus, the last weight of 1 is split between the jurors J3, J4, and j5 equally. For each of those jurors, 1/3 of their scores is removed. So, secondly, their scores are multiplied by 2/3. Table 3 presents the resulting weighting vector.

ii) *Integer and fractional parts method.* In this method, the whole number 3.4 is distributed across the jurors. Firstly, the integer part of 3.4 is divided among jurors as in the integer part method. The remainder part 0.4 is equally divided among jurors in the next distance group. Thus, in this case, scores of jurors J6 and J7 are multiplied by 0.8. Table 3 presents the resulting weighting vector. □

Theorem 3. *The anti-manipulation methods for the Manhattan and Euclidean distances with the integer part weighting are not consistent.*

Proof. The proof relies on specific counterexamples. We use the jurors' scores in the Wieniawski Competition, given in Table 1, and take all jurors as the set V.
For the Manhattan distance, we define

$$V' = \{J7, J9, J11\} \quad \text{and} \quad V'' = \{J1, J2, J3, J4, J5, J6, J8, J10\}.$$

The winner over V' and over V'' is B while the winner over the whole set V is A.

For the Euclidean distance, we define

$$V' = \{J5, J6, J7, J8, J10\} \quad \text{and} \quad V'' = \{J1, J2, J3, J4, J9, J11\}.$$

The winner over V' and over V'' is B while the winner over the whole set V is A. $\square$

Theorem 4. *The anti-manipulation methods for the Manhattan and Euclidean distances with the integer and fractional parts weighting are not consistent.*

Proof. The proof relies on specific counterexamples. We use the jurors' scores in the Wieniawski Competition, given in Table 1, and take all jurors as the set V.

For the Manhattan distance, we define

$$V' = \{J7, J10, J11\} \quad \text{and} \quad V'' = \{J1, J2, J3, J4, J5, J6, J8, J9\}.$$

The winner over V' and over V'' is A while the winner over the whole set V is B.

For the Euclidean distance, we define

$$V' = \{J5, J6, J7, J8, J10\} \quad \text{and} \quad V'' = \{J1, J2, J3, J4, J9, J11\}.$$

The winner over V' and over V'' is B while the winner over the whole set V is A. $\square$

Remark 1. There are 11 jurors, so there are 1023 bi-partitions. All the bi-partitions were analyzed. In the case of the integer method, there are 14 (about 1.4%) inconsistent cases for the Euclidean metrics and 78 (about 7.6%) for Manhattan metrics. In the case of the integer and fractional parts method, there are 54 (about 5%) inconsistent cases for the Manhattan metrics and 13 (about 1,2%) for the Euclidean metrics. Computations were done with a computer program written in R (see Appendix). $\square$

Remark 2. Different ways of computing 20% of a number of jurors may lead to different results. For the Manhattan metrics and bi-partition $V' = \{J7, J10, J11\}$, $V'' = \{J1, J2, J3, J4, J5, J6, J8, J9\}$ the winner by the integer part method is C, while for the integer and fractional parts method it is A. $\square$

Corollary 1. *The anti-manipulation method is not equivalent to any ranking.*

Proof. It is implied by Theorem 2. If the anti-manipulation method were a scoring method, A would be the winner over V for the Manhattan distance and B for the Euclidean distance. $\square$

Corollary 2. *A winner of voting by the anti-manipulation method may be different for the Manhattan and Euclidean metrics.*

Proof. It is implied by the proof of Theorem 3. $\square$

4 Inconsistent Methods and Their Properties

In this section, we use some examples from the "Consistency Criterion" entry on Wikipedia about various voting methods that do not satisfy the consistency conditions[2]. The examined group consists of very different voting methods. Some of them are quite popular and old, but the last two are rather new, complicated, and rarely used. The following social choice functions are considered:

1. Copeland,
2. Instant-runoff voting,
3. Kemeny-Young method (see proof of Proposition 3 for a strict definition),
4. Majority Judgement (Balinski–Laraki),
5. Minimax,
6. Ranked pairs,
7. Schulze method,
8. Litvak method.

For each of these methods, the mentioned Wikipedia entry presents an example of a bi-partition, for which the method fails[3] the consistency condition (1). Interestingly, the anti-manipulation method with the Manhattan distance and the integer part weighting satisfies the consistency condition in these cases. Consequently, the anti-manipulation method is not equivalent to any of the methods listed above. We further examine the anti-manipulation method in the context of these cases in the following propositions.

Proposition 1. *There exist profiles, for which the Copeland method does not satisfy the consistency condition, but the anti-manipulation does.*

Proof. Let us consider 5 candidates A, B, C, D, E and 27 voters. Preference are presented in Table 4. The Copeland method computes the difference between the number of pairs where a candidate wins and the number of pairs where the candidate loses. Candidate with greatest such difference wins [16].

In the Copeland method, A is the winner for V' and V'' while C is the winner over the whole set V. Thus, this profile is a counterexample for the Copeland method satisfying the consistency condition. Using the anti-manipulation method gives B as the winner over V' and C as the winner over V''. Thus, the premise of the implication is false. Therefore, whatever the value of the conclusion, the implication is true. Concluding, this profile cannot be a counterexample for the anti-manipulation method satisfying the consistency condition.   □

Proposition 2. *There exist profiles, for which the instant-runoff method does not satisfy the consistency condition, but the anti-manipulation does.*

---

[2] The data in Tables 4–10 are taken from https://en.wikipedia.org/wiki/Consistency_criterion.

[2] The data in Tables 4–10 are taken from https://en.wikipedia.org/wiki/Consistency_criterion.
[3] Authors verified calculations.

Table 4. Copeland method.

Preferences of voters from V'	Number of voters from V'	Preferences of voters from V''	Number of voters from V''
$A > D > B > E > C$	3	$A > D > C > E > B$	3
$A > D > E > C > B$	2	$A > D > E > B > C$	1
$B > A > C > D > E$	3	$B > D > C > E > A$	3
$C > D > B > E > A$	3	$C > A > B > D > E$	3
$E > C > B > A > D$	3	$E > B > C > A > D$	3

Proof. In the instant–runoff voting method, a candidate with the lowest number of votes is eliminated, and voting with such a diminished number of candidates is repeated till one of the candidates gets the majority [17]. This method is quite old and frequently used. There are 3 candidates A,B,C and 23 voters. Preferences of voters are presented in Table 5.

Table 5. Instant-runoff method.

Preferences of voters from V'	Number of voters from V'	Preferences of voters from V''	Number of voters from V''
$A > B > C$	4	$A > B > C$	4
$B > A > C$	2	$B > A > C$	6
$C > B > A$	4	$C > A > B$	3

In the instant-runoff method, A is the winner over both V' and V'', while B is the winner over the whole set V. Thus, this bi-partition is a counterexample for the instant-runoff method satisfying the consistency condition. Using the anti-manipulation method gives B as the winner for all V', V'' and V. Thus, this profile cannot be a counterexample for the anti-manipulation method satisfying the consistency condition. □

Proposition 3. *There exist profiles, for which the Kemeny-Young method does not satisfy the consistency condition, but the anti-manipulation does.*

Proof. The Kemeny–Young method consists of two steps. In the first step, pairwise voter preferences are calculated. Next, scores for all possible rankings are determined based on the results of the first step. The best candidate in the ranking with the highest score is a winner [7]. We consider the case with 3 candidates A, B, C and 38 voters. Table 6 presents preferences.

In the Kemeny-Young method, A is the winner over both V' and V'' while B is the winner over the whole set V. Thus, this profile is a counterexample for the Kemeny-Young method satisfying the consistency condition.

Table 6. Kemeny-Young method.

Preferences of voters from V'	Number of voters from V'	Preferences of voters from V''	Number of voters from V''
$A > B > C$	7	$A > C > B$	8
$B > C > A$	6	$B > A > C$	7
$C > A > B$	3	$C > B > A$	7

The anti-manipulation method gives B as the winner for all sets V', V'' and V. Thus, this profile cannot be a counterexample for the anti-manipulation method satisfying the consistency condition. We should note, however, that there is a generalization of the Kemeny-Young method, where a social choice function determines the ranking, not only the winner. In such a case, the method satisfies the consistency condition [11]. □

Proposition 4. *There exist profiles, for which the majority judgment method does not satisfy the consistency condition, but the anti-manipulation does.*

Proof. The majority judgment method was introduced by Balinski and Laraki, 2010, [1]. In this method, voters grade candidates as Excellent, Very Good, Good, Acceptable, Poor, or Reject, perhaps with ties. The candidate with the highest median wins the vote. We consider a case with 2 candidates, A, B, and 10 voters. Table 7 presents the voters' preferences.

Table 7. Majority judgment.

A	B	Number of voters from V'	A	B	Number of voters from V''
Excellent	Good	3	Good	Poor	3
Poor	Good	2	Poor	Good	2

For the majority judgment method, A is the winner over both V' and V'', while B is the winner for the whole set V. Thus, this profile is a counterexample for the majority judgment method fulfilling the consistency condition.

In order to use the anti-manipulation method, we label "Poor" as 1, "Good" as 2, and "Excellent" as 3 and deal with ranking instead of the Borda Count. The method gives A and B as winners for the whole set V, and A as the winner for both sets V' and V'. Thus, the methods are not equivalent. □

Proposition 5. *There exist profiles, for which the minimax method does not satisfy the consistency condition, but the anti-manipulation does.*

Proof. In the minimax method, pairwise scores score(y, x) of x against y are computed. The winner is given by the following formula, [9],

$$\arg\min_{x}\left(\max_{y} \text{score}(y, x)\right).$$

We consider the case with 4 candidates, A, B, C, D and 43 voters. Table 8 presents voters' preferences.

Table 8. Minimax voting method.

Preferences of voters from V'	Number of voters from V'	Preferences of voters from V''	Number of voters from V''
$A > B > C > D$	1	$A > B > D > C$	8
$A > D > B > C$	6	$A > D > C > B$	2
$B > C > D > A$	5	$C > B > D > A$	9
$C > D > B > A$	6	$D > C > B > A$	6

For the minimax method, A is the winner over both sets V' and V'', while C is the winner over the whole set V. Thus, this profile is a counterexample for the minimax method satisfying the consistency condition. The anti-manipulation method gives D as the winner for V' and C as the winner over the set V''. Thus, the premise of the implication is false, and consequently, the implication is true. Concluding, this profile cannot be a counterexample for the anti-manipulation method satisfying the consistency condition.   □

Proposition 6. *There exist profiles, for which the ranked pair method does not satisfy the consistency condition, but the anti-manipulation does.*

Proof. The ranked pair voting is a very complicated method which was introduced by Tideman, [20]. In this method, an acyclic graph with one source is constructed based on a pairwise comparison of candidates. The source is a winner. We consider a case with 3 candidates A, B, C, and 39 voters. Table 9 shows voters' preferences.

Table 9. Ranked pair method.

Preferences of voters from V'	Number of voters from V'	Preferences of voters from V''	Number of voters from V''
$A > B > C$	7	$A > C > B$	9
$B > C > A$	6	$B > A > C$	8
$C > A > B$	3	$C > B > A$	6

For the ranked pair method, A is the winner for both sets V' and V'', while B is the winner for the whole set V. Thus, this profile is a counterexample for the ranked pair method satisfying the consistency condition.

The anti-manipulation method gives B as the winner for the set V', and A for the set V''. Thus, the premise of the implication is false, and the implication is true. Consequently, this profile cannot be a counterexample for the anti-manipulation method fulfilling the consistency condition. □

Proposition 7. *There exist profiles, for which the Schulze method does not satisfy the consistency condition, but the anti-manipulation does.*

Proof. The Schulze method, [18], is very complicated. The method uses pairwise comparisons, builds a graph, and solves the widest path problem. We consider a case with 3 candidates A, B, C and 39 voters. Table 10 presents the voters' preferences.

Table 10. Schulze method.

Preferences of voters from V'	Number of voters from V'	Preferences of voters from V''	Number of voters from V''
$A > B > C$	7	$A > C > B$	9
$B > C > A$	6	$B > A > C$	8
$C > A > B$	3	$C > B > A$	6

In the Schulze method, A is the winner for both sets V' and V'', while B is the winner for the whole set V. Thus, this profile is a counterexample for the Schulze method satisfying the consistency condition. In the case of the anti-manipulation method, voters' preferences are the same as in the ranked pair method, so reasoning from the proof of Proposition 6 completes the proof. □

The following proposition investigates the Litvak method. This method was proposed by Litvak, [10], and analyzed by Bury and Wagner, [2], and Nurmi, [15]. Let k be a number of ordered alternatives. Each voter has his preference ranking. Generally, ties are allowed, but in this paper, we restrict our considerations to cases where preference rankings have no ties. This assumption is justified by the fact that we want to compare the Litvak method and anti-manipulation method, and the latter one is based on the Borda Count, where ties are not allowed. Each preference ranking P assigns a preference vector with k components. The component i of the preference vector indicates how many alternatives are placed ahead of the i-th one in ranking under consideration. Each such vector consists of numbers $0, 1, \ldots, k-1$. Litvak rule looks for the k-component vector V that is closest to the observed preferences in the sense that the sum of component-wise absolute differences between the reported preference vectors and V is minimal. The Litvak method is intended for expert group decision making, [15]. The following example presents the method.

Example 3. This example is taken from [15]. Let us consider 3 alternatives A, B, C and 5 persons where 3 of them have preference $A > B > C$ and 2 have preference $B > C > A$. The Litvak sums for all six rankings are: $A > B > C : 8$, $A > C > B : 14$, $B > A > C : 10$, $B > C > A : 12$, $C > A > B : 20$, $C > B > A : 16$. So, the Litvak ranking is $A > B > C$.   □

Proposition 8. *The Litvak method is not equivalent to anti-manipulation method.*

Proof. Let us consider the example from Table II, [15], presented here in Table 11. It was demonstrated, using this example, that the Condorcet winner is not the Litvak winner. Moreover, we show that the Litvak winner is not a winner determined by the anti-manipulation method.

Table 11. The Condorcet winner, the Litvak Winner and the anti-manipulation winner do not coincide Source: [15].

Preferences	Number of voters
$A > B > C$	4
$B > C > A$	3
$C > A > B$	2

In this example, C is the Condorcet winner, $A > B > C$ is the Litvak ranking, and $B > A > C$ is the anti-manipulation ranking. If we also deal with ties and ranking with ties is the Litvak winner, then it cannot be an anti-manipulation ranking because the last one has no ties.   □

5   Conclusions

We show, Sect. 3, that the anti-manipulation method is not equivalent to any scoring method. In Sect. 4, we show that this method is not equivalent to any from a group of the various methods. So, it may suggest that this method has its specific properties, which are not used for characterization of known up to now methods.

There are some further interesting questions regarding the anti-manipulation algorithms. The proposed and studied algorithm removes jurors. The alternative to that is eliminating scores, not jurors. It is not immediately clear which one of these fundamental principles is better in some given sense.

Once this fundamental principle is fixed, many algorithms can be used to decide which jurors or scores should be removed. In the current paper, we analyzed the particular algorithm that uses the 20% threshold. This decision was informed by the results of experiments, as mentioned in the text. There are, however, other possibilities. First, we can use a different weighting scheme. Secondly, jurors or scores can be classified as outliers and then removed.

This approach requires a strict definition of an outlier, which leads to many possibilities. Another possibility still is classifying a juror or a score as an influential observation, with the meaning of influential observation in econometrics. Perhaps such influence means manipulation. Thus, such observation should be carefully considered.

Still, another question concerns consistency between different voting methods. It is well known that different voting methods lead to different results. Perhaps an algorithm that removes either jurors or scores could eliminate this disparity, at least for a specific subset of voting methods. We leave these issues for future research.

A   Algorithm Description

As was mentioned in the main text, the set of alternatives is denoted by A, V is a finite subset of a set of voters N. Any function from V into a set of linear orders on A is a profile, denoted by w. Any function f assigning to a profile w a nonempty subset of A is called a social choice function. The task of the algorithm is to check if for a given profile w the choice function described in the paper (with variants) is consistent. Consistency is defined as the following condition

$$f(w') \cap f(w'') \neq \emptyset \Rightarrow f(w') \cap f(w'') = f((w', w'')), \tag{2}$$

where (w', w'') is a concatenation of profiles leading to a new joint profile. In practice, the data contain a single profile (w', w'') and the algorithm checks consistency condition (2) for all possible bi-partitions.

The main algorithm, Algorithm 1, is relatively simple. First, it reads the data that contain a single profile (w', w''). Then, it computes the winner for the whole profile. Finally, the consistency condition is checked for all possible bi-partitions. There are two elements of the algorithm that require further explanation. One of these elements is the procedure used to calculate a winner for a given profile w, that is an algorithm used for the social choice function f. The other is a way to efficiently create all possible bi-partitions.

Data: a single profile (w', w'')
Result: reports with inconsistent examples
1 read in data;
2 compute winner for the whole profile (w', w''), add to the final report;
3 compute indices $i \in I$ for all bi-partitions;
4 **for** $i \in I$ **do**
5   create profiles w' and w'' based on an index i;
6   compute winners for both profiles w' and w'';
7   **if** $f(w') = f(w'') \neq f((w', w''))$ **then**
8   add example based on w' and w'' to the final report;
9   **end**
10 **end**
11 save reports;

Algorithm 1: Main algorithm

All bi-partitions are created using Algorithm 2. It takes a number of voters k. There are exactly $2^{k-1} - 1$ bi-partitions. First, the algorithm creates a list of integers from 1 to $2^{k-1} - 1$. Then, each integer is written to the binary and converted into a logical vector, that is used as an index.

Data: a number of voters
Result: a list of Boolean vectors
1 create a list I of integers from 1 through $2^{k-1} - 1$;
2 **for** $i \in I$ **do**
3 | write an integer i to the binary;
4 | cast into a logical vector;
5 **end**

Algorithm 2: Generating all bi-partitions

The last element of the main algorithm that requires an explanation is a procedure calculating a winner for a given profile w. This procedure depends on a metric and a type of algorithm used to trim the set of voters. There are two types of metric considered: the standard Euclidean metric and the Manhattan metric. The trimming algorithm has two variants. In all variants 20% of voters are assigned 0 weight. In one variant of the algorithm, only the whole part of $k/5$ is used while in the other also the fraction part is removed. Thus, there are four variants of the procedure used to calculate a winner. Algorithm 3 is used for the procedure calculating a winner.

Algorithm 3 is straightforward, however, one step requires an explanation. The whole algorithm is based around distance groups. If distances between all voters and a mean are all different, then distance groups are just numbers $1, 2, \ldots, k$. However, if some distances between a mean and some voters are equal, then all voters with equal distances are assigned the same distance group. As an example consider the following distances $5, 5, 4, 4, 1$. The distance groups for such a vector of distances are $1, 1, 2, 2, 3$.

Data: a profile w, metric $d(\cdot)$

Result: a list containing a profile w, original means, weighted means for both trimming variants, metric $d(\cdot)$, weights for both trimming variants, winners for both trimming variants

1 mean0 ← calculate standard means based on w;
2 dist1 ← calculate distances between voters and mean0 using the provided metric $d(\cdot)$ and a profile w;
3 M ← $\lfloor k/5 \rfloor$;
4 Mrest ← $k/5 - \lfloor k/5 \rfloor$;
5 sort1 ← sort dist1 in decreasing order and return an index;
6 sort1DG ← calculate distance groups based on sort1;
7 breakGroup ← sort1DG[M];
8 ws1 ← vector of weights 1 for voters;
9 indBreak ← sortDG == breakGroup;
10 indBefore ← sortDG < breakGroup;
11 indNext ← sortDG == breakGroup + 1;
12 Mbefore ← number of voters in group indBefore;
13 Mbreak ← number of voters in group indBreak;
14 Mnext ← number of voters in group indNext;
15 ws1 ← assign weight 0 for each voter in group indBefore;
16 ws1 ← assign weight 1 - (M - Mbefore) / Mbreak for each voter in group indBreak;
17 ws2 ← ws1;
18 ws2 ← assign weight 1 - Mrest / Mnext for each voter in group indNext;
19 mean1 ← calculate means with weights ws1;
20 mean2 ← calculate means with weights ws2;
21 winner1 ← index of a maximum mean1;
22 winner2 ← index of a maximum mean2;
23 return a list containing w, mean0, mean1, mean2, dist1, ws1, ws2, winner1, winner2;

Algorithm 3: Calculating a winner

References

1. Balinski, M., Laraki, R.: Majority Judgment: Measuring, Ranking, and Electing. MIT Press, Cambridge (2011)
2. Bury, H., Wagner, D.: Use of preference vectors in group judgement: the median of Litvak. In: Kacprzyk, J., Wagner, D. (eds.) Group Decisions and Voting, pp. 102–120. Exit, Warsaw (2003)
3. Fine, B., Fine, K.: Social choice and individual rankings ii. Rev. Econ. Stud. **41**(4), 459–475 (1974)
4. Fine, B., Fine, K.: Social choice and individual ranking i. Rev. Econ. Stud. **41**(3), 303–322 (1974)
5. Hołubiec, J., Mercik, J.W.: Inside voting procedures, vol. 2. Accedo Verlagsgesellschaft (1994)

6. Januszkiewicz, M., Chorościak, E.: Konkurs skrzypcowy im. Wieniawskiego w Poznaniu (Wieniawski Violin Competition in Poznań). Ruch Muzyczny, pp. 50–55 (2016)
7. Kemeny, J.G.: Mathematics without numbers. Daedalus 88(4), 577–591 (1959)
8. Kontek, K., Sosnowska, H.: Specific tastes or cliques of jurors? Available at SSRN 3297252 (2018)
9. Levin, J., Nalebuff, B.: An introduction to vote-counting schemes. J. Econ. Perspect. 9(1), 3–26 (1995)
10. Litvak, B.G.: Information Given by Experts. Methods of Acquisition and Analysis. Radio and Communication, Moscow, Russian (1982)
11. Merlin, V.: The axiomatic characterizations of majority voting and scoring rules. Mathématiques et sciences humaines 163 (2003). https://doi.org/10.4000/msh.2919, http://journals.openedition.org/msh/2919
12. Moulin, H.: Axioms of Cooperative Decision Making. Econometric Society Monographs, Cambridge University Press (1988). https://doi.org/10.1017/CCOL0521360552, https://www.cambridge.org/core/books/axioms-of-cooperative-decision-making/481FCBCDD15F3CCEE2FE381E7BF17B3D
13. Myerson, R.B.: Axiomatic derivation of scoring rules without the ordering assumption. Soc. Choice Welfare 12(1), 59–74 (1995). https://doi.org/10.1007/BF00182193
14. Nurmi, H.: Comparing Voting Systems. Theory and Decision Library A. Springer, Dordrecht (1987). https://doi.org/10.1007/978-94-009-3985-1. https://books.google.pl/books?id=qA-CAAAAMAAJ
15. Nurmi, H.: A comparison of some distance-based choice rules in ranking environments. Theor. Decis. 57, 5–24 (2004). https://doi.org/10.1007/s11238-004-3671-9
16. Pomerol, J.C., Barba-Romero, S.: Multicriterion Decision in Management: Principles and Practice, vol. 25. Springer, Heidelberg (2012)
17. Robert, H.: Robert's Rules of Order Newly Revised, 11th edn. Da Capo Press, Cambridge (2011)
18. Schulze, M.: A new monotonic, clone-independent, reversal symmetric, and condorcet-consistent single-winner election method. Soc. Choice Welfare 36(2), 267–303 (2011). https://doi.org/10.1007/s00355-010-0475-4
19. Smith, J.H.: Aggregation of preferences with variable electorate. Econometrica: J. Econom. Soc. 41, 1027–1041 (1973)
20. Tideman, T.N.: Independence of clones as a criterion for voting rules. Soc. Choice Welfare 4(3), 185–206 (1987). https://doi.org/10.1007/BF00433944
21. Woodall, D.: Properties of preferential election rules. Voting Matters 3, 8–15 (1994)
22. Young, H.P.: An axiomatization of Borda's rule. J. Econ. Theory 9(1), 43–52 (1974)
23. Young, H.P.: Social choice scoring functions. SIAM J. Appl. Math. 28(4), 824–838 (1975)

Pairwise Voting Rules in Restricted Domains: The Disappearance and Persistence of Some Monotonicity Paradoxes

Hannu Nurmi$^{(\boxtimes)}$

Department of Contemporary History, Philosophy and Political Science,
University of Turku, Turku, Finland
hnurmi@utu.fi

Abstract. The property of participation is satisfied by a voting rule if under no circumstances it is to the benefit of a voter to abstain rather than vote according to his/her preferences. By Moulin's result of 1988 all voting rules that always elect a Condorcet winner when one exists fail on the property of participation [16]. Focusing on preference profiles that are restricted to those having a Condorcet winner we ask whether Moulin's result holds under these preference profiles. It turns out that while some types of monotonicity paradoxes vanish in the Condorcet domains, others persist.

1 Introduction

The incompatibility of the Condorcet winner criterion and the condition known as participation is certainly an important finding [16]. The latter condition has an interesting historical background. In the context of discussing the single transferable vote system in single- member constituencies in early 20'th century Ireland, James Creed Meredith [14, p. 93] made the following puzzling observation:

> Suppose that D (Nationalist), M (Ind. Unionists) and Z (Unionist) are three continuing candidates and that one seat remains to be filled. The quota is, say, 800 and D has 410 votes, M 400 and Z 500. Then M is eliminated and his votes may be supposed to be transferred to Z, who is declared elected. But if D were eliminated before M, we may easily suppose that his votes would go to M, who would be elected. The injustice of the result appears even more striking when we reflect that if D had 11 votes less, his supporters would have succeeded in returning M instead of Z, as they desired to.

H. Nurmi—The author is indebted to the late Dan S. Felsenthal for numerous conversations in which the problems touched upon in this article were discussed. Those conversations culminated in the joint monograph [5] which this article largely draws upon. The constructive comments of the referees on an earlier version are gratefully acknowledged.

© Springer-Verlag GmbH Germany, part of Springer Nature 2020
N. T. Nguyen et al. (Eds.): TCCI XXXV, LNCS 12330, pp. 38–51, 2020.
https://doi.org/10.1007/978-3-662-62245-2_3

In the case of multi-member constituencies Meredith [14, p. 93, fn] quotes The Report of the Royal Commission:

> ... the representation of a party might be so much at the mercy of the order of elimination, that while it would only obtain one seat with 19,000 votes of its own, it would obtain two with 18,000, because in the latter case the order of elimination would be reversed.

It took a while – about 70 years – before these observations became a subject of systematic study [6]. Fishburn and Brams introduced the important distinction between the no-show paradox and the more-is-less paradox. The former coincides with the one referred to by Meredith in his first quote above, while the latter occurs whenever a procedure that in a given profile of preference rankings ends up in alternative x being chosen, results in y when a group voters each ranking x first joins the electorate, *ceteris paribus*. Both the no-show and more-is-less paradoxes exhibit failures of participation, *i.e.* a property that characterizes procedures where abstaining, *ceteris paribus*, never yields a unanimous voter group an outcome that it prefers to the one ensuing from its voting according to its preferences [16]. Participation so defined is clearly a desirable property of voting rules. Indeed, failure on participation casts a shadow over the whole idea of voting: why vote if you can reach a better outcome by abstaining? Worse still, why encourage people to exercise their right to express their views about candidates or policies if it is known that sometimes doing so may harm the voter?

Another widely supported desideratum of voting rules is Condorcet consistency, *i.e.* the requirement that whenever a Condorcet winner[1] exists in a voter preference profile, it must be elected. To those subscribing to the plausibility of Condorcet consistency, Moulin's [16] incompatibility theorem must have been a piece of bad news. According to the theorem no Condorcet consistent voting rule can guarantee the condition of participation when four or more candidates are competing. The theorem has subsequently been refined by Pérez [20,21].

The proof of the theorem is basically constructive, but the device whereby the examples demonstrating the emergence of the no show paradox involve highly specific constellations of preferences. This naturally raises the question of empirical relevance of the theorem itself. This is the main subject of this article. Moulin's result is of general nature and, consequently, makes no assumptions regarding the preference profiles. The applications, on the other hand, may be intended for rather specific types of profiles. Of particular interest to this article are those where a Condorcet winner exists.

The article is organized as follows. Since the Condorcet consistency is the primary virtue of voting rules based on pairwise comparison of candidates, we start with a discussion of these rules. We then restate the main definitions and results pertaining to participation whereupon we move on to the possible profile restrictions and their impact on the incidence of participation paradoxes.

---

[1] A Condorcet winner is a candidate that would defeat all others in pairwise majority votes.

2 Some Virtues and Vices of Binary Rules

The voting rules are customarily divided into pairwise (or binary), positional and hybrid classes (see e.g. [18]). The first class consists of procedures that subject the candidates or other decision alternatives to pairwise comparisons and determine the overall winners on the basis of these. Usually the pairwise winners are determined on the basis of the simple majority principle. The second class includes voting rules that determine the winners on the basis of their position in the individual preference rankings that the voters report when submitting their ballots. The hybrid procedures, in turn, are combinations or repetitions of pairwise and positional rules.[2] Since the Condorcet consistency is most obviously related to the pairwise rules, we shall mainly focus on them in this article.

The main virtues of the binary rules are:

1. Simplicity for voters: these rules call for simple comparisons. Comparing two candidates at a time is certainly easier than ranking or grading them.
2. They are intended to elect 'obvious' winners: Condorcet winners. Given an exhaustive set of pairwise comparisons, it seems natural to elect the candidate that beats each one of the others.
3. When a Condorcet winner exists, it is the winner in all subsets of alternatives as well. Since the Condorcet winner is determined by performing all pairwise comparisons, it remains the Condorcet winner also in every subset of candidates.

Some main flaws of binary rules are:

1. The Condorcet winner may not be first ranked by any voter, *i.e.* it is possible that no one gets his/her top candidate elected. See Table 1.
2. There are Condorcet extensions that may elect a Condorcet loser, *i.e.* despite the emphasis on pairwise comparisons, the candidate that is defeated by all others may be elected. See Table 2 and Table 3.
3. Some extensions may even elect an absolute loser, *i.e.* even the candidate that is ranked last by an absolute majority of voters may be elected. See Table 2 and Table 3.
4. They may behave strangely under adding or removing of Condorcet components. This is shown in Table 4.

In Table 1 candidate C is the Condorcet winner, but none of the three voters ranks it first. This can be seen as an instance of thwarted-majorities paradox discussed by Fishburn and Brams [6]. The paradox occurs when a candidate who could win every other candidate in pairwise votes does not win the election.

Table 2 focuses on Dodgson's method, a Condorcet consistent rule that elects a Condorcet winner whenever one exists (thereby guaranteeing Condorcet consistency). When the profile under study does not contain a Condorcet winner,

---

[2] This division is not a partition as some rules, notably the Borda count, can be implemented in both binary and positional manner. Moreover, there are voting rules that are based on neither binary nor positional principles, *e.g.* a randomized dictatorship.

Table 1. Condorcet winner C has the smallest number of first ranks

1 voter	1 voter	1 voter
A	B	D
C	C	C
B	A	B
D	D	A

Table 2. Dodgson's method results in the absolute loser D

10 voters	7 voters	1 voter	7 voters	4 voters
D	B	B	C	D
A	C	A	A	C
B	A	C	B	A
C	D	D	D	B

Dodgson's method elects the candidate(s) that is (are) closest to being a Condorcet winner. The closeness is measured in terms of the minimum number of binary preference reversals required to make a given candidate the Condorcet winner.[3] In Table 2 D is the absolute loser, but is elected by Dodgson's method as it requires a smaller number of binary preference reversals than any other candidate to become the Condorcet winner.

Another Condorcet consistent rule, the minimax method, can also result in a Condorcet loser, even in an absolute loser candidate. This method elects a candidate whose maximum opposition in all pairwise contests is the smallest [12]. Table 3 provides an example of the said possibility, *viz.* that the absolute (and *a fortiori* a Condorcet) loser is elected. D, the absolute loser, is the minimax choice in the example.

Table 3. Minimax method elects the absolute loser D

2 voters	3 voters	3 voters	1 voter	2 voters
D	D	C	B	A
A	B	B	A	C
C	A	A	C	B
B	C	D	D	D

---

[3] Dodgson's method is discussed in some detail e.g. in [19]. Due to its computational properties, this method has been of particular interest among the computational social choice scholars. See e.g. [3].

Table 4. A profile with a strong Condorcet winner (l) and a Condorcet component (r)

4 voters	3 voters		2 voters	2 voters	2 voters
A	B		A	B	C
B	C	+	C	A	B
C	A		B	C	A

One advantage of the Condorcet consistent rules is that when a Condorcet winner exists, it remains the Condorcet winner also in all subsets of candidates. However, the Condorcet winner is not robust under additions or removals of sets of voters whose preferences constitute a perfect tie as Table 4 illustrates. The two left columns represent a 7-voter profile over candidates A, B and C where A is the strong Condorcet winner, *i.e.* a candidate ranked first by more than half of the electorate. The profile to the right of the '+' sign constitutes a Condorcet paradox profile with the defining property that every candidate is ranked first, second and third by equally many voters. Should pairwise comparisons be conducted in the latter profile, each candidate would defeat one of the other candidates by a 4 to 2 margin and lose to one of the others by a 2 to 4 margin. So, the latter profile represents a perfect tie.

Now, combine the two profiles to get a 13-voter one. In this combined profile B is the Condorcet winner. Thus, adding a perfect tie profile to one with a Condorcet winner disposes the latter and replaces it with another candidate. It is worth noticing that the Borda count winner remains the same, *viz.* B, in both the original and combined profiles.[4]

In sum, Condorcet consistent voting rules have both virtues and drawbacks. Of the latter a particularly significant one pertains to the very rationale of voting, viz. participation. Its incompatibility with Condorcet consistency will be discussed in the following.

3   Condorcet vs. Participation

In his important article Moulin defines participation as a condition requiring that 'the voter never loses by joining the electorate and reporting (sincerely) his preferences' [16]. This definition encompasses a variety of forms of 'losing'. When such a loss occurs or could occur, it is customary to say that a participation paradox has or could have occurred. In their path-breaking article Fishburn and Brams distinguish two such paradoxes, *viz.* the more-is-less paradox and the no show paradox [6]. Strictly speaking, only the latter is a participation paradox since the former, as defined by Fishburn and Brams, is a fixed electorate paradox,

---

[4] This is not an accident, but happens every time a Condorcet paradox profile is added to another profile. This is because the Borda scores of each candidate in a Condorcet paradox profile are equal and, thus, the Borda score of each candidate in the original profile is added by the same number keeping the score differences unchanged.

while participation paradoxes, *sensu stricto*, pertain to variable electorates. It is, however, not difficult to modify Fishburn and Brams's definition of the more-is-less paradox so that it becomes a variable electorate paradox at least in spirit. This is done in the following definition adapted from [21].

Definition 1. *Positive strong no-show paradox occurs when a group of like-minded voters get their first-ranked alternative elected when abstaining, ceteris paribus, while if they voted according to their preferences, something else would win.*

This paradox is also known as upward monotonicity failure in variable electorates [15]. Procedures avoiding this type of paradox are also called procedures that satisfy the top property [10].

The no show paradox of Fishburn and Brams can be defined as follows.

Definition 2. *Negative strong no show paradox occurs when an alternative, say A, wins in a profile, but, when a group of like-minded voters ranking B last in their preferences joins the electorate, B wins.*

This paradox belongs to class of downward monotonicity failures in variable electorates [15]. Procedures that avoid this type of paradox are also called procedures that satisfy the bottom property [10].

The main result connecting Condorcet consistency and participation is due to Moulin and states the following.

Theorem 1. *If there are more than three candidates and at least 25 voters, no voting rule satisfies both the Condorcet consistency and the participation condition [16].*

The lower bound of the number of voters has subsequently been reduced to 12 by Brandt, Geist and Peters [2]. A somewhat more nuanced picture of the vulnerability of Condorcet consistent voting rules to various types of participation paradoxes is given by the following result of Pérez.[5]

Theorem 2. *All commonly known Condorcet extensions are vulnerable to positive strong and negative no-show paradoxes, except for two extensions, namely the minimax rule and Young's rule [21].*

Young's rule tallies, for each candidate, the minimum number of voter removals that are needed to make this candidate the Condorcet winner. The candidate associated with the smallest number of such removals is the winner [23].

---

[5] Duddy has generalized the incompatibility to profiles where the preference rankings are weak instead of strict [4]. Other variations of the incompatibility are discussed in [17].

4 Profile Restrictions

Moulin's and Pérez's theorems are of general nature; i.e. they say that *if no restrictions are made* and Condorcet extensions are resorted to, then *some profiles* will be found where some like-minded voters are better off abstaining. As such they say nothing about the kinds of profiles that are susceptible to the participation paradoxes. This raises the questions: what if it is known that the profiles always satisfy some general restrictions? Is it possible that the participation failures are encountered under those restrictions?

Some profile restrictions have played an important role in the history of voting theory. To wit, single-peakedness of preferences was a concept invented and utilized by Black in the analysis of the cyclic majorities [1]. Black discovered that the culprit of cyclic majorities is a profound disagreement in the voting body regarding candidates: each alternative is ranked last by at least one voter. If in all triplets of candidates one could find one candidate who is not ranked last by any voter, then the pairwise majority voting would produce a complete and transitive collective ranking of candidates. In other words, this minimal consensus would be a sufficient condition for the avoidance of the majority cycles.

Now, single-peakedness implies that there is a nonempty core in the profile, *i.e.* a set of majority non-dominated candidates. When this set is a singleton, we have a profile with a Condorcet winner. How common are such profiles? This depends on the way the profiles emerge in the situations one wants to study. Overall, however, there is a widespread contention that the probability of a Condorcet paradox is quite small in 'random' environments [7, p. 21] and empirically based simulations. Furthermore, it has been shown that both the homogeneity of voter preferences and interdependence of opinions reduce the probability of encountering a Condorcet paradox profile [8, p. 55]. Hence, it makes sense to have a look at the relevance of the participation paradox results in the profile domain characterized by the presence of a Condorcet winner at the outset. The profiles that have a Condorcet winner constitute the Condorcet domain.

A couple of observations about Condorcet consistent rules summarize our findings:

- In an original profile where a Condorcet winner exists, all Condorcet extensions - by definition - end up with the same winner. Adding its support, *ceteris paribus*, retains its status as the Condorcet winner. Hence, these systems are invulnerable to the more-is-less paradoxes in variable electorates.
- If the original profile *does not* contain a Condorcet winner, there are Condorcet extensions that are vulnerable to the more-is-less paradoxes (see Table 5, and Table 6).
- In unrestricted domains nearly all Condorcet extensions are vulnerable to the no show paradox (see Table 9).
- In Condorcet domains some vulnerable Condorcet extensions that are vulnerable to the no show paradox turn out to be invulnerable, but some don't (see Table 10).

Table 5. Strong no show and amendment

2 voters	3 voters	2 voters	2 voters
A	B	C	C
B	C	A	B
C	A	B	A

5   Condorcet Consistency in Unrestricted Domains

The strong positive involvement paradox occurs when a group of unanimous voters ranking x in their top position makes y the winner even though without their presence x would have won. This is the positive involvement paradox of Pérez [21, p. 605–606]. Three examples of Condorcet consistent procedures that are vulnerable to this paradox are the amendment procedure, Copeland's method and Black's method. The first one is based on pairwise comparisons of candidates according to a predetermined agenda so that out of k candidates $k-1$ pairwise comparisons are conducted. The loser of each comparison is eliminated whereas the winner takes on the next candidate in the agenda. The winner of the $k-1$'th comparison is the overall winner. Suppose that in Table 5 profile the agenda is: (i) A vs. B, (ii) the winner vs. C. This yields B as the winner. If the rightmost two voters abstain, the winner is C, their first ranked candidate.

A similar paradox can occur when Copeland's procedure is in use. We recall that this procedure counts the number of victories in pairwise comparisons and declares the candidate with the largest number of victories the Copeland winner. An instance of the paradox can be seen in Table 6.

Table 6. Strong no show and Copeland

2 voters	1 voter	1 voter
E	C	D
D	B	C
A	A	B
B	E	A
C	D	E

The corresponding pairwise comparison matrix is in Table 7. The latter shows that candidate D beats three other candidates, more than any other candidate, thus becoming the Copeland winner. Suppose now that this electorate is augmented with one voter whose preference ranking is: $D \succ E \succ A \succ B \succ C$. In this augmented profile, E is the Condorcet and thus Copeland winner. So, with the additional voter absent, his/her most preferred D wins, but if he/she joins the electorate, E wins.

Table 7. Pairwise comparison matrix of Table 6

	A	B	C	D	E
A	–	2	2	1	2
B	2	–	2	1	2
C	2	2	–	1	2
D	3	3	3	–	1
E	2	2	2	3	–

Black's method is a hybrid one, but at the same time a Condorcet consistent one. It elects a Condorcet winner when one exists. Otherwise it elects the Borda winner. Table 8 demonstrates that Black's method is vulnerable to the strong positive no show paradox. Since there is no Condorcet winner, the Borda winner

Table 8. Strong positive no show paradox in Black's method

3 voters	3 voters	4 voters	3 voters	1 voter
D	E	C	D	E
E	A	D	E	B
A	C	E	B	A
B	B	A	C	D
C	D	B	A	C

E is elected. Suppose that two voters with the $E \succ B \succ A \succ D \succ C$ ranking join the electorate. In the new profile, D emerges as the Condorcet – and hence Black – winner. Thus with the two last mentioned voters absent, their favourite candidate wins, but if they vote according to their preferences, another, by them less preferred, candidate wins.

Bucklin's method is not a Condorcet extension. It elects an absolute winner if one exists. Otherwise, for each candidate the number of voters ranking it first or second are summed. If there now is a candidate with a sum larger than 50% of the electorate, it is declared the winner. Otherwise, one continues by including the third ranks etc. until a winner is found [9,22]. Should at any stage more than one candidate become the winner in the above sense, the tie is broken by electing the candidate with the largest sum.

Table 9 summarizes the performance of a set of voting procedures to strong positive and negative involvement paradoxes under unrestricted domains (see [5] for further examples and proofs).

Table 9. Summary of vulnerability of some systems to strong no show paradoxes under unrestricted domains

Method	Vulnerable to strong positive involvement paradox	Vulnerable to strong negative Involvement paradox
Successive elimination	Yes	Yes
Bucklin	No	Yes
Majority judgment	No	Yes
Minimax	No	No
Black	Yes	Yes
Copeland	Yes	Yes
Kemeny	Yes	Yes
Schwartz	Yes	Yes
Young	Yes	No

6 Ten Condorcet Extensions and Participation Failures in Condorcet Domain

Keeping in mind (i) the incompatibility results of Moulin and Pérez cited above and (ii) the assumption stemming from probabilistic and simulation studies of Gehrlein and Lepelley also cited above according to which profiles with a Condorcet winner are more common than those without it, we now take a look at what happens to the incompatibility between Condorcet consistency and participation in the Condorcet domain. Table 10 lists the performance of ten Condorcet consistent rules in the Condorcet domain. We recall that Nanson's method resorts to elimination of candidates on the basis of their Borda scores so that on each round all those candidates with at most the average Borda score are eliminated and Borda scores are computed for the remaining candidates until the winner is found. Baldwin's method is similar to Nanson's but eliminates on each round only the candidates with the smallest Borda score. Schwartz's method determines the smallest set of candidates such that every candidate in the set is unbeaten by any candidate outside the set. The first thing to observe is that the vulnerability to the more-is-less paradox is avoided by all ten procedures. This obviously follows from the observation that Condorcet winner x remains the Condorcet winner if a set of unanimous voters all ranking x first enters the fray, *ceteris paribus*. To wit, x defeats all the candidates it defeats in the original profile, *i.e.* it defeats all others. It is, therefore the Condorcet winner also in the expanded electorate. Since all Condorcet consistent rules, by definition, elect the Condorcet winner, x must be elected in the expanded electorate as well. So, if we can rest assured that the profiles we will be confronted with are in the Condorcet domain, the Condorcet consistent systems can be adopted without fear of encountering the more-is-less paradox in expanding electorates.

Table 10. Ten Condorcet extensions in Condorcet domains

Procedure	Vulnerable to strong negative involvement paradox	Vulnerable to strong positive involvement paradox
Amendment	Yes	No
minimax	No	No
Dodgson	Yes	No
Nanson	Yes	No
Baldwin	Yes	No
Copeland	Yes	No
Black	Yes	No
Kemeny	Yes	No
Schwartz	Yes	No
Young	No	No

With respect to the no show paradox as defined by Fishburn and Brams, *i.e.* the failure to satisfy the strong negative involvement condition, the picture is completely different. Consistent with the result of Pérez, only minimax and Young's rules are invulnerable to this types of paradox. A couple of examples illustrate how the incompatibility between Condorcet consistency and the bottom property is established. Firstly, we consider the case of Kemeny's method in the Condorcet domain (the example is from [5, p. 30]). It will be recalled that, given a preference profile, this rule determines the ranking that is closest to the profile in the sense of requiring the smallest number of binary switches between adjacent candidates in the voters' rankings to become universally adopted [11]. The winner is the candidate ranked first in the closest ranking. The Condorcet consistency of Kemeny's rule was shown by Levenglick [13]. In Table 11 A is the strong Condorcet winner and is thus elected under Kemeny's rule. Now suppose that, *ceteris paribus*, four additional voters whose preference ordering is $B \succ C \succ A \succ D$ join the electorate. The ensuing Kemeny ranking is now: $D \succ B \succ C \succ A$. Hence the lowest ranked candidate of those 4 voters becomes the winner. In other words, the bottom property is not satisfied by Kemeny's rule.

Table 11. Kemeny fails on the bottom property in Condorcet domain

5 voters	3 voters	3 voters
D	A	A
B	D	D
C	C	B
A	B	C

Table 12. Copeland and the bottom property

5 voters	4 voters
B	C
C	D
D	A
A	B

Table 10 shows that vulnerabilities of Condorcet consistent rules to the no show paradox in the sense of Fishburn and Brams persist in the Condorcet domain. So, participation failure is, indeed, an essential characteristic of those procedures. The more-is-less paradox, on the other hand, is excluded in this domain.

What about even more 'stable' profiles than those containing a Condorcet winner? Can one expect the vulnerabilities to no show paradoxes to vanish completely in Condorcet consistent rules? Not necessarily. To wit, Kemeny's rule exhibits vulnerability to the strong negative involvement even in a profile where a strong Condorcet winner (or an absolute winner) exists as shown in Table 11. A similar example involving Copeland's method is presented in Table 12 where a strong Condorcet winner (B) exists in the original profile of nine voters. B, thus, wins.

Suppose now that three voters with ranking $A \succ D \succ B \succ C$ join in. Now both C and D become Copeland winners. Thus, the worst-ranked C of the entrants is now included in the choice set showing the vulnerability of Copeland to the strong negative involvement paradox, albeit in a somewhat milder form.

The work on other Condorcet consistent voting rules and their vulnerability to the strong negative involvement paradox is yet to be completed, but it seems that Condorcet's intuition of winning has a profound incompatibility with the participation.

7 Concluding Comments

In the age-old contest between rules that emphasize pairwise comparisons and those that take a more holistic view over the voter preferences, Condorcet consistent methods seem to attract a larger following. Hence the results demonstrating the incompatibility between the Condorcet consistency and some other desiderata gain additional dramatic value just because of the often felt plausibility of the former property. Our focus has been on one such result: the incompatibility of Condorcet consistency and participation. The result has been discussed above from a somewhat nuanced perspective by distinguishing upward and downward monotonicity in variable electorates. Particular attention has been paid to profiles where a Condorcet winner exists, *i.e.* to the Condorcet domain. Unsurprisingly, the upward monotonicity failures of Condorcet consistent voting rules vanish in this domain. However, the downward monotonicity failures are unaffected by the restriction of the domain. We have seen that two intuitively plausible Condorcet consistent rules (Kemeny and Copeland) exhibit vulnerability to the strong negative involvement paradox even under the stronger restriction that there exists a strong Condorcet winner in the original profile. This suggest that the incompatibility between Condorcet consistency and participation is quite fundamental.

References

1. Black, D.: The Theory of Committees and Elections. Cambridge University Press, Cambridge (1958)
2. Brandt, F., Geist, C., Peters, D.: Optimal bounds for the no show paradox via SAT solving. Math. Soc. Sci. **90**, 18–27 (2017)
3. Caragiannis, I., Hemaspaandra, E., Hemaspaandra, L.: Dodgson's rule and Young's rule. In: Brandt, F., Conitzer, V., Endriss, U., Lang, J., Procaccia, A. (eds.) Handbook of Computational Social Choice, pp. 103–126. Cambridge University Press, New York (2016)
4. Duddy, C.: Condorcet's principle and the strong no show paradoxes. Theor. Decis. **77**, 275–285 (2014)
5. Felsenthal, D.S., Nurmi, H.: Voting Procedures Under a Restricted Domain. An Examination of the (In)Vulnerability of 20 Voting Procedures to Five Main Paradoxes. SE. Springer, Cham (2019). https://doi.org/10.1007/978-3-030-12627-8
6. Fishburn, P.C., Brams, S.J.: Paradoxes of preferential voting. Math. Mag. **56**, 207–214 (1983)
7. Gehrlein, W.V., Lepelley, D.: Voting Paradoxes and Group Coherence. The Condorcet Efficiency of Voting Rules. Springer, Heidelberg (2011). https://doi.org/10.1007/978-3-642-03107-6
8. Gehrlein, W.V., Lepelley, D.: Elections, Voting Rules and Paradoxical Outcomes. SCW. Springer, Cham (2017). https://doi.org/10.1007/978-3-319-64659-6
9. Hoag, C.G., Hallett, G.H.: Proportional Representation. The Macmillan Co., New York (1926)
10. Kasper, L., Peters, H., Vermeulen, D.: Condorcet consistency and the strong no show paradoxes. Math. Soc. Sci. **99**, 36–42 (2019)
11. Kemeny, J.: Mathematics without numbers. Daedalus **88**, 577–591 (1959)
12. Kramer, G.H.: A dynamical model of political equilibrium. J. Econ. Theory **16**, 310–333 (1977)
13. Levenglick, A.: Fair and reasonable election systems. Behav. Sci. **20**, 34–46 (1975)
14. Meredith, J.C.: Proportional Representation in Ireland. Edward Ponsonby Ltd., Dublin, Simpkin, Marshall, Hamilton, Kent, & Co, London (Reprint from the collections of the University of California Libraries) (1913)
15. Miller, N.R.: Closeness matters: monotonicity failure in IRV elections with three candidates. Public Choice **173**, 91–108 (2017)
16. Moulin, H.: Condorcet's principle implies the no-show paradox. J. Econ. Theory **45**, 53–64 (1988)
17. Núñez, M., Sanver, M.R.: Revisiting the connection between the no-show paradox and monotonicity. Math. Soc. Sci. **90**, 9–17 (2017)

18. Nurmi, H.: Voting procedures: a summary analysis. Br. J. Polit. Sci. **13**, 181–208 (1983)
19. Nurmi, H.: Reflections on two old condorcet extensions. Trans. Comput. Collective Intell. **XXXI**, 9–21 (2018)
20. Pérez, J.: Incidence of no-show paradoxes in Condorcet choice functions. Investigaciones Económicas **XIX**, 139–154 (1995)
21. Pérez, J.: The strong no show paradoxes are a common flaw in Condorcet voting correspondences. Soc. Choice Welfare **18**, 601–616 (2001)
22. Tideman, N.: Collective Decisions and Voting: The Potential for Public Choice. Ashgate, Aldershot (2006)
23. Young, H.P.: Extending Condorcet's rule. J. Econ. Theory **16**, 335–353 (1977)

Group Decision Making Based on Constructing a Short List

David M. Ramsey[✉]

Department of Operations Research, Wrocław University of Science and Technology,
Wrocław, Poland
david.ramsey@pwr.edu.pl

Abstract. This article considers several aspects of a multi-person household making an important consumer decision, e.g. buying a new flat. In such situations, normally several members of the household have input in the decision making process. Also, when there are a large number of offers, search can be facilitated via the use of the Internet. Basic information about offers, e.g. price, location, number of rooms and size, can be found on the Internet at very little cost. However, in order to make a final decision, members of the household should physically view a number of offers. The costs involved at this stage of the search process are much higher. In such scenarios, search based on the short list heuristic are efficient. Search via the Internet is used to find a relatively small number of promising offers from a large number of propositions. These promising offers are then more closely inspected, before a final decision is made. Results from simulations indicate that group decision procedures based on each decision maker ranking offers and the short list heuristic can be highly effective and robust.

1 Introduction

This paper considers procedures used by multiple decision makers to search for a valuable good using short lists of promising offers to be inspected more closely. For example, suppose a family is looking for a new flat in a large city. Thanks to the Internet, basic information on a large number of flats, e.g. price, floor space and location, can be found very quickly. Purchasing a flat just on the basis of information from the Internet would be highly risky (without physically viewing a flat, it is difficult to assess how appropriate an offer is). On the other hand, viewing all the flats that meet predetermined conditions based on size, price and location may well involve prohibitive search costs. For these reasons, a strategy based on the concept of a short list, i.e a relatively small number of promising offers that are inspected more closely before a purchasing decision is made, is a potentially useful heuristic in such scenarios. This article applies concepts of group decision making to heuristic search procedures based on a short list. To the author's knowledge, this is the first academic article to combine these two approaches.

© Springer-Verlag GmbH Germany, part of Springer Nature 2020
N. T. Nguyen et al. (Eds.): TCCI XXXV, LNCS 12330, pp. 52–75, 2020.
https://doi.org/10.1007/978-3-662-62245-2_4

Due to the cognitive limitations of decision makers (DMs), heuristics can be very useful tools. Successful heuristics are adapted to both the cognitive abilities of DMs and the form of the information gained during search (see Simon (1955; 1956), Todd and Gigerenzer (2000), as well Bobadilla-Suarez and Love (2018)). Short lists are practical when the costs of exhaustive search are excessive or the amount of information available exceeds the cognitive abilities of DMs (see Masatlioglu et al. (2012) and Lleras et al. (2017)). For example, someone wishing to go on holiday to a new destination can construct a short list of attractive propositions using information from friends and colleagues (see Bora and Kops (2019)). Short lists may also be practical when offers can be categorized (Armouti-Hansen and Kops (2018)). When searching for offers via the Internet, filters can be used to search a set of offers with multiple attributes by ordering offers according to the traits that are judged to be the most crucial in the decision process (see Rubenstein and Salant (2006) and Mandler et al. (2012)). Kimya (2018) presents a similar model where offers that are assessed the least positively based on a given trait are eliminated, in decreasing order of the importance of traits. Such a strategy can be interpreted as a procedure based on constructing short lists of ever decreasing dimensions until a final decision is made.

The model presented here differs from Kimya's (2018) model, since the search procedure is split into two stages of a clearly different nature. Kimya's model does not explicitly consider search costs and hence should be applied to search procedures where search costs are low, e.g. purely carried out using the Internet, or at least uniform. The model presented here assumes that the search costs involved in the first stage are low, but that search is costly in the second stage. Such a procedure is often applied by employers when searching for a specialist employee. The employer first invites written applications (often via the Internet). The costs of this invitation and appraising the written applications are assumed to be low. However, these written applications only give a rough estimate of the value of the applicants and hence the employer commonly then invites the most promising candidates for interview. The costs of these interviews are generally relatively high, since they involve using a panel of experts for a relatively long time and the travel costs of the interviewees are reimbursed. One important aspect of such problems is determining the appropriate size of the short list (the number of candidates to invite for interview) according to the structure of the information gained at each stage of the search process and the search costs. Ramsey (2019) was the first to propose such a model of an individual DM searching for a valuable resource using a short list. Analytis (2014) presents a similar model with two rounds of inspection which involves what might be called prioritising, rather than constructing a short list. In the first round (parallel search), offers are ranked on the basis of an initial signal. In the second round (sequential search), the DM closely observes offers starting with the highest ranked and stops when the value of an offer exceeds the expected reward from future search. This article generalizes the model of Ramsey (2019) to take into account that such procedures often involve several decision makers.

Using a game-theoretic procedure, various concepts of a solution to a decision problem can be applied. Using the concept of Nash equilibrium, it is assumed that the actions of the DMs are independent and the outcome of the game results from the combined actions of the players and possibly random factors. Under such an equilibrium, it does not pay any of the players to unilaterally change their strategy. Alpern and Baston (2016) consider such an equilibrium for a model in which two members of a committee must choose a single employee from a set of candidates who appear sequentially. The members of the committee have their own preferences, but a cost is incurred when there is no unanimous decision regarding whether a particular candidate should be employed or not. A similar model was considered by Sakaguchi and Mazalov (2004). When the members of such a committee have common interests, it seems reasonable that DMs should communicate when making their decisions. The concept of correlated equilibrium (see Aumann (1987)) allows the possibility of communication (either before a decision process is carried out or at each stage of such a process). At such a correlated equilibrium, a player is free to ignore the communication process, but should not unilaterally change his/her strategy given the agreement achieved via communication. Ramsey and Szajowski (2008) consider such a model when two DMs from a single organization each wish to appoint an employee and candidates appear sequentially. These models assume that offers appear sequentially. However, the search process considered here is a two-stage process in which offers can be assessed in parallel, but only partial information on the offers is available in the first stage.

Classical game-theoretical models assume that each player is economically rational, i.e. only considers his/her own payoff from the game. However, when households are making purchasing decisions, it is natural to assume that the players involved take into account the payoff of other players (see Fehr and Schmidt (2006)). Such an approach is adopted in Ramsey (2020), which considers a game-theoretical model of a pair of DMs searching for a valuable resource based on the short list heuristic. One of the DMs constructs the short list, while the other makes the final decision. This model is essentially game theoretic, rather than a group decision making procedure, since the two players individually make decisions that affect the search process. However, the player choosing the short list can show altruism to the other player - in the form of placing more offers on the short list than would be optimal if he/she only considered his/her own payoff.

According to classical models of group decision making, each of the DMs ascribes a score to each of the offers (or ranks the offers) based on full information about the offers. These scores (or rankings) are then used to define the attractiveness of an offer to the group as a whole (see e.g. Taha (2017)). Classically, it is assumed that DMs honestly assess the attractiveness of an offer. However, one may interpret the method a DM uses to ascribe scores as his/her strategy (i.e. interpret the decision process as a type of game). In this context, an important aspect of such decision making processes is the robustness of the process to dishonesty. Under a robust process, it pays the DMs to present an honest assessment of the attractiveness of each offer (see Taylor and Pacelli (2008)). However, when the DMs can communicate or have information regarding the preferences of others, even such voting procedures can be manipulated (see Gibbard (1973), Kontek and Sosnowska (2018)).

Section 2 presents the model of an individual decision maker searching for a valuable good presented by Ramsey (2019). Some key results from this model are presented in Sect. 3. Possible extensions to group decision making are considered in Sect. 4. This section considers both approaches based on procedures for group decision making (Sect. 4.1) and game theoretic approaches (Sect. 4.2). Section 5 describes a model of group decision making using the short list heuristic. Section 6 considers three desirable properties for decision making procedures. The first is the Weak Axiom of Revealed Preferences (WARP, see Lleras et al. (2017)), the second is the property of inducing honesty (see Taylor and Pacelli (2008)) and the third is the property of dominance consistency (previously undefined). The procedures described in Sect. 5 do not satisfy WARP, but satisfy the conditions of inducing honesty and dominance consistency. Section 7 describes the simulations used to investigate the effectiveness of various procedures for group decision making involving short lists. The results from these simulations are presented in Sect. 8. Conclusions and directions for future research are given in Sect. 9.

2   A Model of Search with an Individual Decision Maker

This model was first presented in Ramsey (2019). A decision maker (DM) must choose one of n offers. The DM first observes in parallel an initial signal of the value of each offer. It is assumed that the DM cannot precisely measure these signals, but can rank these signals according to their attractiveness. This ranking will be called the initial ranking. Based on this ranking, the DM chooses k offers for further inspection, where $1 \leq k \leq n$. The strategy of the DM is defined by the length of this short list. In the second round, the DM further inspects the k offers on the short list and obtains another signal of the value of each offer. The DM then chooses one of them. It is assumed that when the DM observes all of the offers closely, then he/she can rank these offers based on the two signals combined. Such a ranking will be called the overall ranking. However, after closer inspection, the DM can only compare the k offers on the short list with each other (the DM's partial ranking). It is assumed that this partial ranking agrees completely with the overall ranking, i.e. offer i is ranked below offer j in a partial ranking if and only if offer i is ranked below offer j in the overall ranking.

It is assumed that the two signals of the value of an offer to the DM come from a continuous joint distribution. These signals may be correlated, but the pair of signals observed for offer i is independent of the pair of signals observed for offer j, $i \neq j$. The value of an offer is a function of these two quantitative signals. Let X_m be the value of the m-th signal ($m = 1, 2$) and W the value of an offer. It is assumed that given $x > y$, then the random variable $W|X_1 = x$ stochastically dominates the random variable $W|X_1 = y$. Also, the value of an offer is increasing in the realization of the second signal. In short, high values of the signals correspond to high values of offers.

The goal of the DM is to maximize his/her expected reward from search. This is defined as the value of the offer accepted minus the search costs. Search costs are divided into the costs of initial inspection and the costs of closer inspection. The costs of initial inspection, given by $f_1(k, n)$, are strictly increasing in both the number of offers and the length of the short list, n and k respectively. These costs reflect the effort required for initial inspection of the offers and maintaining the short list. Also, it is assumed that f_1 is convex in k, i.e. $f_1(k, n) - f_1(k-1, n)$ is non-decreasing in k. Such a cost function reflects the cognitive effort necessary to control short lists of long length. It should be noted that this is a simplification, since when $k = n$ the DM automatically inspects all of the offers closely. Hence, in this case, the search costs should not include the costs of controlling the short list. The costs of inspecting the offers on the short list, given by $f_2(k)$, are assumed to be increasing and convex in the length of the short list. It may be natural to assume that these costs are linear in k (when $k \geq 2$, then each successive offer on the short list is inspected and only needs to be compared with the best ranked of the offers previously inspected). Let $f(k, n) = f_1(k, n) + f_2(k)$ be the total search costs and $C_k = f(k, n) - f(k-1, n)$ be the marginal costs of increasing the length of the short list from $k-1$ to k.

It should be noted that a short list of length k should consist of the k highest ranked offers based on the initial round of observations. This results directly from the fact that the reward obtained by selecting from these offers stochastically dominates the reward obtained by choosing from any other set of k offers given the initial ranking.

3   Some Results

These results are given in Ramsey (2019). Let W_i be the value of the i-th ranked offer according to the initial ranking and V_k be the value of the offer accepted when the length of the short list is k, i.e. $V_k = \max_{1 \leq i \leq k}\{W_k\}$. It follows that when $i < j$, then V_i is stochastically dominated by V_j. Denote by M_k the marginal increase in the expected value of the offer accepted when the length of the short list is increased from $k-1$ to k, i.e. $M_k = E[V_k - V_{k-1})$. The criterion determining the optimal length of the short list is based on the following theorem:

Theorem. The marginal increase in the expected value of the offer accepted, M_k, is non-increasing in k.   □

Proof. By definition

$$M_k = E[\max\{0, W_k - V_{k-1}\}]; \qquad M_{k+1} = E[\max\{0, W_{k+1} - V_k\}].$$

The fact that $M_k \geq M_{k+1}$ follows directly from the facts that W_k stochastically dominates W_{k+1} and V_k stochastically dominates V_{k-1}.   □

Theorem. Suppose that $M_2 > C_2$. The optimal length of the short list, k^*, is the largest integer k, such that $k \leq n$ and $M_k > C_k$.   □

This theorem follows from the fact that M_k is non-increasing in k and C_k is non-decreasing in k. The condition $M_2 > C_2$ ensures that it is better to create a short list of length two than automatically accept the offer that is ranked might highly according to the initial inspection. For all $k \leq k^*$, it follows that $M_k > C_k$ and for $k > k^*$, then $M_k \leq C_k$. Hence, the DM always gains by increasing the length of the short list when $k < k^*$, but when $k \geq k^*$ the costs of increasing the length of the short list always outweigh the gains. Hence, the optimal length of the short list is given by k^*.

Note that when $M_k = C_k$, then the DM is indifferent between using a short list of length $k - 1$ and using a short list of length k. The condition given above assumes that when the optimal length of the short list is not unique, then the smallest length from the set of optimal lengths is used.

4   Possible Extensions of the Model to Group Decision Making

In this section, we consider two general approaches to solving problems faced by a group of DMs who have to make a common decision, often after a set of intermediate decisions: a) procedures for group decision making and b) game theoretic approaches. Suppose a procedure for group decision making is used to choose a single offer from a set of n offers. It is assumed that at each stage of the decision process each DM assesses the offers currently under consideration and they make a common decision according to a procedure that is defined prior to the decision-making process. On the other hand, classical game theoretic models assume that each DM makes his/her own decisions based on his/her assessments of the offers currently under consideration and the outcome of the game depends on the set of decisions made by the DMs. For example, consider a procedure in which two individuals jointly choose an offer. One DM might choose which offers should be placed on the short list and the other DM then chooses which offer should be finally picked. Based on the above discussion, such a procedure should be interpreted as game theoretic approach, since the two decisions are made by individual DMs.

On the other hand, consider a procedure in which a set of DMs define a function that provides a single measure of the attractiveness of an offer to the group as a whole based on the current rankings of the offers by the DMs. After an initial inspection, the k offers with the largest measures of attractiveness are placed on the short list. After closer inspection, the offer with the largest measure of attractiveness to the group as a whole is accepted. From the discussion made above, this should be interpreted as a procedure for group decision making.

4.1   Procedures for Group Decision Making

Classical mathematical procedures for group decision making assume that the DMs observe a set of n offers in parallel. The DMs fully inspect these offers and ascribe a measure of attractiveness to each offer (or rank the offers). These measures (or rankings) are used to define an overall measure of the attractiveness of an offer to the group as a whole and the offer with the greatest attractiveness is accepted (see Taha (2017)). Such models do not explicitly consider the search costs. Since a set of n offers is fully inspected, one can assume that the search costs are fixed. Also, classical models assume that the DMs give honest assessments of the values of the offers. However, depending on the information available during a decision process and the preferences of the players, it may pay a DM to give dishonest assessments (see e.g. Kontek and Sosnowska (2018)). This will be further considered in the subsection on game theoretical models.

It is assumed that players do not observe the precise values of signals, but can rank them. Also, the attractiveness of an offer to the group as a whole is measured by a function of the ranks ascribed to that offer by the DMs. It is assumed that there are m decision makers. In order to adapt such a procedure to the short list heuristic, the following components of the decision rule are required:

1. The function $g_1(r_1, r_2, \ldots, r_m)$ measuring the overall attractiveness of an offer based on initial information, where r_i is the rank ascribed to the offer by the i-th decision maker in the first round of inspection.
2. The length of the short list to be used, k.
3. The function $g_2(s_1, s_2, \ldots, s_m)$ measuring the overall attractiveness of an offer on the short list based on all the information gained in both rounds, where s_i is the rank ascribed to the offer by the i-th decision maker in the second round of inspection.

The functions g_1 and g_2 are by definition non-increasing in each of their arguments. These two functions will be called the assessment functions. The k offers associated with the highest values of g_1 are selected for closer inspection. After the second round, the group accepts the offer associated with the highest value of g_2.

In this article, we consider assessment functions that are symmetric and additive.

Definition. An assessment function $g(r_1, r_2, \ldots, r_m)$ is said to be symmetric and additive when there exists a function g_c such that

$$g(r_1, r_2, \ldots, r_m) = \sum_{i=1}^{m} g_c(r_i).$$

Hence, the measure of overall attractiveness can be interpreted as a sum of the measures of attractiveness to the individual DMs (according to the function g_c) and this overall measure is independent of the way in which the DMs are labelled (i.e. the identity of the DMs is not important). The function g_c will be called the inducing function.

The three following types of inducing functions are natural within this framework:

1. Linear: $g_c(r) = n_0 - r$, where n_0 is the number of offers currently under consideration.
2. Exponential: $g_c(r) = \alpha^{r-1}$, where $0 < \alpha < 1$.
3. Hyperbolic $g_c(r) = \frac{1}{1+\beta(r-1)}$, where $\beta > 0$.

It should be noted that a wide range of linear inducing functions are admissible for the decision procedures considered here. The only necessary condition is that the inducing function is decreasing in r. However, it is relatively simple to show that all of these functions are equivalent, since maximization of the assessment function is always equivalent to minimization of the sum of the ranks ascribed by the DMs.

The choice of the inducing function depends on whether it is assumed better to ensure that all the DMs are relatively happy or to ensure that at least some of the DMs are very happy. In the first case, it seems more natural to use a concave inducing function (the overall attractiveness is lower when the ranks ascribed to an offer by two DMs are 1 and $r - 1$ than when both DMs ascribe a rank of $\frac{r}{2}$, where r is an even number such that $r \geq 4$). In the second case, it seems more natural to use a convex inducing function (the overall attractiveness is greater when the ranks ascribed to an offer by two DMs are 1 and $r - 1$ than when both DMs ascribe a rank of $\frac{r}{2}$). The exponential and hyperbolic functions given above are both convex.

Note that the linear inducing function is from the following family of inducing functions: $g_c(r) = (n_0 - r)^\gamma$, where $\gamma > 0$. When $\gamma < 1$, this function is concave and when $\gamma > 1$, this function is convex.

4.2   Game Theoretic Models

In classical models of game theory, the DMs involved in a game choose their strategies independently of each other and any DM, denoted by DMi, aims to maximize his/her own expected payoff, either under the assumption that other DMs behave in an analogous manner (see Nash (1950)), or assuming that other DMs aim to minimize the payoff of DMi (the minimax approach, see von Neumann and Morgestern (1944)).

The minimax approach is unsuitable when the DMs involved have common interests and/or share good will towards each other (e.g. when a family are looking for a new flat). However, it might be appropriate when the DMs are e.g. representatives of two disciplines within an academic department which is looking for a single new employee. There can be applicants from each discipline and candidates from one discipline are less attractive to DMs from the other discipline.

The classical approach of Nash can be adapted to model the good will shown by DMs to others by assuming that DMs do not look simply at their own payoffs, but also take into account the payoffs of the other DMs involved in the game. Such an approach was used to define a game-theoretic model of search using the short list heuristic by Ramsey (2020).

Such good will may lead to greater coordination between the decisions of the DMs, but such coordination may be also enabled by adopting the concept of a correlated strategy (see Aumann (1987)). When the DMs use a correlated strategy, they can correlate their actions on the basis of a signal that is observed before each decision is made or on just one signal that is observed before any decision is made (see Ramsey and Szajowski (2008)). Another approach to coordinating the actions of the DMs is to define the decision problem as a cooperative game where payoffs are transferable. Using such an approach, the individual DMs can form coalitions with other DMs in order to promote an outcome which is favourable to the coalition as a whole. If this outcome is bad for a single member of the coalition, then the remaining members of the coalition can recompensate him/her in some way. It is assumed that different coalitions are antagonistic towards each other (see Shapley (1953)). A very common type of such a cooperative game is given by the class of voting games. Such games assume that an appropriate majority of the DMs are required to implement a decision and the payoff from implementing this decision (normalised to be equal to one) is split between the players. The decision process described for employing a specialist by committee could be decided by such a voting procedure. However, the formation of different majorities may well lead to different candidates being employed. Hence, although such a problem would be similar to a classical voting game, it would be essentially different from a mathematical point of view.

As described in the introduction, a classical group decision approach to the type of problems considered here can be generalised to a game theoretic approach by assuming that the DMs do not necessarily report their preferences honestly. In the future, The authors intends to compare game-theoretic approaches with group decision procedures.

5   A Model of Group Decision Making Using the Short List Heuristic

This section considers a model of a decision procedure with two DMs. However, the ideas presented here can be easily extended to a larger number of DMs. A model of choice where a single DM uses a short list is given in Ramsey (2019). In that model, the DM first observes a signal, X_1, of the value of each of n offers. Based on these signals, the DM chooses a short list of k candidates and then observes a second signal of the value of these offers, X_2. These signals are i.i.d. realisations from a bivariate normal distribution. It is assumed that X_1 comes from the standard normal distribution, i.e. with mean zero and standard deviation one. It is further assumed that the coefficient of correlation between X_1 and X_2 is ρ. Also, X_2 has a mean of 0 and a residual variance of σ^2 (this is the variance of X_2 given than $X_1 = x$ for any given x). It follows from this that the overall variance of X_2 is given by $\frac{\sigma^2}{1-\rho^2}$. The value of an offer is given by $V = X_1 + X_2$. Hence, the parameter σ^2 can be interpreted as a measure of the importance of the information given by the second signal relative to the first signal.

The following model is a particular case, which assumes symmetry between the two players, of the model presented by Ramsey (2020). Assume that two DMs, DM1 and DM2, together must choose one of n offers using a procedure based on forming a short list. Let $X_{i,j}$ be the value of the i-th signal as observed by the j-th DM and let $\mathbf{X} = (X_{1,1}, X_{2,1}, X_{1,2}, X_{2,2})$ denote the set of signals of the value of an offer that can be observed by the two DMs. Generalizing the model for a single DM, the signals of the values of an offer to the DMs are given by a four-dimensional normal distribution. In general, this might lead to a complex correlation structure between the signals observed by the DMs. In order to keep this correlation structure relatively simple, the following assumptions are made:

1. The correlation between the two signals observed by a single DM is ρ_1 independently of the DM (this is analogous to the parameter ρ in the model with a single DM).
2. The correlation between the value of a signal as observed by the two DMs is ρ_2 (independently of the signal).
3. Given the value of the first signal as observed by a DM, the value of the second signal observed by this DM is conditionally independent of the value of the first signal as observed by the other DM.
4. Analogously, given the value of the second signal as observed by a DM, the value of the first signal observed by this DM is conditionally independent of the value of the second signal as observed by the other DM.

The parameter ρ_2 can be interpreted as a measure of the level of coherence between the preferences of the DMs. It is assumed that $\rho_i \geq 0$, $i = 1, 2$. The structure of the correlation between the signals is illustrated by Fig. 1.

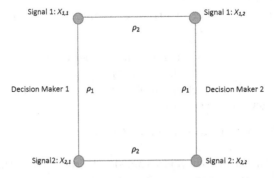

Fig. 1. Structure of the correlations between the signals observed by the decision makers.

It follows that the correlation matrix for these signals is given by

$$\rho = \begin{pmatrix} 1 & \rho_1 & \rho_2 & \rho_1\rho_2 \\ \rho_1 & 1 & \rho_1\rho_2 & \rho_2 \\ \rho_2 & \rho_1\rho_2 & 1 & \rho_1 \\ \rho_1\rho_2 & \rho_2 & \rho_1 & 1 \end{pmatrix}. \tag{1}$$

Analogously to the model with a single DM, it is assumed that $X_{1,j}$ has a standard normal distribution and $X_{2,j}$, $j = 1, 2$, has a mean of 0 and a residual variance of σ^2 (given the realisation of $X_{1,j}$). The value of an offer to the j-th DM is given by $V_j = X_{1,j} + X_{2,j}$. Hence, this model assumes symmetry between the preferences of the DMs in the sense that they give the second signal the same relative weight and have the same overall strength of preferences (the distribution of V_j is independent of j). It follows that

$$\mathrm{Var}(V_1) = textVar(X_{1,1}) + \mathrm{Var}(X_{2,1}) + 2\rho_1\sqrt{\mathrm{Var}(X_{1,1})\mathrm{Var}(X_{2,1})}$$

$$= 1 + \frac{\sigma^2}{1 - \rho_1^2} + \frac{2\rho_1\sigma}{\sqrt{1 - \rho_1^2}}. \tag{2}$$

It is assumed that, prior to observing the offers, the decision players agree to jointly use a group decision rule which is defined by the inducing functions used in each round of inspection and the length of the short list to be used, k. For convenience, it will be henceforth assumed that the inducing function used is $f_c(r) = (n - r)^\gamma$ in round one and $f_c(r) = (k - r)^\gamma$ in round two, where n, k and r denote the total number of offers, the length of the short list and the rank of an offer, respectively. Note that when $\gamma = 1$, any offer maximisation of the assessment function corresponds to minimisation of the sum of the ranks ascribed to an offer by the DMs.

It is assumed that the cost functions for search are the same for both DMs. The search costs are composed of:

1. The costs for initially inspecting an offer: c_1 per offer.
2. The costs for controlling the short list: $c_2 k^2$.
3. The costs for closely inspecting an offer on the short list: c_3 per offer, where c_3 is much larger than c_1 and c_2.

It follows that the total costs are given by $C(k, n)$, where $C(k, n) = c_1 n + c_2 k^2 + c_3 k$.

The payoff of the i-th DM, R_i, is assumed to be the value of the offer obtained minus the search costs. Hence, $R_i = V_i - C(k, n)$, where V_i is the value of the offer accepted to the i-th DM. As described above, decision makers first apply a decision rule based on the rankings of the offers according to initial information to choose a short list of k offers. After gaining additional information about the offers on the short list, the decision makers then apply a decision rule to make the final choice of the offer to be selected based on their rankings of the offers on the short list. We consider decision rules of this form (i.e. defined by functions measuring the overall attractiveness of an offer according to the information currently available and the length of the short list to be used) that are best designed to achieve one of the following two goals:

1. To maximize the sum of the payoffs of the DMs: $\max(R_1 + R_2)$.
2. To maximize the minimum of the payoffs of the DMs: $\max[\min\{R_1, R_2\})$.

A summary of the parameters used is given in Table 1.

Table 1. Summary of the parameters used in the model for group decision making

Parameter	Description
σ	Relative importance of the second signal to DMs
ρ_1	Correlation between the two signals of the value of an offer observed by a single DM
ρ_2	Correlation between the values of a single signal as seen by the two DMs
c_1	Cost of initial inspection per offer
c_2	Coefficient of costs for short list control
c_3	Cost of close inspection per offer
γ	Exponent in the inducing function
k	Length of the short list

Due to the mathematical difficulty of solving these problems, particularly when the signals are correlated, various realisations of the decision problem are solved with the aid of simulation. This requires simulating the values of the signals observed by the DMs. Firstly, a set of four signals, $\mathbf{Y} = (Y_{1,1}, Y_{2,1}, Y_{1,2}, Y_{2,2})$, whose covariance matrix is given by ρ is generated using the Cholesky decomposition (see Horn and Johnson (1985)). Using the Cholesky decomposition, the correlation matrix ρ can be written as $\rho = \mathbf{L}\mathbf{L}^T$, where T denotes transposition and

$$\mathbf{L} = \begin{pmatrix} 1 & 0 & 0 & 0 \\ \rho_1 & \sqrt{1-\rho_1^2} & 0 & 0 \\ \rho_2 & 0 & \sqrt{1-\rho_2^2} & 0 \\ \rho_1\rho_2 & \rho_2\sqrt{1-\rho_1^2} & \rho_1\sqrt{1-\rho_2^2} & \sqrt{1-\rho_1^2-\rho_2^2+\rho_1^2\rho_2^2} \end{pmatrix}. \tag{3}$$

Let $\mathbf{Y} = \mathbf{L}\mathbf{Z}$, where $\mathbf{Z}^T = (Z_1, Z_2, Z_3, Z_4)$ is a vector of independent realisations from the standard normal distribution, i.e. with mean and standard deviation equal to 0 and 1, respectively. The components of the vector $\mathbf{Y}$ have the appropriate correlation matrix, but the standard deviation of each component is equal to one. Hence, in order to obtain the components of $\mathbf{X}$, it is necessary to multiply the components corresponding to the second signal by the appropriate standard deviation. Analogous to the model with one DM, it follows that

$$X_{1,1} = Z_1; \quad X_{2,1} = \frac{\sigma Z_2}{\sqrt{1 - \rho_1^2}}; \quad X_{1,2} = Z_3; \quad X_{2,2} = \frac{\sigma Z_4}{\sqrt{1 - \rho_1^2}}. \quad (4)$$

6   Desirable Properties of Short Lists

It is assumed that the DMs gain information on the offers in two stages. In the first stage, basic information about all of n offers is observed. Each of the DMs ranks the offers on the basis of this information. A short list of k promising offers is formed, where $k < n$. The DMs then observe more information about each of the offers on the short list before making a final choice from amongst these offers. Let S denote the set of traits of the offers and S_i be the set of traits observed in stage i, $i = 1, 2$. It is assumed that S_1 and S_2 are mutually exclusive and $S_1 \cup S_2 = S$.

For convenience, it will be said that the DMs have information set T when they have observed all of the traits in the set T for all the offers and nothing else. If $T_1 \subset T_2$, then T_2 is said to be a richer information set than T_1. A linear ranking of n offers made on the basis of the information set T by a decision maker is defined by a permutation $\{a_1(T), a_2(T), \ldots a_n(T)\}$, such that offer $a_i(T)$ has ranking i. We write $r(a_i; T) = i$. It is assumed that offer i_1 is preferred to offer i_2 on the basis of information T if and only if $r(i_1; T) < r(i_2; T)$. It is assumed that the rankings of a DM based on information set T correspond perfectly to a ranking of the expected values to that DM of the offers based on T.

The following definition can be interpreted as an extension of the concept of Pareto domination when a set of decision makers define a linear ranking of offers.

Definition. Suppose each of a set of m decision makers constructs a linear ranking of n offers on the basis of information T. Let $r(i, j; T)$ be the ranking of offer i according to decision maker j. Offer i_1 dominates offer i_2 on the basis of information T if and only if $r(i_1, j; T) < r(i_2, j; T)$ for all $j \in \{1, 2, \ldots, m\}$. Offer i is said to be "k-dominated", $k = 0, 1, \ldots, m - 1$ on the basis of information T if and only if there are exactly k offers that dominate offer i on the basis of information T. Offer i is said to be "at least k-dominated" on the basis of information T if and only if there are at least k offers that dominate offer i on the basis of information T. $\square$

Remark 1. Any offer that is 0-dominated on the basis of information T is by definition Pareto optimal on the basis of information T.

The following definitions describe desirable properties of a procedure for making a short list by committee, when each member of the committee defines their own ranking of the offers available on the basis of information S_1.

Definition. A decision procedure is said to be honesty inducing if the following condition is satisfied: when all of the DMs honestly report their assessments of the offers, then it does not pay any of them to unilaterally change their report.   □

Theorem. Suppose that DMs do not have any information (additional to that resulting from the mathematical definition of the decision problem) regarding the assessments made by the other DMs. The decision procedure described in Section 4.1 is honesty inducing.   □

Proof. Suppose that there exist a pair of offers i and j, such that a DM prefers offer i to offer j based on the current information, but reports that j is ranked immediately above offer i. Suppose that this DM swaps the position of these two offers in the ranking. The value of the assessment function for offer i in the current round of voting increases, while this value for offer j decreases. Hence, if this occurs in round one, the probability of offer i being placed on the short list increases, while the probability of offer j being placed on the short list decreases. In this case, the expected reward from search of this DM will increase. Similarly, if this occurs in round two, the probability of offer i being ultimately chosen increases, while the probability of offer j being ultimately chosen decreases. Again, the expected reward from search of this DM will increase. It follows that the offer reported to have rank i must be preferred to the offer reported to have rank $i+1$ for all $i = 1, 2, \ldots, n-1$ in round one and for all $i = 1, 2, \ldots, k-1$ in round 2. Only reports which honestly rank the offers satisfy this condition.   □

Remark 2. It should be noted that this theorem does not contradict the results obtained by e.g. Gibbard (1973), Kontek and Sosnowska (2018), since in the situations considered in those papers it is assumed that a DM can gain additional information by communicating with other DMs.

Definition. A procedure for defining a short list of k offers from an initial set of n offers, where $n > k$, on the basis of information S_1 is said to be dominance-consistent (DC) if and only if no offer that is at least k-dominated can ever be chosen to be on the short list for any $k < n$.   □

Remark 3. This is a desirable property, since when offer i is k-dominated, there are exactly k offers that are preferred to offer i by all of the DMs. Hence, all of the DMs will prefer to put these k offers on the short list rather than include offer i.

Theorem. The procedure described in Section 4.1 is dominance-consistent.   □

Proof. Suppose that offer i is at least k-dominated in round one. From the definition of the assessment function, there exist at least k offers associated with a higher value of the assessment function. Hence, offer i will not be placed on the short list.   □

Remark 4. Using a similar argument, the offer ultimately chosen must be 0-dominated, i.e. Pareto optimal, amongst the offers on the short list.

Definition. The Weak Axiom of Revealed Preferences (WARP, see Lleras et al. [2017]) states that when offers i and j belong to both of the sets of offers A and B and i is chosen from the set A, then j is never chosen from the set B. In mathematical terminology, when $c(A)$ denotes the offer chosen from the set A, then

$$[c(A) = i, j \in A, i \in B] \Rightarrow [c(B) \neq j].$$

The following example shows that a search procedure based on forming a short list of fixed length does not satisfy WARP. Suppose i and j are two offers such that initial inspection results in i being dominated by j, but closer inspection reveals that offer i dominates offer j. One may define sets of offers A and B, such that both i and j would be on the short list of offers from the set A and i is chosen, but i is not on the short list of offers from set B and the offer j is chosen. It should be noted that this argument is a simple adaptation of the proof that choice using a short list implemented by a single decision maker does not satisfy WARP.

7   Description of the Simulations

The effectiveness of group decision rules with two DMs in search problems based on the model presented in Sect. 5 were investigated using a program written in R. The total number of offers available was assumed to be $n = 100$. The search costs incurred in the two rounds of search are assumed to be $f_1(n, k) = c_1 n + c_2 k^2$ and $f_2(k) = c_3 k$, respectively, where $c_1 = c_2 = 0.0001$ and $c_3 = 0.1$. The parameters of the function defining the search costs are defined to reflect the fact that search in the second round is much more expensive than in the first round.

The quartet of signals, $(X_{1,1}, X_{2,1}, X_{1,2}, X_{2,2})$, describing the value of an offer, were assumed to be independent realisations from a multivariate normal distribution, where $X_{j,i}$ is the j-th signal of the value of an offer as observed by DMi (as described in Sect. 5).

The inducing function used in the first round of inspection was assumed to be of the form $g_c(r_i) = (n - r_i)^\gamma$, where r_i is the rank ascribed to an offer in the first round of inspection by DMi and $\gamma \in \{1/3, 1/2, 1, 2, 3\}$. Hence, the assessment function applied in the first round is $g(r_1, r_2) = (n - r_1)^\gamma + (n - r_2)^\gamma$. The offers associated with the k largest values of the assessment function are placed on the short list. When the k-th and $k + 1$-th ordered values of the assessment function are both equal to some value y, then the appropriate number of offers associated with an assessment function of value y are chosen at random in order to obtain a short list of length k.

In the second round of inspection, the assessment function used is $g(s_1, s_2) = (k - s_1)^\gamma + (k - s_2)^\gamma$, where s_i is the rank ascribed to an offer in the second round of inspection by DMi. If there exists a unique offer on the short list that maximises the corresponding assessment function, then this is the offer chosen. Otherwise, an offer is chosen at random from the set of offers maximising the value of the assessment function.

The aims of the simulations were to estimate the optimal length of the short list according to the following two criteria: a) maximisation of the expected sum of the payoffs of the DMs, b) maximisation of the expected value of the minimum payoff obtained over the set of DMs, for the set of parameters given by the vector $(\sigma, \rho_1, \rho_2, \gamma)$. These optimal values are denoted by $w_1(\sigma, \rho_1, \rho_2, \gamma)$ and $w_2(\sigma, \rho_1, \rho_2, \gamma)$, respectively. These expected values were estimated on the basis of 100 000 simulations of the search procedure. These estimates are denoted by $\hat{w}_1^G(\sigma, \rho_1, \rho_2, \gamma)$ and $\hat{w}_2^G(\sigma, \rho_1, \rho_2, \gamma)$, respectively. The empirically derived optimal lengths of the short lists are given by $\hat{k}_1^G(\sigma, \rho_1, \rho_2, \gamma)$ and $\hat{k}_2^G(\sigma, \rho_1, \rho_2, \gamma)$, respectively. The corresponding group decision rules are denoted as G_1 and G_2, respectively.

In order to assess the efficiency of the decision procedures described above, the following search procedures were also simulated:

1. A single DM faces an analogous set of offers and signals in which the search costs and standard deviances of the signals are doubled, while the correlation between the signals is unchanged. This makes the reward from search of the single searcher comparable with the sum of the rewards gained in the group decision procedure. Hence, the search costs are defined by $c_1 = c_2 = 0.0002$ and $c_3 = 0.2$. The coefficient of correlation between the two signals observed is ρ_1, the variance of the first signal is 4 and the residual variance of the second signal is $4\sigma^2$. The estimate of the optimal expected reward in such a search problem is denoted by $\hat{w}^I(\sigma, \rho_1)$. The corresponding empirically derived optimal length of the short list is given by $\hat{k}^I(\sigma, \rho_1)$. The corresponding decision rule is denoted by I.

2. A pair of DMs face the same set of offers and signals. In the first round of inspection, the procedure for choosing the short list is identical to the group decision procedure described above. However, it is assumed that in the second round of inspection each of the DMs observe precisely the value of an offer to themselves and they maximise the expected sum of the payoffs obtained by the DMs. The estimate of the optimal expected reward in such a search problem is denoted by $\hat{w}_3^G(\sigma, \rho_1, \rho_2, \gamma)$. The corresponding empirically derived optimal length of the short list is given by $\hat{k}_3^G(\sigma, \rho_1, \rho_2, \gamma)$. The simulations also considered the length of a short list for such rules which maximises the expected value of the minimum payoff obtained over the set of DMs. The estimate of the expected minimum reward for such a decision procedure is denoted by $\hat{w}_4^G(\sigma, \rho_1, \rho_2, \gamma)$. The corresponding empirically derived optimal length of the short list is given by $\hat{k}_4^G(\sigma, \rho_1, \rho_2, \gamma)$. The corresponding decision rules are denoted by G_3 and G_4.

Remark 5. It should be noted that one may find a more effective rule for maximising the minimum reward obtained by a DM than G_4 by assuming that in the second round of the search procedure the DMs choose the offer which maximises the minimum payoff of the DMs (rather than maximising the sum of the payoffs). The approach used here is adopted in order to investigate the robustness of decision rules based on ranks in both rounds of inspection. Such a decision rule is deemed to be robust when the expected value of the lowest payoff obtained by a DM is high.

On the basis of these simulations, we can estimate the following two measures of the efficiency of the group decision procedure:

1. The efficiency with respect to the decision of a single DM, $\epsilon_1(\sigma, \rho_1, \rho_2, \gamma)$. This is defined as $\epsilon_1(\sigma, \rho_1, \rho_2, \gamma) = \frac{\hat{w}_1^G(\sigma, \rho_1, \rho_2, \gamma)}{\hat{w}^I(\sigma, \rho_1)}$, i.e. a measure of the expected sum of payoffs from the decision procedure relative to the expected payoff obtained by a single DM in an analogous problem where the costs incurred and benefits obtained by the individual are doubled.

2. The efficiency with respect to the group decision procedure in which the abilities of the DMs to measure the value of an offer on the basis of close inspection is perfect, $\epsilon_2(\sigma, \rho_1, \rho_2, \gamma)$. This is defined as $\epsilon_2(\sigma, \rho_1, \rho_2, \gamma) = \frac{\hat{w}_1^G(\sigma, \rho_1, \rho_2, \gamma)}{\hat{w}_3^G(\sigma, \rho_1, \rho_2, \gamma)}$. It should be noted that in order to realise such a strategy, the DMs should report their assessments of the value of an offer honestly. However, such a decision procedure may not be honesty inducing.

Remark 6. The above definitions of efficiency are reasonable, since one may interpret the payoffs defined above as the expected gain in payoff relative to the payoff from choosing a random offer (whose expected value is defined to be zero). The efficiency measure ϵ_2 is by definition bounded above by one as seen from the following argument. Consider a decision rule of the same form as G_3 in which the players use the same rule as G_1 in the first round of inspection. Call this rule G_5. Since under G_5, the DMs accept the offer on the short list that maximises the sum of the payoffs to the players, it follows that the expected reward under G_5 cannot be less than the expected reward under G_1. Also, by definition, the expected reward under G_5 cannot exceed the expected reward under G_3. The fact that the efficiency measure ϵ_1 is bounded above by one follows from an analogous argument.

The results from these simulations are described in the following section.

8   Results from the Simulations

This section looks at the effect on the efficiency of the group decision procedure considered of a) the structure of the correlations between the signals, b) the form of the assessment function, and c) the relative importance of the second signal. With regard to the structure of the correlations between the signals, ρ_2 is a measure of the coherence of the preferences of the DMs. Hence, it is expected that the efficiency of the group decision procedure is increasing in ρ_2. With regard to the form of the assessment function, defined by the parameter γ, as explained in Sect. 4.1 when $\gamma < 1$, the decision procedure is expected to more highly adapted to maximising the minimum of the payoffs of the rewards obtained by the DMs than to maximising the sum of the payoffs. These hypotheses will be investigated in the following subsections.

These search problems are characterised by four parameters: $(\sigma, \rho_1, \rho_2, \gamma)$. Both σ and γ are chosen from the set $\{1/3, 1/2, 1, 2, 3\}$, while ρ_1 and ρ_2 are chosen from the set $\{0, 1/3, 2/3\}$. This gives a total of $5^2 \times 3^2 = 225$ search problems. The total number of offers available is assumed to be $n = 100$. The search costs in the first round are given by $f_1(n, k) = c_1 n + c_2 k^2$, where $c_1 = c_2 = 0.0001$ and k is the length of the short list. The search costs in the second round are assumed to be $f_2(k) = c_3 k$, where $c_3 = 0.1$. In order to restrict the number of realisations considered, the number of offers available and the search costs are assumed to be fixed. Previous research indicates that, under the assumptions of the model, as long as the total number of offers is relatively large, the optimal length of the short list is very robust to the total number of offers available. The optimal length of the short list is decreasing in the relative cost of search in the second round (see Ramsey (2019)).

8.1   Search by a Single Decision Maker

The search procedure faced by a single searcher can be characterised by two parameters: a) σ, the relative importance of the second signal, and b) ρ_1 the coefficient of correlation between the two signals. It follows that there are 15 search problems with a single DM corresponding to the 225 group decision problems considered, where $\sigma \in \{1/3, 1/2, 1, 2, 3\}$ and $\rho_1 \in \{0, 1/3, 2/3\}$. The empirically derived optimal expected rewards and optimal lengths of the short list are presented in Table 2. As noted before, to make this problem comparable to the group decision problem with two searchers, the standard deviation and search costs are multiplied by 2 in the simulations. Such a search problem can also be interpreted as two clones jointly searching for a valuable resource.

Table 2. Empirically derived optimal expected reward (first entry) and optimal length of short list (second entry) for the corresponding search problems with one DM when 100 offers are available.

	$\rho_1 = 0$	$\rho_1 = 1/3$	$\rho_1 = 2/3$
$\sigma = 1/3$	(4.7936, 1)	(5.3839, 1)	(6.2884, 1)
$\sigma = 1/2$	(4.9157, 2)	(5.7833, 2)	(7.1099, 2)
$\sigma = 1$	(5.5885, 4)	(7.2236, 3)	(9.7763, 3)
$\sigma = 2$	(7.8531, 7)	(10.7905, 6)	(15.5758, 4)
$\sigma = 3$	(10.7318, 11)	(14.8180, 8)	(21.6331, 6)

It can be seen that the optimal length of the short list is increasing in the relative importance of the second signal. Fixing the residual variance in the second signal, the optimal length of the short list is decreasing in the level of correlation between the two signals (this is most visible when the residual variance in the second signal is large). This is due to the fact that when the residual variance of the second signal is fixed, as the coefficient of correlation between the two signals increases, the first signal contains relatively more information about the overall value of an offer.

8.2   Effect of the Structure of Correlations Between the Signals

Table 3 gives results for the simulation of the group decision process when $\sigma = 2$ and $k = 1$. In each cell, the first two rows relate to the group decision process where in the second round the DMs choose the offer which maximises the sum of the payoffs (the expected sum of payoffs and the expected minimum payoff, respectively). The final two rows in each cell relate to the group decision rule where the choices in both rounds are based on the appropriate assessment functions (i.e. based on the rank ascribed to offers by the DMs). The first entry in each vector gives the appropriate maximum expected value. The second entry gives the corresponding length of the short list. When appropriate, the third and fourth entries give the efficiencies ϵ_1 and ϵ_2, respectively.

It can be seen that the efficiency of the rank-based decision rules are weakly increasing in ρ_1 and strongly increasing in ρ_2. As ρ_2 increases, the coherence of the preferences of the DMs increases. Intuitively, as ρ_2 tends to one, the preferences of the DMs converge (hence ϵ_1 tends to one, since the two players act more and more like clones) and the probability that the offer which maximises the sum of the payoffs simultaneously maximises the assessment function will tend towards one (hence ϵ_2 also tends to one). This is reflected in the results. The optimal length of the short list is decreasing in ρ_1 and almost independent of ρ_2.

In addition, it can be seen that the rank-based rule which maximises the expected sum of payoffs is always very similar to the rank-based rule which maximises the expected minimum of the payoffs. This is not the case for rules based on accepting the offer which maximises the sum of payoffs after the second round. In fact, when the variance of the second signal is sufficiently large to ensure that a short of at least moderate size (4 or more) is used, then the expected value of the minimum payoff is larger under a rank-based rule G_1 or G_2 than under either of the rules G_3 or G_4. This suggests that such rank-based rules are robust.

It should also be noted that the optimal length of the short list is virtually independent of whether there is a single DM or pair of DMs.

8.3   Effect of the Form of the Assessment Function

As argued above, it is expected that a concave assessment function should be used when the goal is to maximise the minimum of the payoffs rather than maximise the sum of the payoffs. Table 4 gives results for the realisations of the decision process with $\sigma = 2$ and $\rho_1 = 1/3$. It can be seen that concave assessment functions ($\gamma < 1$) are slightly more effective at maximising the minimum of the payoffs obtained, particularly when the preferences of the DMs are independent ($\rho_2 = 0$). The effect of the form of the assessment function on the expected sum

Table 3. Effect of the correlation structure: $\sigma = 2, \gamma = 1$. Empirically derived optimal expected reward (first entry) and optimal length of short list (second entry) for search procedures with two DMs when 100 offers are available. When appropriate, the third and fourth entries give the efficiency measures for the ranked-based decision rule.

		$\rho_2 = 0$	$\rho_2 = 1/3$	$\rho_2 = 2/3$
$\rho_1 = 0$	G_3: max. sum	(5.0929, 6)	(6.1134, 6)	(7.0228, 7)
	G_4: max. min.	(1.0091, 2)	(1.6079, 2)	(2.2353, 2)
	G_1: max. sum.	(4.7435, 6, 0.6040, 0.9314)	(5.8393, 6, 0.7436, 0.9552)	(6.8445, 7, 0.8716, 0.9746)
	G_2: max. min.	(1.4188, 7)	(2.1003, 7)	(2.7948, 7)
$\rho_1 = 1/3$	G_3: max. sum	(7.1849, 5)	(8.5170, 5)	(9.7048, 6)
	G_4: max. min.	(2.0562, 2)	(2.8478, 2)	(3.6611, 2)
	G_1: max. sum.	(6.7938, 5, 0.6296, 0.9456)	(8.2035, 5, 0.7603, 0.9632)	(9.4978, 6, 0.8802, 0.9787)
	G_2: max. min.	(2.3217, 6)	(3.1707, 6)	(4.0304, 6)
$\rho_1 = 2/3$	G_3: max. sum	(10.5389, 4)	(12.4094, 4)	(14.0505, 4)
	G_4: max. min.	(3.5943, 2)	(4.6978, 2)	(5.7948, 2)
	G_1: max. sum.	(10.0625, 4, 0.6460, 0.9548)	(12.0068, 4, 0.7709, 0.9676)	(13.7753, 4, 0.8844, 0.9804)
	G_2: max. min.	(3.7116, 5)	(4.8470, 5)	(5.9704, 5)

of the payoffs is even weaker. However, the expected sum of payoffs tends to be greatest when the assessment function is linear or quadratic (i.e. somewhat convex).

The optimal length of the short list is virtually unaffected by the form of the assessment function.

8.4   Effect of the Relative Importance of the Second Signal

Table 5 illustrates the effect of the relative importance of the second signal. It should be noted that as σ increases both the overall variance of the value of an offer and the relative importance of the second signal increase. It is thus unsurprising that the optimal length of the short list is increasing in σ. The relative efficiency of the group decision procedure is almost independent of σ. There is some variation when the residual variance in the second signal is small, but this is likely to be related to the fact that in such cases the short list heuristic is inappropriate (the optimal short list is of length one, i.e. the DMs should choose the best offer on the basis of the first signal). Also, note that when the optimal length of the short list is one under decision rules of both type G_1 and G_3, then the second measure of efficiency is equal to one by definition.

Table 4. Effect of the form of the assessment function: $\sigma = 2, \rho_1 = 1/3$. Empirically derived optimal expected reward (first entry) and optimal length of short list (second entry) for search procedures with two DMs when 100 offers are available. When appropriate, the third and fourth entries give the efficiency measures for the ranked-based decision rule.

		$\rho_2 = 0$	$\rho_2 = 1/3$	$\rho_2 = 2/3$
$\gamma = 1/3$	G_3: max. sum	(7.1723, 5)	(8.5033, 5)	(9.6990, 5)
	G_4: max. min.	(2.0591, 2)	(2.8497, 2)	(3.6604, 2)
	G_1: max. sum.	(6.7304, 5, 0.6237, 0.9384)	(8.1568, 5, 0.7559, 0.9593)	(9.4738, 5, 0.8780, 0.9768)
	G_2: max. min.	(2.3701, 6)	(3.2009, 6)	(4.0442, 6)
$\gamma = 1/2$	G_3: max. sum	(7.1727, 5)	(8.4992, 5)	(9.6955, 6)
	G_4: max. min.	(2.0502, 2)	(2.8381, 2)	(3.6576, 2)
	G_1: max. sum.	(6.7329, 5, 0.6240, 0.9387)	(8.1476, 5, 0.7551, 0.9586)	(9.4670, 6, 0.8773, 0.9764)
	G_2: max. min.	(2.3754, 6)	(3.1983, 6)	(4.0476, 6)
$\gamma = 1$	G_3: max. sum	(7.1849, 5)	(8.5170, 5)	(9.7048, 6)
	G_4: max. min.	(2.0562, 2)	(2.8478, 2)	(3.6611, 2)
	G_1: max. sum.	(6.7938, 5, 0.6296, 0.9456)	(8.2035, 5, 0.7603, 0.9632)	(9.4978, 6, 0.8802, 0.9787)
	G_2: max. min.	(2.3217, 6)	(3.1707, 6)	(4.0304, 6)
$\gamma = 2$	G_3: max. sum	(7.1899, 5)	(8.5169, 5)	(9.7083, 5)
	G_4: max. min.	(2.0460, 2)	(2.8412, 2)	(3.6602, 2)
	G_1: max. sum.	(6.7843, 5, 0.6287, 0.9436)	(8.2132, 5, 0.7612, 0.9643)	(9.5081, 5, 0.8812, 0.9794)
	G_2: max. min.	(2.1543, 5)	(3.0839, 5)	(3.9960, 6)
$\gamma = 3$	G_3: max. sum	(7.2330, 5)	(8.5233, 5)	(9.7076, 6)
	G_4: max. min.	(2.0555, 2)	(2.8442, 2)	(3.6608, 2)
	G_1: max. sum.	(6.7407, 5, 0.6247, 0.9319)	(8.1819, 5, 0.7583, 0.9599)	(9.4957, 6, 0.8800, 0.9782)
	G_2: max. min.	(2.3217, 6)	(3.1707, 6)	(4.0304, 6)

Table 5. Effect of the form of the relative importance of the second signal: $\gamma = 1, \rho_1 = 1/3$. Empirically derived optimal expected reward (first entry) and optimal length of short list (second entry) for search procedures with two DMs when 100 offers are available. When appropriate, the third and fourth entries give the efficiency measures for the ranked-based decision rule.

		$\rho_2 = 0$	$\rho_2 = 1/3$	$\rho_2 = 2/3$
$\sigma = 1/3$	G_3: max. sum	(3.5780, 1)	(4.2259, 1)	(4.8102,1)
	G_4: max. min.	(1.3886, 1)	(1.7505, 1)	(2.1125, 1)
	G_1: max. sum.	(3.5780, 1, 0.6646, 1)	(4.2259, 1, 0.7849, 1)	(4.8102, 1, 0.8938, 1)
	G_2: max. min.	(1.3886, 1)	(1.7505, 1)	(2.1125, 1)
$\sigma = 1/2$	G_3: max. sum	(3.8379, 2)	(4.5492, 2)	(5.1868, 2)
	G_4: max. min.	(1.4202, 1)	(1.8158, 2)	(2.2359, 2)
	G_1: max. sum.	(3.7791, 1, 0.6535, 0.9847)	(4.4573, 1, 0.7707, 0.9798)	(5.0934, 2, 0.8807, 0.9820)
	G_2: max. min.	(1.4202, 1)	(1.8130, 1)	(2.2078, 1)
$\sigma = 1$	G_3: max. sum	(4.8004, 3)	(5.6966, 3)	(6.4946, 3)
	G_4: max. min.	(1.6396, 2)	(2.1693, 2)	(2.7159, 2)
	G_1: max. sum.	(4.5598, 3, 0.6312, 0.9499)	(5.4975, 3, 0.7610, 0.9650)	(6.3587, 3, 0.8803, 0.9791)
	G_2: max. min.	(1.5978, 3)	(2.1497, 3)	(2.7168, 3)
$\sigma = 2$	G_3: max. sum	(7.1849)	(8.5170, 5)	(9.7048, 6)
	G_4: max. min.	(2.0562, 2)	(2.8478, 2)	(3.6611, 2)
	G_1: max. sum.	(6.7938, 5, 0.6296, 0.9436)	(8.2035, 5, 0.7603, 0.9643)	(9.4978, 6, 0.8802, 0.9794)
	G_2: max. min.	(2.3217, 6)	(3.1707, 6)	(4.0304, 6)
$\sigma = 3$	G_3: max. sum	(9.8713, 7)	(11.7110, 7)	(13.3341, 8)
	G_4: max. min.	(2.4390, 2)	(3.5022, 2)	(4.5892, 2)
	G_1: max. sum.	(9.3404, 7, 0.6303, 0.9462)	(11.2795, 8, 0.7612, 0.9632)	(13.0463, 8, 0.8804, 0.9784)
	G_2: max. min.	(3.1994, 8)	(4.3657, 8)	(5.5325, 8)

9 Conclusions and Future Research

This article has presented a model of a group decision procedure based on a short list. In many practical search problems (searching for a flat, second-hand car or employee), a certain amount of information regarding the appropriateness of an offer may be available at low cost. For example, when searching for a flat a couple may find basic information about offers (e.g. size, price, location) via the Internet. However, in order to accurately assess the value of an offer, it is necessarily to physically view a flat. When facing such a search problem, a two-stage procedure based on a the short list heuristic can be a very successful approach.

This paper has considered such a problem with multiple DMs. Using a group decision procedure, the DMs should define the way in which offers will be assessed in both rounds of the search procedure and how many offers should be considered in the second round (the length of the short list). The precise form of such a decision rule depends on the overall goals of the DMs (e.g. they can aim to maximise the expected sum of the payoffs or maximise the minimum reward obtained over the set of DMs), the coherence of the preferences of the decision makers and the relative value of the information gained at each stage of the search process.

It is assumed that the assessment function used to measure the overall attractiveness of an offer to the DMs is based on each DM's ranking of the offers (as assessed according to initial information and then after closer inspection of the items on the short list). Such functions are quite easy to use and robust, e.g. when DMs do not have private information above the preferences of others, then it is always optimal to report one's preferences honestly. The exact form of the assessment function seems only to have a subtle effect on the effectiveness of such a group decision procedure. For example, concave assessment functions place a higher stress on maximising the minimum payoff obtained over the set of DMs rather than maximising the sum of their payoffs. However, such rules are generally very robust (the rule of this form which maximises the expected sum of payoffs is always very similar to the rule which maximises the expected value of the minimum reward obtained over the set of DMs). Since the assessment function seems to have little effect on the effectiveness of a decision procedure, it might be concluded that it is practical to use a linear assessment function. Using such a procedure, the k items on a short list correspond to the k offers corresponding to the lowest sums of the ranks ascribed by the DMs in the first round of the search procedure. In the second round of the search procedure, the offer chosen corresponds to the minimum sum of the ranks ascribed by the DMs after closer inspection of offers on the short list. Also, the optimal length of the short list seems to be almost independent of whether there is a single DM or a pair of DMs.

It has been shown that such a group decision procedure can be both efficient and robust (attain a high expected sum of payoffs, while ensuring that the DMs accept an offer that is highly attractive to each of them). Such search procedures are particularly effective when the preferences of the DMs are coherent.

Future research should look at what types of decision procedures are efficient when asymmetries exist between the DMs, how other forms of the assessment function affect the efficiency of a decision procedure and investigate other approaches to such decision problems (e.g. game-theoretic, including cooperative games).

Acknowledgements. This research was funded by Polish National Science Centre grant number 2018/29/B/HS4/02857, "Logistics, Trade and Consumer Decisions in the Age of the Internet".   □

References

Alpern, S., Baston, V.: The secretary problem with a selection committee: do conformist committees hire better secretaries? Manag. Sci. **63**(4), 1184–1197 (2016)

Analytis, P.P., Kothiyal, A., Katsikopoulos, K.: Multi-attribute utility models as cognitive search engines. Judgm. Decis. Mak. **95**, 403–419 (2014)

Armouti-Hansen, J., Kops, C.: This or that? Sequential rationalization of indecisive choice behavior. Theory Decis. **84**(4), 507–524 (2018)

Aumann, R.J.: Correlated equilibrium as an expression of Bayesian rationality. Econometrica J. Econ. Soc. **55**(1), 1–18 (1987)

Bobadilla-Suarez, S., Love, B.C.: Fast or frugal, but not both: decision heuristics under time pressure. J. Exp. Psychol. Learn. Mem. Cogn. **44**(1), 24 (2018)

Borah, A., Kops, C.: Rational choices: an ecological approach. Theory Decis **86**(3–4), 401–420 (2019)

Fehr, E., Schmidt, K. M.: The economics of fairness, reciprocity and altruism? Experimental evidence and new theories. In: Kolm, S.C., Ythier, J.M. (eds.) Handbook of the Economics of Giving, Altruism and Reciprocity, vol. 1, pp. 615–691 (2006)

Gibbard, A.: Manipulation of voting schemes. A general result. Econometrica **41**, 587–601 (1973)

Horn, R.A., Johnson, C.R.: Matrix Analysis. Cambridge University Press, Cambridge (1985)

Kimya, M.: Choice, consideration sets, and attribute filters. Am. Econ. J. Microecon. **10**(4), 223–247 (2018)

Kontek, K., Sosnowska, H.: Specific tastes or cliques of jurors? (2018). https://papers.ssrn.com/sol3/papers.cfm?abstract_id=3297252. Accessed 4 Jan 2020

Lleras, J.S., Masatlioglu, Y., Nakajima, D., Ozbay, E.Y.: When more is less: limited consideration. J. Econ. Theory **170**, 70–85 (2017)

Mandler, M., Manzini, P., Mariotti, M.: A million answers to twenty questions: choosing by checklist. J. Econ. Theory **147**(1), 71–92 (2012)

Masatlioglu, Y., Nakajima, D., Ozbay, E.Y.: Revealed attention. Am. Econ. Rev. **102**(5), 2183–2205 (2012)

Nash, J.: Equilibrium points in n-person games. Proc. Natl. Acad. Sci. **36**(1), 48–49 (1950)

von Neumann, J., Morgenstern, O.: Theory of Games and Economic Behavior. Princeton University Press, Princeton (1944)

Ramsey, D.M., Szajowski, K.: Selection of a correlated equilibrium in Markov stopping games. Eur. J. Oper. Res. **184**(1), 185–206 (2008)

Ramsey, D.M.: Optimal Selection from a set of offers using a short list. To appear in Multiple Criteria Decision Making (2019)

Ramsey, D.M.: A game theoretic model of choosing a valuable good via a short list heuristic. Submitted to Mathematics (2020)

Rubinstein, A., Salant, Y.: A model of choice from lists. Theor. Econ. **1**(1), 3–17 (2006)

Sakaguchi, M., Mazalov, V.V.: A non-zero-sum no-information best-choice game. Math. Methods Oper. Res. **60**(3), 437–451 (2004)

Shapley, L.S.: A value for n-person games. Contrib. Theory Games **2**(28), 307–317 (1953)

Simon, H.A.: A behavioral model of rational choice. Q. J. Econ. **69**(1), 99–118 (1955)

Simon, H.A.: Rational choice and the structure of the environment. Psychol. Rev. **63**(2), 129 (1956)

Todd, P.M., Gigerenzer, G.: Précis of simple heuristics that make us smart. Behav. Brain Sci. **23**(5), 727–741 (2000)

Taha, H.A.: Operations Research: An Introduction. Pearson Education Limited, London (2017)

Taylor, A.D., Pacelli, A.M.: Mathematics and Politics: Strategy, Voting, Power, and Proof. Springer, Berlin (2008). https://doi.org/10.1007/978-0-387-77645-3

A Note on Equal Treatment
and Symmetry of Values

Marcin Malawski[1,2]([⊠])

[1] Leon Koźmiński University, Jagiellońska 59, 03-301 Warszawa, Poland
mmn@kozminski.edu.pl
[2] Institute of Computer Science PAS, Jana Kazimierza 5, 01-248 Warszawa, Poland

Abstract. We investigate under what conditions equal treatment property and symmetry of a value for cooperative games are equivalent. For additive values, null player property or efficiency is sufficient for the equivalence. When additivity is replaced by fairness, both equivalences cease to be true. But the marginal contributions condition ensures the equivalence without any additional assumptions.

Keywords: Cooperative games · Value · Symmetry · Equal treatment · Marginal contributions property · Fairness

1 Introduction and Prerequisites

Two notions of "symmetry" of (single-valued) solutions have co-existed for a long time in the theories of axiomatic bargaining and of cooperative games: a stronger one [4,11] requiring the solution of games (bargaining problems) to commute with the re-labellings of players and nowadays often called "anonymity", and a weaker one [5,7] requiring only that symmetries in games (problems) be reflected by symmetries in their solutions.[1] In bargaining theory both of them were called "symmetry" and were often used almost interchangeably. In cooperative game theory Lehrer [5] explicitly distinguished the weaker equal treatment property from Shapley's symmetry and applied it to characterize axiomatically the Banzhaf value.

In this note the term "symmetry" will be used in its stronger (anonymity) meaning, to be distinguished from the equal treatment property. However, it should be kept in mind that much of the literature (e.g. [1,10]) uses this term to denote equal treatment and to be distinguished from anonymity.

It is obvious that symmetry implies equal treatment, but not conversely. However, in cooperative game theory it can often be traced directly from the

---

[1] For *multivalued* solutions an alternative stronger version of equal treatment is discussed by Aumann [2].

M. Malawski—I am grateful to two anonymous referees for their helpful remarks and for correcting some minor errors in the paper. Any remaining errors are, of course, my own.

N. T. Nguyen et al. (Eds.): TCCI XXXV, LNCS 12330, pp. 76–84, 2020.
https://doi.org/10.1007/978-3-662-62245-2_5

proofs that the equal treatment property is sufficient in standard axiomatizations of solutions that originally include the symmetry condition. It is therefore of interest to study when the two conditions are equivalent, aiming at general theorems. For additive values one such theorem assuming dummy player property was proved in [6]; it is recalled in a slightly stronger version as Theorem 1 in this note. Further, it is shown that the null player condition in Theorem 1 can be replaced by efficiency of the value; this is Theorem 2. One direct corollary of the two results is the equivalence of fairness (as defined by van den Brink [12]) and symmetry under the same assumptions.

It was also observed in [6] that in various axiomatic characterizations of values linearity can be replaced by the "marginal contributions" condition à la [14] (this itself being a marginal contribution added to earlier ones by Young [14] and Nowak [8]). Therefore, a natural question arises whether this observation applies also to Theorems 1 and 2. Theorem 4 provides a positive answer to this question. Moreover, it turns out that the marginal contributions alone implies the equivalence – no additional normalizing assumption like efficiency or null player property is needed.

Recall that an n-person (transferable utility) <u>cooperative game</u> is a pair (N, v) where $N = \{1, 2, \ldots, n\}$ is the set of players and v is the <u>characteristic function</u> – a real-valued function defined on the set $\mathcal{N} = 2^N$ of all <u>coalitions</u>, fulfilling $v(\emptyset) = 0$. The value of this function on a coalition T, $v(T)$, is often called the <u>worth</u> of the coalition T. Whenever it causes no confusion, the game will be identified with its characteristic function, and so (N, v) will be replaced by just v; thus, the games will henceforth be usually denoted by v, w, ... Let $\mathcal{G}_n$ denote the set of all n-person cooperative transferable utility games, and $\mathcal{G}^* = \bigcup_{n=1}^{\infty} \mathcal{G}_n$. A <u>value</u> is any function $\psi : \mathcal{G}^* \to \bigcup_{n=1}^{\infty} R^n$ such that $\psi(\mathcal{G}_n) \subset R^n$ for every n; the individual values of players in a game v are components of $\psi(v)$.

Given the set $N = \{1, 2, \ldots, n\}$ of players and a player $i \in N$, the notation $\mathcal{N}_{-i} = \mathcal{N} \cap 2^{N \setminus \{i\}}$ will be used for the set of all coalitions which do not contain player i. For brevity, braces in one-element sets – e.g. in $T \cup \{j\}$ – will be omitted (to obtain $T \cup j$), and the marginal contribution of player i in the game v to a coalition T not containing i, $v(T \cup i) - v(T)$, will be denoted by $v_i'(T)$.

For sake of completeness, all properties of values used in what follows are recalled below.

NP *Null player property*: If for every $S \in \mathcal{N}_{-i}$ $v_i'(S) = 0$, then $\psi_i(v) = 0$.

MC *Marginal contributions*: If for two games $v, w \in \mathcal{G}_n$ the equality $v_j'(S) = w_j'(S)$ holds for every coalition $S \in \mathcal{N}_{-j}$, then $\psi_j(v) = \psi_j(w)$.

ET *Equal treatment property*: If for every coalition $S \in \mathcal{N}_{-i} \cap \mathcal{N}_{-j}$ $v(S \cup j) = v(S \cup i)$ (and thus $v_i'(S) = v_j'(S)$), then $\psi_i(v) = \psi_j(v)$.

S *Symmetry*: For any permutation Π of N and any game $v \in \mathcal{G}_n$, denote by $\Pi^* v$ the game given by $\Pi^* v(S) = v(\Pi(S))$ for each $S \subset N$. Then $\psi_i(\Pi^* v) = \psi_{\Pi(i)}(v)$ $\forall i \in N$.

A *Additivity*: For any two games $v, w \in \mathcal{G}_n$ we have $\psi(v + w) = \psi(v) + \psi(w)$.

EF *Efficiency*: For every n and every game $v \in \mathcal{G}_n$, $\sum_{i=1}^{n} \psi_i(v) = v(N)$.

F *Fairness*: If $v, w \in \mathcal{G}_n$ and for every $S \in \mathcal{N}_{-i} \cap \mathcal{N}_{-j}$ $v(S \cup j) = v(S \cup i)$, then $\psi_i(v + w) - \psi_i(w) = \psi_j(v + w) - \psi_j(w)$.

Notice that **NP**, **ET** and **EF** are "punctual" properties of values (cf. [3]) – implications of the form $\mathcal{P}(v) \Rightarrow \mathcal{Q}((\psi(v))$ asserting that some property $\mathcal{P}$ of a game implies some property $\mathcal{Q}$ of value of this game, while the other four are "relational" properties stating that some relation $\mathcal{R}$ between (in their case) two games implies some relation $\mathcal{Q}$ between their values. It is clear that, if **ET** (a punctual property) is to imply **S** (a relational one), then some additional relational property of the value must be assumed. In the next two sections we investigate equivalence of equal treatment, fairness and symmetry for additive values, and extensions with fairness replacing additivity. In the last section we prove the equivalence of equal treatment and symmetry for values having the marginal contributions property.

2   Equal Treatment and Symmetry for Additive Values

In this section we study the case when the assumed additional relational property of the value is additivity (**A**) and show that, under **A** and some of punctual normalizing assumptions, equal treatment is equivalent to symmetry.

Theorem 1. *Every additive value satisfying conditions* **NP** *and* **ET** *is symmetric.*

This is theorem 4(b) in [6] with the stronger dummy player condition replaced by null player property. However, it is only **NP** that is used in the original proof, so it is not repeated here.

Theorem 2. *Every efficient additive value with the* **ET** *property is symmetric.*

Proof. Let us fix the player set N. It is well-known that every game $v \in \mathcal{G}_n$ can be expressed as a (unique) linear combination of unanimity games:

$$v = \sum_{T \subset N, T \neq \emptyset} c_T u_T,$$

where for every nonempty coalition T, c_T is a real number and the game u_T given by

$$u_T(S) = \begin{cases} 1 & \text{if } S \supseteq T \\ 0 & \text{if } T \setminus S \neq \emptyset \end{cases}$$

is the unanimity game of coalition T.

Now let ψ be any additive and efficient value on $\mathcal{G}_n$ satisfying **ET**, and let Y be any coalition in $\mathcal{N}$. We first note that by equal treatment $\psi_k(u_Y) = \psi_l(u_Y)$ for every $k, l \in Y$, and $\psi_k(u_Y) = \psi_l(u_Y)$ for every $k, l \notin Y$. Thus, the numbers

e_Y = the value of any non-null player in u_Y (member of Y), and
z_Y = the value of any null player in u_Y (non-member of Y)

are well defined, and by efficiency

$$\sum_{k \in N} \psi_k(u_Y) = ye_Y + (n - y)z_Y = u_Y(N) = 1 \quad \text{(where } y = \#Y\text{)}.$$

Second, we show that for any two coalitions S and T of equal size, $e_S = e_T$ and $z_S = z_T$. When S and T differ by just one player, i.e. $S = U \cup i$, $T = U \cup j$, $i \neq j$, consider the game $w = u_S + u_T$. In this game we have for every coalition $Z \in \mathcal{N}_{-i} \cap \mathcal{N}_{-j}$

$$w_i'(Z) = w_j'(Z) = \begin{cases} 1 & Z \supseteq U \\ 0 & U \setminus Z \neq \emptyset, \end{cases}$$

so, again by equal treatment, $\psi_i(w) = \psi_j(w)$. By additivity, this implies $\psi_i(u_S) + \psi_i(u_T) = \psi_j(u_S) + \psi_j(u_T)$, so (as $i \in S \setminus T$ and $j \in T \setminus S$)

$$e_S + z_T = z_S + e_T. \tag{1}$$

But since ψ is efficient, we have $\sum_{k \in N} \psi_k(u_S) = \sum_{k \in N} \psi_k(u_T) = 1$, thus

$$se_S + (n - s)z_S = te_T + (n - t)z_T \tag{2}$$

where $s = \#S, t = \#T$. Since $s = t$ and $n - s > 0$, (1) and (2) give $nz_T = nz_S$ and so $e_T = e_S$. For other pairs (S', T') of coalitions of equal size, we obtain $e_{S'} = e_{T'}$ and $z_{S'} = z_{T'}$ by $r = \#(S \setminus T)$ successive replacements of single players.

Third, notice that the above argument is also valid for games of the form $c \cdot u_Y$ where c is any non-zero constant. Therefore, the numbers $e_{c,Y}$ and $z_{c,Y}$ – the values of any non-null player and of any null player in cu_Y are well defined, and whenever $\#S = \#T$, $e_{c,S} = e_{c,T}$ and $z_{c,S} = z_{c,T}$. (When c is rational, additivity implies that $e_{c,Y} = ce_Y$ and $z_{c,Y} = cz_Y$, but for non-rational constants this need not be true).

Therefore, we obtain for every permutation Π of the set N and every game of the form $w = c \cdot u_T$

$$\psi_i(\Pi^* w) = \begin{cases} ce_T & \text{when } \Pi(i) \in T \\ cz_T & \text{when } \Pi(i) \notin T \end{cases}$$

(because $\Pi^* w(S) = w(\Pi(S)) = c$ for $\Pi(S) \supseteq T$ and $\Pi^* w(S) = w(\Pi(S)) = 0$ for $T \setminus \Pi(S) \neq \emptyset$), and employing additivity once again we obtain symmetry for all games in $\mathcal{G}_n$.

$$\text{QED}$$

Remark 1. When the additivity assumption in theorems 1 and 2 is strenghtened to linearity by adding the homogeneity condition ($\psi(cv) = c \cdot \psi(v)$ for any real number c), it can be proved that the values satisfying all assumptions are of

80   M. Malawski

specific forms. This was done for values having the dummy player property by
Weber [13][2] and for efficient values by Ruiz et al. [10]. However, in both cases
"full" linearity is necessary, because without homogeneity nothing can be said
about relation between $\psi(c \cdot u_T)$ and $\psi(u_T)$ when c is not rational.

Remark 2. It might be asked whether an additional normalization condition like
NP or **EF** is indeed necessary in theorems 1 and 2, i.e. whether additivity (or
maybe linearity) itself is not sufficient for the equivalence of equal treatment and
symmetry. The answer is positive: it is not difficult to construct non-symmetric
linear values with equal treatment property. In particular, one simple sufficient
condition for a linear value to fulfill **ET** is

$$\forall S, T \subset N \quad (\#S = \#T \quad \Rightarrow \quad e_S - z_S = e_T - z_T)$$

(notation e. and z. as in the proof of Theorem 2), while symmetry **S** is equivalent
to

$$\forall S, T \subset N \quad (\#S = \#T \quad \Rightarrow \quad e_S = e_T \text{ and } z_S = z_T).$$

3   Fairness as a Substitute for Additivity or Equal Treatment

In an interesting axiomatization of the Shapley value van den Brink [12] introduced the fairness property of values, **F**. In comparison to the original characterization by Shapley [11], the **F** condition in that axioms system appears to
work as a substitute for both equal treatment (symmetry) and linearity.

The first rôle is obvious, since it follows immediately from the definition that
under **NP** fairness implies equal treatment. Moreover, another straightforward
observation on fairness is the following

Remark 3. For additive values the conditions **ET** and **F** are equivalent.

Therefore, an equivalent result follows at no cost from Theorems 1 and 2:

Theorem 3. *Every additive value satisfying fairness and either **NP** or **EF** is
symmetric.*

The second rôle of the **F** condition is more interesting, and it raises a question
whether fairness can substitute *additivity* in Theorems 1 and 2. The answer, however, is negative, as demonstrated by two examples below. For simplicity, they
are both on the space $\mathcal{G}_2$ of *two-person* games, but at an expense of some compli-
cation can also be generalized to $\mathcal{G}_n$. The values in both examples satisfy **ET** and
F; moreover, the value in Example 1 has the null player property (actually, even
the stronger dummy player property), and the value in Example 2 is efficient.
None of them, however, is symmetric.

---

[2] Weber actually assumes symmetry instead of equal treatment, but theorem 1 ensures
that the two are equivalent.

Example 1. Denote for every two-person game v

$$\sigma(v) = v(12) - (v(1) + v(2))$$

and

$$a_{12} = \text{sgn}\,(v(1) - v(2))$$

(sgn is the sign function: $\text{sgn}(0) = 0$ and $\text{sgn}(x) = \frac{x}{|x|}$ for $x \neq 0$), and consider the following value γ on $\mathcal{G}_2$:

$$\gamma_1(v) = v(1) + a_{12} \cdot \sigma(v), \quad \gamma_2(v) = v(2) + a_{12} \cdot \sigma(v).$$

Clearly, γ is fair, because adding a game in which players are interchangeable increases both $v(i)$s by the same amount and does not affect a_{12}. Also, γ satisfies null player and equal treatment conditions: if any player is a null player (in fact, even if he is a dummy player), then $\sigma(v) = 0$, and if they are interchangeable, then $a_{12} = 0$, and so in both cases $\gamma_i(v) = v(i)$ for $i = 1, 2$. But obviously γ is not symmetric, because renumbering the players usually changes the *set* of individual values: depending on the sign of the difference $v(1) - v(2)$, either both players gain or both lose in comparison to their worths as one-person coalitions.

Example 2. Consider the value ξ on $\mathcal{G}_2$ defined by

$$\xi_1(v) = \frac{v(12) - |v(1) - v(2)|}{2} + \frac{2\,(v(1) - v(2))^+}{3} + \frac{(v(2) - v(1))^+}{4},$$

$$\xi_2(v) = \frac{v(12) - |v(1) - v(2)|}{2} + \frac{(v(1) - v(2))^+}{3} + \frac{3\,(v(2) - v(1))^+}{4}.$$

where $c^+ = \max(c, 0)$ denotes the positive part of the number c. This value is obtained as follows: The smaller of worths of one-person coalitions and the smaller of marginal contributions to the grand coalition are divided equally. The rest of $v(12)$ – i.e., the difference between the larger and smaller worth of one-person coalitions – is divided between players 1 and 2 in proportion 2:1 if $v(1) > v(2)$, and in proportion 1:3 if $v(1) < v(2)$. (These proportions can be modified at will). It is obvious that ξ is efficient and satisfies **ET**; it is also fair, since adding a game in which the two players are interchangeable does not affect $v(1) - v(2)$. But, clearly, ξ is not symmetric.

Finally, notice that fairness, efficiency *and* null player property *together* do imply the equivalence between equal treatment and symmetry. But it is so because they simply characterize the Shapley value – this is precisely the main theorem of [12].

4   Equal Treatment and Symmetry for Marginalistic Values

As mentioned in the introduction, the marginal contributions condition can successfully replace linearity/additivity in quite a few axioms systems for values.

In this section we show that this is also the case for the results on **ET** $\Leftrightarrow$ **S** equivalence of Sect. 2. In fact, the **MC** condition turns out to be even more powerful in this context: assuming it, we can even dispose of *any* normalizing assumptions (like efficiency or null player property).

Theorem 4. *Every value satisfying conditions* **MC** *and* **ET** *is symmetric.*

The proof proceeds through a sequence of lemmata. We have to show that $\psi_i(\Pi^* v) = \psi_{\Pi(i)}(v)\ \forall i \in N$. To this end, we first introduce two operators on the set $\mathcal{G}_n$ and establish some of their properties used thereafter to prove the required equality for Π being a transposition of two players. Then we use the well-known fact that each permutation is a composition of transpositions to prove symmetry.

For the set of players N and two players $i, j \in N$, let $T_{i/j}$ be the transposition interchanging players i and j:

$$T_{i/j}(k) = \begin{cases} k & \text{for } k \neq i, j\,, \\ i & \text{for } k = j\,, \\ j & \text{for } k = i\,; \end{cases}$$

and let $I_{ij} : \mathcal{G}_n \to \mathcal{G}_n$ be the operator defined by

$$I_{ij}(v)(U) = v((T_{i/j}(U))\quad \forall U \subset N.$$

Also, define the following operator $S_{ij} : \mathcal{G}_n \to \mathcal{G}_n$:

$$S_{ij}(v)(T) = \begin{cases} v(T) & \text{when } i \notin T, \\ v(T \cup j \setminus i) & \text{when } i \in T, j \notin T, \\ v(T) - v(T \setminus j) + v(T \setminus i) & \text{when } i, j \in T. \end{cases}$$

I_{ij} is the operator of *interchange* of players i and j, and S_{ij} – of *substitution* for player i another player whose rôle in the game is exactly the same as that of player j while preserving the worths of all coalitions which do not include player i.

Denote:

$$v_{i/j} = I_{ij}(v),\quad v_{i\to j} = S_{ij}(v).$$

Lemma 1. *For every game $v \in \mathcal{G}_n$ and every $k, l, m \in N$,*

(a) $\forall T \in \mathcal{N}_{-k} \cap \mathcal{N}_{-l}\quad (v_{k\to l})'_k(T) = (v_{k\to l})'_l(T)$,
(b) $\forall T \in \mathcal{N}_{-l}\quad (v_{k\to l})'_l(T) = v'_l(T)$,
(c) $\forall T \in \mathcal{N}_{-k}\quad (v_{k\to l})'_k(T) = (v_{k/l})'_k(T)$,
(d) *if $k, l, m \in N$ are all distinct, then* $I_{kl} \circ S_{km} = S_{lm} \circ I_{kl}$,
     or equivalently $\quad (v_{k\to m})_{k/l} = (v_{k/l})_{l\to m}\quad \forall v \in \mathcal{G}^*$.

Proof. (a) and (b) follow directly from the definition of the game $v_{k\to l}$. To prove (c), observe that $(v_{k\to l})'_k(T) = v'_l(T)$ when $k, l \notin T$, and

$$(v_{k\to l})'_k(T) = (v(T \cup k) - v(T \cup k \setminus l) + v(T)) - v(T) =$$
$$= v(T \cup k) - v(T \cup k \setminus l) = (v_{k/l})'_k(T)$$

when $k \notin T$, $l \in T$. The proof of (d) is somewhat tedious but in fact quite straightforward – we have to check that both games $(v_{k \to m})_{k/l}$ and $(v_{k/l})_{l \to m}$ take the same values on every coalition T depending on which of the players k, l, m belong to T. For instance, when $l, m \in T$ but $k \notin T$, we have

$$(v_{k \to m})_{k/l}(T) = v_{k \to m}(T \cup k \setminus l) = v(T \cup k \setminus l) - v(T \cup k \setminus \{l, m\}) + v(T \setminus l)$$

and

$$(v_{k/l})_{l \to m}(T) = v_{k/l}(T) - v_{k/l}(T \setminus m) + v_{k/l}(T \setminus l) =$$
$$= v(T \cup k \setminus l) - v(T \cup k \setminus \{l, m\}) + v(T \setminus l).$$

In exactly the same way (but usually easier) it is shown that in other cases both $(v_{k \to m})_{k/l}(T)$ and $(v_{k/l})_{l \to m}(T)$ are equal to

$$
\begin{array}{ll}
v(T) & \text{for } k, l \notin T, \\
v(T \cup l \setminus k) & \text{for } k \in T, \ l \notin T, \\
v(T \cup m \setminus k) & \text{for } k, l \in T, \ m \notin T, \\
v(T) - v(T \setminus m) + v(T \setminus k) & \text{for } k, l, m \in T, \\
v(T \cup m \setminus l) & \text{for } l \in T, \ k, m \notin T, \\
v(T \cup k \setminus l) - v(T \cup k \setminus \{l, m\}) + v(T \setminus l) & \text{for } l, m \in T, \ k \notin T.
\end{array}
$$

QED

Lemma 2. *Let ψ be any value satisfying conditions* **MC** *and* **ET**. *Then for every game v and every two distinct players k, l in v we have*

$$\psi_m(v_{k/l}) = \psi_{T_{k/l}(m)}(v) \quad \forall m \in N.$$

Proof. We need to show that:

(a) $\psi_k(v_{k/l}) = \psi_l(v)$,   (b) $\psi_l(v_{k/l}) = \psi_k(v)$,
(c) $\psi_m(v_{k/l}) = \psi_m(v)$ for $m \neq k, l$.

To prove (a), consider the game $z = v_{k \to l}$. Lemma 1 (a) and **ET** imply that $\psi_k(z) = \psi_l(z)$, Lemma 1 (c) and **MC** – that $\psi_k(z) = \psi_k(v_{k/l})$, and Lemma 1 (b) and **MC** – that $\psi_l(z) = \psi_l(v)$. The three equations together give (a). (b) is proved in the same way using the game $v_{l \to k}$, and (c) is obtained from the following sequence of equations:

$$
\begin{array}{ll}
\psi_m(v) = \psi_m(v_{k \to m}) & \text{(by } \mathbf{MC} \text{ and lemma 1 (b))} \\
= \psi_k(v_{k \to m}) & \text{(by } \mathbf{ET} \text{ and lemma 1 (a))} \\
= \psi_l((v_{k \to m})_{k/l}) & \text{(by (b))} \\
= \psi_l((v_{k/l})_{l \to m}) & \text{(by lemma 1 (d))} \\
= \psi_m((v_{k/l})_{l \to m}) & \text{(by } \mathbf{ET} \text{ and lemma 1 (a))} \\
= \psi_m(v_{k/l}) & \text{(by } \mathbf{MC} \text{ and lemma 1 (b)).}
\end{array}
$$

QED

Lemma 3. *Let Π_1, Π_2 be two permutations of the set N, and let $\Pi = \Pi_2 \circ \Pi_1$. Then every value ψ satisfying*

$$\psi_j(\Pi_1^* v) = \psi_{\Pi_1(j)}(v) \quad and \quad \psi_j(\Pi_2^* v) = \psi_{\Pi_2(j)}(v) \quad \forall j \in N, \ v \in \mathcal{G}_n$$

satisfies also $\psi_j(\Pi^* v) = \psi_{\Pi(j)}(v) \quad \forall j \in N, \ v \in \mathcal{G}_n.$

Proof. Straightforward: keeping in mind that $(\Pi_2 \circ \Pi_1)^* = \Pi_1^* \circ \Pi_2^*$, we immediately obtain

$$\psi_j(\Pi^* v) = \psi_j(\Pi_1^*(\Pi_2^* v)) = \psi_{\Pi_1(j)}(\Pi_2^* v) = \psi_{\Pi(j)}(v).$$

Proof of the Theorem. Lemma 2 assures the "anonymity" of values having the **ET** and **MC** properties in the case of permutation Π being a transposition. To obtain the same for any permutation Π and thus to complete the proof of the theorem it remains to combine Lemma 2 with Lemma 3 and with the fact that every permutation can be decomposed into a finite number of transpositions.

QED

Remark 4. In some axiomatic characterizations of Shapley and Banzhaf values, the equal treatment condition is further weakened, being assumed only for some specific pairs instead of all pairs of players – namely, for *mutually dependent* or *mutually independent* players (see [9] and [6]). In view of this, it might be an interesting problem to check also under what additional conditions, or sets of conditions, these weaker versions of equal treatment imply **ET** or even symmetry.

References

1. Algaba, E., Fragnelli, V., Sánchez-Soriano, J.: The Shapley value, a paradigm of fairness. In: Algaba, E., Fragnelli, V., Sánchez-Soriano, J. (eds.) Handbook of the Shapley Value. CRC Press, Boca Raton (2019)
2. Aumann, R.: Value, symmetry and equal treatment: a comment on Scafuri and Yannelis. Econometrica **55**, 1461–1464 (1987)
3. Béal, S., Casajus, A., Huettner, F., Rémila, E., Solal, P.: Characterizations of weighted and equal division values. Theory Decis. **80**(4), 649–667 (2015). https://doi.org/10.1007/s11238-015-9519-7
4. Kalai, E., Smorodinsky, M.: Other solutions to Nash bargaining problem. Econometrica **43**, 513–518 (1975)
5. Lehrer, E.: An axiomatization of the Banzhaf value. Int. J. Game Theory **17**, 89–99 (1988)
6. Malawski, M.: Equal treatment, symmetry and Banzhaf value axiomatizations. Int. J. Game Theory **31**, 47–67 (2002)
7. Nash, J.F.: The bargaining problem. Econometrica **18**, 155–162 (1950)
8. Nowak, A.: On an axiomatization of the Banzhaf value without the additivity axiom. Int. J. Game Theory **26**, 137–141 (1997)
9. Nowak, A., Radzik, T.: On axiomatizations of the weighted Shapley values. Games Econ. Behav. **8**, 389–405 (1995)
10. Ruiz, L.M., Valenciano, F., Zarzuelo, J.M.: The family of least square values for transferable utility games. Games Econ. Behav. **24**, 109–130 (1998)
11. Shapley, L.S.: A value for n-person games. In: Kuhn, H., Tucker, A.W. (eds.) Contributions to the Theory of Games, vol. 2. Princeton University Press (1953)
12. van den Brink, R.: An axiomatization of the Shapley value using a fairness property. Int. J. Game Theory **30**, 309–319 (2001)
13. Weber, R.J.: Probabilistic values for games. In: Roth, A.E. (ed.) The Shapley Value: Essays in Honor of Lloyd Shapley, pp. 101–119. Cambridge University Press, Cambridge (1988)
14. Young, H.P.: Monotonic solutions of cooperative games. Int. J. Game Theory **14**, 65–72 (1985)

Decision-Driven Model for Building IoT Architecture in Environmental Engineering

Cezary Orłowski$^{(\boxtimes)}$ ⓘ, Adam Czarnecki ⓘ, Tomasz Sitek ⓘ, and Artur Ziółkowski ⓘ

WSB University in Gdańsk, Gdańsk, Poland
{corlowski,aczarnecki,tsitek,aziolkowski}@wsb.gda.pl

Abstract. The subject of the article is the presentation of building the model of the Internet of Things (IoT) architecture in environmental engineering. The starting point is the existing four-stage IoT architecture models. The article suggests adding the fifth stage - managing the IoT system construction process, including the creation of three additional layers. The approach proposed in this article was verified in the construction of the air quality assessment system in Gdańsk in which the system architecture integrates the management stage. The developed model is the basis for the ontological model of IoT architecture developed by the authors and presented in this article, easy to implement in the construction of system architectures in environmental engineering.

Keywords: Internet of Things · IoT · System architecture · Measurement network · Knowledge base systems · Environmental engineering · Domain ontology

1 Introduction

Measurement networks are one of the most important elements of an urban infrastructure consistent with the paradigm of "smart cities". The biggest agglomerations (e.g. Singapore, Mexico) use data from measurement networks in the process of decision taking on various levels. Based on a long-term analysis of the data strategic decisions regarding infrastructure development are made, e.g. the location of industrial centers or ring roads. In turn, based on current data (provided as often as every second) it is possible to make ad hoc, operational decisions, such as counteracting any threats to the health caused by local pollution or pollination (e.g. firefighters pouring water over road surface).

Because of an important role (both from the inhabitants' and the city government's point of view) that measurement networks and the data they provide play, the complex and complicated task of designing these networks based on architecture became an important issue in modern IT. It seems to be a complex matter, which is proven by the fact that network designing consists of a number of interdisciplinary problems, from engineering (e.g. in terms of network architecture, software used or sensors standard), through managing (in terms of the localization of particular network elements) to social (in terms of the credibility of the results from the network). It is also a complicated

© Springer-Verlag GmbH Germany, part of Springer Nature 2020
N. T. Nguyen et al. (Eds.): TCCI XXXV, LNCS 12330, pp. 85–98, 2020.
https://doi.org/10.1007/978-3-662-62245-2_6

issue, which is proven by the fact that modern measurement networks are built of elements (sensors) that differ in the quality of measurements, which makes it necessary to standardize them based on additional, dedicated methods. Furthermore, it seems that in many agglomerations the networks develop in an uncontrolled way (i.e. by turning on different sensors), which makes it more difficult to make a decision later on.

All of the problems that are discussed above, connected to the process of creating and managing the network, lead to thinking about methods that both make the data credible and allow designing effective and high-quality networks. That is why, while considering the issue of building measurement networks in agglomerations one that is complex technically and socially, the following questions should be asked in this article:

- What design decisions (managing and engineering) determine a successful implementation of a measurement network, while providing credible data based on which decisions can be made in urban agglomerations?
- What should be the configuration (architecture?) of a hybrid network, for it to provide credible data (ipso facto what determines a successful network construction project)?
- What quality criteria should be applied to evaluate the network, its purpose and effectiveness as a final result of a project?

To answer these questions it is vital to consider the issue of IoT management, which should be divided into two problem areas:

- Managing IoT devices;
- Managing data processed by these devices.

First area—managing the devices—can be called an indirect aim of the project. It focuses on design issues of the target solution. Two basic decision-making problems are noticeable here:

- Regarding the choice of sensors: the choice of a type/technology used has a direct influence on the quality of the measurements, which the device will provide;
- Establishing the right localization for each of these devices.

Second area is the direct aim of the project, supporting management decisions. Properly designed IoT sensors network will gather measurement data—both considering the pollution and the weather conditions. Based on this kind of data the development of decision-making rules is planned, which then provide the decision makers with suggestions as to how to act (e.g. the reaction to measuring anomalies or preventing activities of any kind).

It should be noted that both decision-making areas discussed above are connected by a cause and effect relationship. The measurements—their quality—depend on the decisions made at the stage of designing. It affects the final actions of the decision maker, which the project supports.

2   State of Art - Existing IoT Architecture Frameworks

In this paper, however, authors would like to take into consideration a specific subdomain of the IoT knowledge: it's architecture. There are at least several public models of IoT architecture, but the review of published articles on this matter doesn't bring any formal ontology dedicated in particular to the IoT architecture.

2.1   IoT-A/ARM

One of the IoT architecture models in question is called Internet of Things – Architecture (IoT-A) with its Architectural Reference Model (ARM) [1]. It consists of the IoT Reference Model that provides the highest abstraction level for the definition of the IoT Architectural Reference Model, IoT Reference Architecture that is the reference for building compliant IoT architectures, and The Guidelines that presents how Models, Views and Perspectives described in the first two parts of the document can be concretely used.

In the context of further ontology development this model serves a solid foundation for semantics with its UML models (see: Fig. 1) and detailed descriptions (500 pages as the final deliverable). Also, some references to the possible ontology were being made by the authors [1, p. 184].

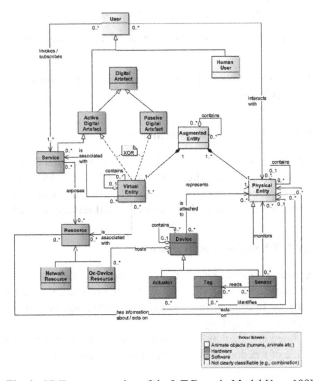

Fig. 1. UML representation of the IoT Domain Model [1, p. 199]

2.2 The IoT Architectural Framework

The IoT Architectural Framework [2] puts stress on the technology layers (see: Fig. 2). The main goal of this architecture is to bring standardization of the network protocols within the 5-layer model: physical, data link, network, transport, and application.

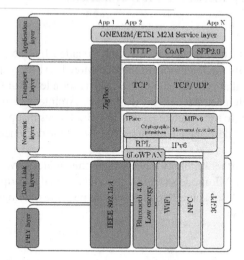

Fig. 2. The overview of IoT layered architecture [2, p. 130]

While this framework serves its purpose, it lacks the rich semantics provided by the aforementioned IoT-A/ARM model.

2.3 Microsoft Azure IoT Reference Architecture

While the IoT-A/ARM is strictly generic and the IoT Architectural Framework is based on communication standards, the Microsoft Azure IoT Reference Architecture [3] is strictly related to one specific technology. The 3-layered architecture (see: Fig. 3) is tailored to the cloud environment of the Microsoft cloud services named Azure.

2.4 The 4 Stage IoT Solution Architecture

The last IoT architecture model recalled in this paper may lack the semantics and the detailed description of the IoT-A/ARM, as well as the references to the network standards or support by the leading software vendor. The advantage of 4 Stage IoT Solution Architecture [4, 16] is its simplicity (see: Fig. 4).

This IoT architecture depicts main concepts of the domain, while leaving a considerable degree of freedom in developing a detailed solution.

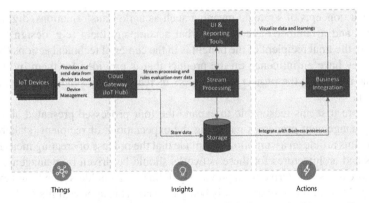

Fig. 3. Core subsystems of the Microsoft Azure IoT Reference Architecture [3, p. 4]

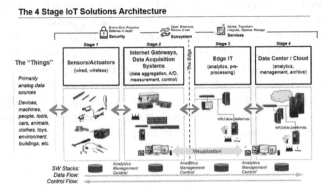

Fig. 4. The 4 Stage IoT Solution Architecture [4]

3   Extended Model of IoT Architecture—Additional Level of Management Processes

The issue of building an IoT network in urban agglomerations should be considered a complex technical and social issue, engaging both engineers designing particular elements of the network, stakeholders and managers providing an appropriate quality of management processes. Therefore this article undertakes the challenge of finding answers as to what management processes should be included in designing and constructing a network and which project decisions lead to creating and implementation of a measurement network that provides credible, high-quality data used in decision making in urban agglomerations.

It seems that because of the social aspect and the significance for recipients (stakeholders) the construction of IoT measurement networks should be considered more widely, that is to say as a project. In that case besides the four engineering processes, a set of management processes should be included, especially initiating, planning, realization, monitoring, closing which lead to achieving a goal (product) that meets the quality expectations of the stakeholders [5]. Even more so that in the era of the agility paradigm and popular concepts of strategic meaning such as agile transformations, digital trans-formations and a number of techniques that accompany them (e.g. design thinking, co-design), the final recipient of the benefit is in the center of technical actions (business value). They have an influence on the product that is provided for them by the engi-neers. The role of all the project stakeholders increases at the stage of realization and production.

Therefore it seems reasonable to expand the four processed presented above with a set of management processes gathering the expectations of recipient (stakeholders) groups. In this article an assumption was made that the process of creating measurement networks and architectures for these networks should be driven by management deci-sions. Those decisions derive from previously defined stakeholders' needs and expected benefits (values) of the network that is being created. This approach fits in the modern agility paradigm as applied not only to software development projects but also to the functioning of entire organizations, including organization such as cities in which city governments are the primary stakeholders in IoT network construction projects.

The approach that is presented in Fig. 5 assumes including particular groups of recip-ients of the IoT network construction project's results. It also assumes that management processes (managing the project) are immanent to processes of constructing an IoT net-work. Therefore management processes should not be treated separately but as ones that integrate the four classic stages of constructing an IoT network. It should be assumed that the process of constructing an IoT network and architecture is not only a technical process but a social and technical one, which is why it should be carried on with both good engineering practice and good management practice.

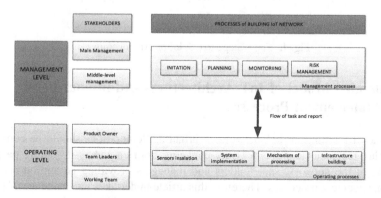

Fig. 5. Levels of building IoT network

Considering the necessity of engaging stakeholders and their representatives in the process of network construction and viewing management processes as those that inte-grate all the actions, it seems reasonable to base the quality criteria on providing useful and valuable solutions to target stakeholders rather than on technical parameters (e.g. computing power). This approach is closer to the agility paradigm mentioned before, which means that instead of putting pressure on the realization of a project from the beginning to the end, it should be put on an incremental construction of IoT measurement networks including the level of fulfilling the stakeholders' needs.

Therefore assuming that the measurement networks will be constructed based on best agility practice [6], the attention to the measurements quality will increase simultaneously with the concern for meeting the expected benefits. The construction of networks should be driven by appropriate decisions in terms of both engineering (in regard to network construction processes) and management (helping to achieve the result of the project close to the needs/benefits).

4 Extended Model of IoT Architecture—Additional Decision-Making Layer

The research carried out by the authors is focused on the process of managing the building of IoT systems. In particular, their aim is to manage the network of air quality sensors. One of the main parameters taken into consideration is location of such devices in the agglomeration. These activities are significant part of the broadly understood Smart City development.

Data collected from properly selected and located sensors can be used to make decisions either for the city (as an organization directly responsible for the quality of life of residents) or for individual decision-makers, who want to consciously function in their closest environment (place of living or work), and shape it.

At this point it should be clarified how the phrase "management of sensor/IoT network" is understood, as it is being frequently recalled in this article. All the activities that qualify as IoT network management were divided into two decision areas:

- Decision Area DA-I: management of physical IoT devices.
- Decision Area DA-II: management of data processed by these devices.

4.1 Decision-Making Layer—Decision Areas

Decision area I—concerning management of devices—was established for the realization of the indirect project objective. It concentrates on the design problems of the final solution. In particular, two elementary decision problems which the IoT network designer faces were identified:

- Problem (1A): how to make a proper selection of sensors? The choice of model/technology used has a crucial impact on the quality of measurements that the device will provide.
- Problem (1B): how to determine the correct locations for each of these devices?

The second Decision Area (DA-II) aims to archive the primary goal of the project, supporting management decisions. A properly designed and then calibrated network of IoT sensors will collect measurement data—both regarding pollution and weather factors. Based on these data, it is planned to create decision based system. Such solutions, based on if-then rules would give decision makers specific suggestions for actions (e.g. reactions to detected measurement anomalies or all preventive activities).

It should be noted that both decision areas described above are interrelated with a cause-effect relationship. These dependencies are shown in Fig. 6. The measurements themselves—their validity and quality—depend on the decisions made at the stage of designing and constructing the sensor network. This has a significant impact on the final actions of the decision maker, which the project supports.

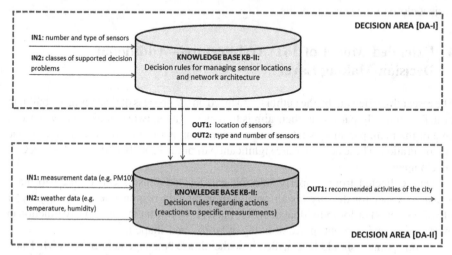

Fig. 6. Relationships between the identified Decision Areas DA-I and DA-II

The areas presented in Fig. 6 constitute a complex knowledge-based system. Its core are two knowledge bases, each containing acquired knowledge in the form of rules (if-then) and facts (triplets). For each of them, input variables (INx) and output decisions (OUTx) were proposed. These knowledge bases are:

- Knowledge Base KD-I: dedicated to store knowledge on the physical aspects of IoT sensor management in the agglomeration, i.e. the number and location of sensors.
- Knowledge Base KD-II: containing rules defining actions suggested by decision-makers (reactions) depending on the collected data in the context of the reference values defined for them (e.g. maximum or minimum thresholds).

4.2 Decision-Making Layer—Key Problems

Having the research environment presented as above, the aim of this article should be established. It is strongly related to the DA-I Decision Area and the KB-I Knowledge Base. It means, that it concerns decisions related to the IoT sensor network project from the perspective of their physical placement. In this context two key questions arise:

- What are the factors that determine the location of sensors?
- What are the limitations that should be taken into account?

In the field of city management, there are two constraints in the DA-I Decision Area. They are de facto two dimensions, which constitute the boundary conditions for the authors:

- Vast area of each agglomeration;
- Limited number of available sensors.

Therefore, this should lead to an obvious assumption that sensors can be installed in selected locations only and their selection will always be a compromise. It is important to consider the proper criteria for the selection of such locations. Based on the authors' experience a number of initial assumptions can be made here. It was agreed that the validity of measurements is the highest for the following categories of locations:

- Category 1: clusters of inhabitants—these are the places with high population density; residents are interested in measuring air quality; in particular, districts with the largest number of inhabitants and areas with a large number of employees (e.g. office parks) should be taken into account.
- Category 2: commonly known or frequently indicated places of air pollution in a given agglomeration; in particular: single-family housing districts (solid fuel stoves) and main communication arteries (fuel combustion by vehicles).

5 Verification - Building a Civic Measurement Network in Gdańsk Based on the Extended Model

The project of building a civic measurement network called "City Breathes" was carried out at the IBM Advanced Research Center (IBM CAS) in Gdańsk. As part of the research conducted by CAS, a project was launched with a non-government organization, Gdańsk Agglomeration Development Forum (Polish: Forum Rozwoju Aglomeracji Gdańskiej, FRAG) under the name "Tri-City Breathes" (Polish: "Trójmiasto Oddycha"). The aim of this project was to build a network of citizen IoT nodes whose main purpose is local monitoring of PM10 dust concentration. A hybrid monitoring network consisting of several networks and IoT nodes was created, larger and more diverse than the existing public network of The Foundation: Agency of Regional Air Quality Monitoring in Metropolitan Area of Gdańsk (ARMAAG) stations.

The assumption of the project is that the IoT civic nodes are to complement the existing monitoring network, enabling detailed measurement in selected locations. As a result, the total number of IoT nodes, including all networks, has doubled. During the construction of the network, the IoT nodes were made available to residents to encourage them to participate in the project. The problem of building this network was the architecture of this system that changed over time. It was the basis for consideration of the need to look at the construction of the archives of IoT systems in a different way.

This network is built using IoT nodes with Arduino Uno and Raspberry PI microcontrollers, selected for their ability to support the sensors used to measure PM10 concentration. The construction process (see: Fig. 7) also showed how complicated the development of such a node is. However, once created, the process of constructing IoT nodes to measure PM10 is relatively simple and repeatable, which allows relatively fast node generation.

Fig. 7. Construction, IoT node and its deployment at the WSB University in Gdańsk campus

6   Ontology Model of IoT Architecture

The role of the ontology in the described model is to provide a semantic structure of concepts and relationships among them in this domain. The rich semantics of the formal ontology goes beyond common vocabulary or taxonomy. With expressiveness provided by the Web Ontology Language (OWL) and first order logic (FOL) ontologies are not mere data structures but one of the artificial intelligence technologies.

6.1   Existing IoT Ontologies

The idea of representing the domain of the Internet of Things in the ontology is not new. A study of existing ontologies [7] recognizes the following types of IoT ontologies:

- Sensor (SSN, Semantic Sensor Network) ontologies: data description, capabilities, discovery, data access and sharing, and extensibility;
- Context-aware ontologies used to describe places, agents, and events;
- Location-based ontologies that describe the spatial context;

- Time-based ontologies to describe temporal dimension.

Because ontology should serve as a common model for the multiple IoT networks linked together, the issues of interoperability [8, 9] and heterogeneous environments [10, 17] are often raised in papers.

Another branch of IoT ontology research is focused on developing such semantic structures. Gyrard et al. [11] list semantic web methodologies, best practices and other ontology engineering aspects, while Xu et al. [12] propose an upper-ontology-based approach for automatic construction of IoT ontology.

6.2   The 4 Stages IoT Solution Architecture Ontology

The ontology described below is a first revision/approximation of the 4 Stages IoT Solution Architecture model.

Classes. Three main primitive concepts are:

- Stage: gathers 4 classes that represent each of the layer.
- Component: all notions that refer to the tangible (physical) and nontangible objects.
- Activity: actions that are performed according to the model.

All classes of the ontology are shown in Fig. 8. No individuals has been (yet) created.

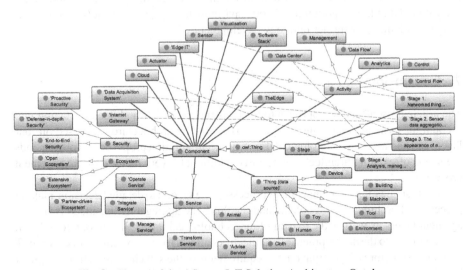

Fig. 8. Classes of the 4 Stages IoT Solution Architecture Ontology

Object Properties. As the original graphical model does not include other relationship than arrows, lines and boxes, the dominant relationship used in the ontology is the inheritance (parent-child). Another relationship used is the isAComponentOfStage property with Component class as its domain and Stage class as its range. There is also a pair of object properties named `isAPredecessorOfStage` and its inverse `isAConsequentOfStage` used to denote the sequence of stages.

A richer set of object properties (and perhaps data properties) is expected to appear in the next version of the ontology.

Competency Questions. At this point of ontology development it serves and answers to the following competency questions:

- What are the stages in this IoT architecture?
- What is the order of stages?
- What are components of the IoT architecture?
- What components are specific to the given stage?
- What are the activities in the model?
- What are the kinds of data sources?

One can also ask about more detailed information on types of services, security or ecosystem.

The ontology layer can also be extended with the air quality domain [13, 14] as the IoT network in questions measures the atmospheric pollution. Furthermore, ontology can be taken into consideration as a knowledge structure for storing decision rules [15].

Ontology Summary. The present revision of the ontology provides only essential knowledge on the 4 Stages IoT Solution Architecture. Authors wish to validate the current model in the air pollution sensors environment to provide a proof-of-concept as well as guidelines for further ontology development.

7   Conclusions

The article presents a new approach to the construction of IoT architectures taking into account the dynamic modeling of layers. IoT's existing architecture was based on four layers and had a strong technological dimension. The solution proposed at work expands the scope of existing architectures by three additional layers focused on management processes.

The first one refers to management processes, the second to detailed decision-making processes of architects' stakeholders and the third one aggregating the added two management layers as well as the existing four technological layers. It's an ontology layer. This approach to the development of architectures allows for any expansion of existing IT system architectures depending on the requirements of the stakeholders. The example of building a civic measurement network presented in the article creates such conditions. It also creates the conditions for building an architect of IoT systems guided by the stakeholder's decisions to include any technological aspects relevant to the design of the network.

In the future, authors plan to make ontologies the basis for both the construction and development of technological layers in the classic IoT architecture. Then it will allow building architectures that meet these requirements taking into account the conditions of the stakeholders. The constituent architectures as well as stakeholder requirements will be classes of ontology built. This approach will simplify the process of building architectures as well as it will create conditions for the construction of any integration bus.

References

1. Bauer, M., et al.: IoT reference architecture. In: Bassi, A., et al. (eds.) Enabling Things to Talk, pp. 163–211. Springer, Heidelberg (2013). https://doi.org/10.1007/978-3-642-40403-0_8
2. Gardašević, G., et al.: The IoT architectural framework, design issues and application domains. Wirel. Pers. Commun. **92**(1), 127–148 (2016). https://doi.org/10.1007/s11277-016-3842-3
3. Microsoft Azure IoT Reference Architecture, Version 2.1, Microsoft, Redmond (2018)
4. Fuller, J.R.: The 4 stages of an IoT architecture. In: Techbeacon. https://techbeacon.com/enterprise-it/4-stages-iot-architecture. Accessed 05 Feb 2020
5. Rose, K.H.: A guide to the project management body of knowledge (PMBOK® Guide)—fifth edition. Project Manag. J. **44**(3), e1 (2013)
6. Schwaber, K., Sutherland, J.: The Scrum Guide: The Rules of the Game. https://www.scrumguides.org/docs/scrumguide/v2017/2017-Scrum-Guide-US.pdf. Accessed 05 Feb 2020
7. Bajaj, G., Agarwal, R., Singh, P., Georgantas, N., Issarny, V.: A Study of Existing Ontologies in the IoT-domain. arXiv preprint arXiv:1707.00112 (2017)
8. Agarwal, R., et al.: Unified IoT ontology to enable interoperability and federation of testbeds. In: IEEE 3rd World Forum on Internet of Things (WF-IoT), pp. 70–75, December 2016
9. Ganzha, M., Paprzycki, M., Pawłowski, W., Szmeja, P., Wasielewska, K.: Semantic interoperability in the Internet of Things: an overview from the INTER-IoT perspective. J. Netw. Comput. Appl. **81**, 111–124 (2017)
10. Kotis, K., Katasonov, A.: An ontology for the automated deployment of applications in heterogeneous IoT environments. Semant. Web J. **4**(3), 47–69 (2013)
11. Gyrard, A., Serrano, M., Atemezing, G.A.: Semantic web methodologies, best practices and ontology engineering applied to Internet of Things. In: IEEE 2nd World Forum on Internet of Things (WF-IoT), pp. 412–417, December 2015
12. Xu, Y., Zhang, C., Ji, Y.: An upper-ontology-based approach for automatic construction of IoT ontology. Int. J. Distrib. Sens. Netw. **10**(4), 594782 (2014)
13. Czarnecki, A., Orłowski, C.: Hybrid approach to ontology specification and development. In: Grzech, A., Borzemski, L., Świątek, J., Wilimowska, Z. (eds.) Information Systems Architecture and Technology: Service Oriented Distributed Systems: Concepts and Infrastructure, pp. 47–57. Wroclaw University of Technology Publishing House, Wrocław (2009)
14. Czarnecki, A., Orłowski, C.: Ontology engineering aspects in the intelligent systems development. In: Setchi, R., Jordanov, I., Howlett, R.J., Jain, L.C. (eds.) KES 2010. LNCS (LNAI), vol. 6277, pp. 533–542. Springer, Heidelberg (2010). https://doi.org/10.1007/978-3-642-15390-7_55
15. Czarnecki, A., Sitek, T.: Ontologies vs. rules—comparison of methods of knowledge representation based on the example of IT services management. In: Borzemski, L., Grzech, A., Świątek, J., Wilimowska, Z. (eds.) Information Systems Architecture and Technology: Intelligent Information Systems, Knowledge Discovery, Big Data and High Performance Computing, pp. 99–109. Wroclaw University of Technology Publishing House, Wrocław (2013)

16. Abdelzaher, T., et al.: Decision-driven execution: a distributed resource management paradigm for the age of IoT. In: 2017 IEEE 37th International Conference on Distributed Computing Systems (ICDCS), Atlanta, GA, pp. 1825–1835 (2017)
17. Song, R., Vanthienen, J., Cui, W., Wang, Y., Huang, L.: Context-aware BPM using IoT-integrated context ontologies and IoT-enhanced decision models. In: 2019 IEEE 21st Conference on Business Informatics (CBI), Moscow, Russia, pp. 541–550 (2019)

The Equity Crowdfunding and Family Firms – A Fuzzy Linguistic Approach

Anna Motylska-Kuźma[(✉)] [iD]

WSB University in Wroclaw, Wroclaw, Poland
`anna.motylska-kuzma@wsb.wroclaw.pl`

Abstract. The purpose of the work is to examine how the equity crowdfunding meets the needs of family firms. For many reasons, the probabilistic approach can be considered inappropriate and too simplistic when explaining the choice of financing source, especially in family businesses which are very heterogeneous. Based on the results of previous research and using the fuzzy linguistic approach, there were assessed the factors influencing the financial decisions and compared the equity crowdfunding to the traditional IPO/issuing shares. The main feature shows that crowdfunding fulfils well the core need of family businesses and using their basic characteristics it minimalizes the weaknesses of social funding.

Keywords: Family business · Financial decisions · Entrepreneurial finance · Equity crowdfunding · Fuzzy approach

1 Introduction

The capital is one of the most needed resources for company [44]. The most frequent source of financing, used in the seed phase of entrepreneurship, is the own savings or loans from family and friends. When these funds are insufficient, the entrepreneur is looking for financial institutions like banks or loan funds [19]. However, each of these sources is limited and cost worthy [51, 52]. The cost is directly proportional to the risk of the idea concerned. The best solution of the problems and needs of entrepreneurs at every stage of a company's development seem to be the alternative sources of capital. Although they are especially dedicated to innovative ideas with very high level of risk, they should be used as well to find the funds for development [2, 61].

Despite the fact, the bank finance is a major source of financing for entrepreneurs [84], in practice the ventures are not very welcome by them as a subject of investments, especially after the global financial crisis [94]. Bankers look for the creditworthiness and prefer establish track record, stable cash flows, and high-quality collateral [85]. Thus, the firms with lacks of this characteristics have the problems with raising debt financing [90, 91].

Entrepreneurs can also search for external equity finance, like venture capital and angel financing. However, this sources are very often unrealistic for the average entrepreneur. They invest in ventures with high growth ambitions and their selection filters are extremely restrictive [94, 96].

© Springer-Verlag GmbH Germany, part of Springer Nature 2020
N. T. Nguyen et al. (Eds.): TCCI XXXV, LNCS 12330, pp. 99–115, 2020.
https://doi.org/10.1007/978-3-662-62245-2_7

The above facts give the possibility to rise the crowdfunding market, especially in the case of the equity crowdfunding and make this new phenomenon a real good alternative to the traditional way of raising funds.

The family business research has been growing over the last decades but is still an emerging field of study [26]. In the literature, family firms have been presented as combinations of two systems that overlap and interact: the emotion–oriented family system that focuses on non–economic goals and the results–oriented business system that focuses on the economic goal [38, 91]. It is the effect of building the family fortune which is in the large part invested in the firm. Thus, the effective separation between the private and business wealth is very difficult in this case and contributes to a specific view on the business.

These two systems have to influence the decision making process and constitute the source of many sophisticated character traits of the family enterprises. Due to Di Giuli [37] most of family firms adopt a wide range of basic financial products and only a limited number utilize non-basic products. Even though the core determinants to use innovative instruments in finance are the generation of family that currently owns the firm, the presence of non-family CEO and the existence of a non-family shareholder, still the lack of capital and the difficulties in its raising make the family businesses eager to urgently look for alternative possibilities to get the funds.

Since the strategic decisions, especially those within the scope of finance, are not only trickled from economic reasons, it is crucial to know if the alternative sources of funding meet the financial logic of family firms or not. Thus, the main objective of this article is to examine if and how the alternative sources of funding, especially the equity crowdfunding, satisfy the needs of family firms.

The fuzzy logic has been widely exploited in the fields of economy and management sciences over the last 20 years. It is a useful tool to represent and analyze inaccurate and qualitative information (which is difficult to define through deterministic or Boolean logics) and above all for structuring complex phenomena. Furthermore, the fuzzy logic is applied to management decision problems [see 10, 48, 62]. Due to the fact, that choosing the financing sources is one of the management decision and it is connected with more or less qualitative determinants, the author decided to use the fuzzy linguistic approach to answer the research question.

This paper makes a number of contributions to the literature. Firstly, it compares the traditional sources of capital with the new phenomenon i.e. crowdfunding, taking into account the most frequent factors influencing the financing decisions. Secondly, it analyses the possibility of using the crowdfunding by the family businesses, contrast the financial logic of such entities with the basic characteristics of crowdfunding. Thirdly, it shows how the weaknesses of crowdfunding could be minimized by the specific characteristics of family businesses and how the sophisticated needs of such entities could be met by using crowdfunding.

The article is structured in the manner as follows. The first section presents the family firms and their basic characteristics which could build the financial logic in such an enterprise. The second section describes the alternative sources of funding, their ideas and types. In the third section the author analyses the possibility of using several sources of funding by the family firms. Using the fuzzy approach, the main characteristics of each source are identified and assessed from the standpoint of family firms need and their particular aims. The article concludes with the summary containing the most important implications.

2 Financial Logic of Family Firms

The scientific observation of family businesses already has its own history, although there is still no clear definition of a family firm, which would not raise doubts as to the affiliation of a given entity to this group of companies [7, 55]. Most often, depending on the research conducted, the methodology used, the data acquisition method and the sample characteristics, a self-definition is adopted [see 6, 12, 21, 37, 42, 59, 77]. However, the common feature of all these definitions is that ownership lies in the hands of the family and the family members have the significant influence on the decisions made in the firm. Due to having a significant stake in the company, the family benefits from the success of the company, but also bears the consequences of wrong decisions. This is the main cause why the maintenance of business control is a very important factor in choosing the source of funding for the activity taken [23]. It is worth asking, therefore, whether family businesses are guided by their own financial logic? Habbershon with others suggests [46] that in family firms there exist complex systems with systematic factors influencing strategy and decision-making processes. Dyer [40] adds, these factors are the set of attributes/values that a family brings into the business and calls it "family effect". The effect has in literature its own measure (F-PEC), introduced by Astrachan with his team [7].

The research shows that family firms focus not only on financial benefits, but also on noneconomic objectives [8, 26], often associated with something which is called socioemotional wealth (SEW), generated by the activity conducted [45]. There are many aspects of family firms directly connected with emotions: protection of the family relationships, independence and continuity of family influence, building the family dynasty, relations with employees, social reputation and identity, relations with a local community, etc. [66, 95, 99]. All those characteristics cause that the family firms are considered as value based [36, 76] and associated relationship, mostly in long term, with the environment that results from trust and altruism [5, 49]. Besides, they reach the market success through the identification of the family with the brand [30] and demonstrate a long perspective of activity [60]. On this basis is built the SEW and the anxiety of making a loss in it is the crucial determinant of strategic behaviour of family firms [25, 34].

The decision making process in such entities is more centralized and focused on culture, values and aims of family [43]. This causes the problems based on agency theory [89]. However, they are not problems of type I, resulting from the superior – subordinate relationship, or owner – agent [54, 68, 78, 82], but more severe problems of type II, resulting from the majority – minority shareholdership [69, 92, 96]. These problems, and in essence striving to avoid them and minimize them, have a big impact on the financial decisions made by family businesses. It should not be forgotten that family firms are very heterogeneous and vary not only because of the attributes of the subject itself, such as size, age or type of activity, but also in terms of certain specific characteristics such as SEW approach [45], risk aversion, norms, attitudes, expectations, experiences, etc. [91].

According to the literature review [73] the current stage of research on the financing of family businesses does not give a clear answer to the question of one consistent logic in shaping the structure of capital. While some argue that family businesses prefer internal sources of funding and family funds (e.g. [84]) running in debts to a less extent than the non-family ones (e.g. [4, 65, 67]), others believe that debt is on the same level (e.g. [27]) or even higher (e.g. [15, 23, 53, 87]).

On the one hand, higher levels of risk aversion may explain less debt exposure. On the other hand, however, a higher level of leverage is consistent with the fear of expropriation or dispersion of control over the company. According to this argument, family businesses will be more likely to engage foreign capital in the form of debt (preferably long-term) than equity from external sources [23]. However, this willingness is different, when we consider the life – cycle of the firm. For example, Keasey et al. [50] found that the relation between the ownership and leverage is positive for mature firms, neutral for revival firms and negative for growth firms (given their different investment opportunities and access to debt financing). Additionally, the conflicts between the family members that often occurs during the succession process (arising from the dilution of family ownership and varying attachments to the family firm: see [29] and [17]) lead to different propensities to dilute control between young family firms (where the succession process has not yet occurred) and old family firms [50].

The above conclusions are in line with López-Gracia's research conducted jointly with Sánchez-Andújar [64], which shows that family firms behave according to the theory of hierarchization of sources of funding. Pindado with the team [79] adds to this the fact that these companies have not only an easier access to foreign capital, but also the average cost of this financing is lower. Hence the gap in the leverage between family and non-family companies is filled much faster, especially in crisis situations. This is why, in situations related to general economic/economics problems, as Crespí&Martín-Oliver [31] claim, family businesses are less exposed to credit restrictions, and thus their capital structure is relatively stable throughout the business cycle.

Looking at the above-described characteristics of family businesses in the scope of choosing the source of funding, it is difficult to clearly articulate the particular logic of the behaviour of these entities. However, there are some specific goals that family firms strive for in terms of capital structure [75, 98]. They are: firstly, the desire to keep the control of the company and thus maintain the business continuity for the future generations and preserve the culture, values and family rules. Secondly, it is the willingness to increase or even maintain the level of SEW, associated with e.g. sustaining the positive relationships not only with the family, but also with employees and the environment. The main cause of eschewing the external sources of capital, especially in the scope of equity financing, is the aversion to losing control of business. Hence, there is reluctance to sell or dilute shares and introduce new investors. In turn, the loss in SEW is the key source of risk aversion visible by avoiding excessive debt.

Both of the objectives mentioned above have little in common with the rational, economic approach to building capital structure. However, the economic goals are not strange to family businesses. Thus, it could be supposed that besides the non-economic aspects, the cost of capital should be considered in choosing the financing model as the most important economic factor.

3 Crowdfunding as an Alternative Source of Funding

For entrepreneurs, internal finance and debt finance are crucial to form and grow a venture [16, 22, 85]. External equity financing, like venture capital or business angels, is usually unavailable. The previous research shows that only 0.10% of start-ups in the US receive venture capital financing [94]. The last financial crisis and the new situation connected with the COVID-19 increase the risk aversion of such investors even higher. Thus, the success rate of raising venture capital or angel financing is really low [13, 80]. On the other site, the entrepreneurs are not willing to attract venture capital or business angels because of fear of dilution the control over the company [28, 87]. Venture capitalists and angels often require important equity stakes in venture and actively involved in their portfolio firms post-investment, which might be in conflict with the self-determination motive of many entrepreneurs [87, 95].

Crowdfunding appeared as an alternative solution to the problem of access to capital among young enterprises in the initial phase of their activity, the so-called start-ups, and it was quickly adapted by entities characterized by above-average pace of development [2]. It is connected with the financing process using online platform through which a sufficiently large number of small investors can support the project by paying small amounts in a predetermined amount of time (usually a few weeks) [52]. Designers, however, use crowdfunding not only to finance their ideas, but also to check the demand and approval of the Internet community regarding proposed solutions [58]. It is assumed that an investor who enjoys the project will also be interested in the products of such a designer, and therefore it is very likely that he will become one of the first clients [20]. Thus, building the right community interested and supporting the project provides the foundation for the future demand for offered products or services. This is one of the biggest advantages of crowdfunding compared to other sources of financing.

It is worth noting that the majority of investors supporting crowdfunding campaigns are not professionals and they are not too demanding, especially in the case of donation models. Therefore, they do not require special business plans, security or they do not verify in detail the creditworthiness and financial condition of a given originator. However, with increasing interest in crowdfunding, "pickup" or "selectivity" of investors also increases. This can be noticed, for example, in the NESTA research on the alternative finance market in the United Kingdom, according to which about 38% of respondents who take active part in crowdfunding campaigns (in the equity model) identify themselves as a sophisticated investor or as HNWI (high net-worth individual) [9].

Currently, online platforms offer four basic crowdfunding models: donation-based crowdfunding with variation without rewarding participants (non-reward-based) and with rewarding participants (reward-based), debt-based crowdfunding, equity-based crowdfunding and the mixed [24, 33, 70, 71].

Equity – based crowdfunding is called share-based social funding or crowdinvesting. In exchange for financial support, investors receive shares in the enterprise. Unlike other crowdfunding models, crowdinvesting does not allow to accumulate an amount higher than the one declared at the beginning of the campaign [32]. This type of financing is very limited by law and, for example, in Poland, due to the fact that the smallest share in the limited company may not be less than PLN 50, the amount requested must be a multiple of this value. Until now, this form of crowdfunding has been used by IT companies, e-commerce (online stores, digital bookshops, group shopping services, etc.), B2B companies whose products are not intended for the consumer market, R&D companies and other companies which have the rights to operate their shares. An example of platforms that implement share projects are StartupValley.com or Crowdcube.pl and in Poland, the most popular is beesfund.pl.

The equity-based crowdfunding is the most sophisticated form of raising social capital. In many countries it still remains legally unregulated. The EU has long been considering the establishment of harmonized crowdfunding legislation. The European Banking Authority ("EBA") as well as the European Securities and Markets Authority ("ESMA") proposed a series of measures to reduce risks connected with crowdfunding, including the possibility of introducing specific registration and regulation of operators of crowdfunding platforms. The European Commission is of the opinion that new regulations could slow down innovations in economies, so it is not interested in introducing such solutions. Few European countries have until now adopted crowdfunding regulations, in particular requirements for developers, crowdfunding platform operators, and investors.

In Poland, the regulations go in another direction [74]. It is supposed that, by its nature, equity crowdfunding is a typical offer to purchase "shares" in limited companies, targeted at an unrestricted recipient. The only problem is that the notion of "participation" does not fall within the definition of securities (in the light of the share of joint-stock company that is a security). This means that the "shares" in limited companies are not subject to a public offering regime within the meaning of the Act on Public Offering and Conditions Governing the Introduction of Financial Instruments to Organized Trading System and Public Companies ("Act on Public Offering"). This frees the limited company from the necessity to complete a number of formalities related to the public issue of securities, in particular as regards preparation and availability of information memorandum or prospectus. There exist a number of legal barriers to limited companies trading in shares, necessitating many other activities before the notary, such as adopting resolutions on capital increase or submitting notifications of shareholdings or, last but not least, regulating the internal organization of the company.

Partially this problem was resolved by the amendment of the Code of Commercial Companies, which entered into force on April 1, 2016. It allows limited companies created by means of a template, in accordance with the provisions of the Code of Commercial Companies, to perform actions connected with the amendment of the company's contract via the teleinformatic system. The new regulations, assessed from the perspective of equity crowdfunding, may have a positive influence on its development in Poland, and thus on the increase in the number of companies that benefit from this method of raising capital. An additional advantage of the amendment, which is the advantage for both sides - the limited company as well as the investor, is a reduction the notary costs.

The Polish government also proposes introducing into the Code of Commercial Companies (from 1st March 2021) a new form of business activity – the simple joint-stock company (PSA), which is based on the French experience with Société par Actions Simplifiée – SAS and the Slovakia solution (Jednoduchá Spoločnosť na Akcie). Thanks to uncomplicated registration and low capital requirements, the proposed solutions should make it easier to raise funds for all those who base their idea on knowledge and have the skills to develop it, but might have neither professional economic or legal knowledge nor high financial means. It is dedicated especially for start-ups and crowdfunding.

Despite legal restrictions, the number of companies which decided to raise the funds through equity crowdfunding is constantly increasing. Till July 2018, with the oldest Polish platform (beesfund.pl) the companies raised about 900.000 EUR, with crowdangels.pl – 450.000 EUR, with crowdway.pl – 550.000 EUR and with FindFunds.pl – 105.000 EUR [72]. Most of the successful campaigns reached the highest possible limit of the raised funds (100.000 EUR). After July 21st, 2018 the limit, which gives the possibility not to prepare the prospectus, has been increased, due to the EU regulations[1]. KNF decided to set this limit on 1mln EUR and we can observe the first campaigns finished with such a big funds (e.g. Lovely.Inc, DoctorBrew or Etno Cafe SA). The last campaign, initiated by Wisła Kraków – one of the football clubs in Poland, raised 4mln PLN (about 1mln EUR) in few days, although the campaign was set for one month.

To date, scholars have focused on the success factors in raising equity crowdfunding (e.g. [1, 81, 93]). They have found that e.g. retaining equity and providing detailed information about the risk make firms more successful. Another line of the research is the assessment of dynamics of internet platforms and outcomes after equity crowdfunding campaigns (e.g. [88]) or the relation between the sustainable development aims, relationship with donors and the success of the campaign (e.g. [72]).

Walthoff-Borm et al. [94] claim that all this firms, listed on equity crowdfunding platform, do not appear on this platform at random. They first need to decide whether they want to seek equity crowdfunding. Thus, the authors have looked for the factors influence firms to search for equity crowdfunding. They found that the more unprofitable the firm is, the more likely it is to search for equity crowdfunding. Moreover, the firms with excessive debt levels and more intangible assets are also more likely to search for equity crowdfunding. Another research, made by Ahlers et al. [1] shows that the entrepreneurs search for equity crowdfunding from a broad pool of small investors and therefore largely retain control over their firms compared with other forms of equity finance.

The results of Motylska - Kuzma research [71] show that crowdfunding could be a real alternative to traditional sources of finance, not only for start-ups, but also for other entities. She has analysed retained profits, bank loans, issue of shares, commercial papers, leasing, venture capital, business angels and private equity and contrasted them against three types of crowdfunding: reward – based, debt and equity. Each source has been assessed by four attributes: cost of capital, impact on the control, complexity of the acquisition process and limitation of use. It can be seen that every type of crowdfunding has its equivalent in a traditional source of funding in the company and in every case it is costless. Particular attention, from the point of view of family businesses, should be paid to equity-based crowdfunding. The cost of this financing model is much lower than the standard share issue or the use of venture capital, private equity or business angels, and the

---

[1] Art. 1 point 3 of the Regulation of the European Parliament and the EU Council 2017/1129 of June 14, 2017 regarding the prospectus to be published in connection with the public offering of securities or admission to trading on a regulated market and the repeal of Directive 2003/71 / EC.

impact on control is considerably smaller. Theoretically, every shareholder has the right to vote for strategic decisions. However, in practice, in the case of equity crowdfunding, the number of new shareholders is very high. It dilutes their voting power. Besides, already at the stage of acquiring funds, the applicant can prepare the campaign so that it will eliminate the possibility of buying the majority of shares by one investor, thus protecting the owner from losing control. The use of such restrictions is hindered by the traditional issue of shares. The above advantages of crowdfunding, regardless of its model, seem to fit perfectly into the financial logic of family businesses.

4 Fuzzy Numbers and Their Arithmetic

The main idea of fuzzy logic is that the world is not black-white, with binary yes-no, 0–1 or true-false decisions [56]. Decisions often involve "notions that cannot be defined precisely, but which depend on their context" [14]. Fuzzy set try to map the degree to which an element belongs to a certain group in the continuous scale between [0, 1] [3]. Lin and Chen [63] suggest that fuzzy set theory provides the useful tool to deal with decisions in which the phenomena are imprecise and vague. It tolerates the blurred boundary of definitions. This gives the opportunity to use the qualitative factors into analysis and decision – making process, which are often vaguely defined or have unclear boundaries. It means, that fuzzy logic in general enables to effectively and efficiently quantifying imprecise information and make decisions based on vague and incomplete data [10].

Let $\mathbb{R}$ be $(-\infty; \infty)$, i.e. the set of all real numbers.

The fuzzy number, denote by $\tilde{X}$ is a fuzzy subset of $\mathbb{R}$ with membership function $u_{\tilde{X}} : \mathbb{R} \to [0, 1]$ satisfying the following conditions:

- There exists at least one number $a_0 \in \mathbb{R}$ such that $u_{\tilde{X}}(a_0) = 1$
- $u_{\tilde{X}}(x)$ is nondecreasing on $(-\infty, a_0)$ and nonincreasing on (a_0, ∞)
- .. (x) is upper semi-continuos, i.e. $\lim_{x \to x_0^+} u_{\tilde{X}}(x) = u_{\tilde{X}}(x_0)$ if $x_0 < a_0$ and $\lim_{x \to x_0^-} u_{\tilde{X}}(x) = u_{\tilde{X}}(x_0)$ if $x_0 > a_0$
- $\int_{-\infty}^{\infty} u_{\tilde{X}}(x)dx < \infty$

Following Zadeh [97] and Dubois and Prade [39], a triangular fuzzy number is an A $= (\alpha, m, \beta)$, where m is the most probable value and the α and β – left and right spread, respectively.

The sum of two triangular fuzzy numbers $\tilde{X} = (\alpha_X, m_X, \beta_X)$ and $\tilde{Y} = (\alpha_Y, m_Y, \beta_Y)$ is a triangular fuzzy number $\tilde{X} + \tilde{Y} = (\alpha_X + \alpha_Y, m_X + m_Y, \beta_X + \beta_Y)$.

The multiplication of two triangular fuzzy numbers $\tilde{X} = (\alpha_X, m_X, \beta_X)$ and $\tilde{Y} = (\alpha_Y, m_Y, \beta_Y)$ is a triangular fuzzy number $\tilde{X} \otimes \tilde{Y} = (\alpha_X \cdot \alpha_Y, m_X \cdot m_Y, \beta_X \cdot \beta_Y)$, if the $\alpha_x, \alpha_y, m_x, m_y, \beta_x, \beta_y$ are the positive numbers, and the subtraction of two triangular fuzzy numbers $\tilde{X} = (\alpha_X, m_X, \beta_X)$ and $\tilde{Y} = (\alpha_Y, m_Y, \beta_Y)$ is a triangular fuzzy number $\tilde{X} \ominus \tilde{Y} = (\alpha_X - \beta_Y, m_X - m_Y, \beta_X - \alpha_Y)$.

The inverse of the fuzzy number $\tilde{Y} = (\alpha_Y, m_Y, \beta_Y)$ is a triangular fuzzy number $1/\tilde{Y} = (1/\beta_Y, 1/m_Y, 1/\alpha_Y)$, where α_x, m_x, β_x, are all the nonzero positive real numbers. If the $\alpha_x, \alpha_y, m_x, m_y, \beta_x, \beta_y$ are all the nonzero positive numbers, then the division of $\tilde{X}$ and $\tilde{Y}$ is $\tilde{X} \oslash \tilde{Y} = (\alpha_X/\beta_Y, m_X/m_Y, \beta_X/\alpha_Y)$.

In the case of assessment the complex phenomenon it is crucial to know the ratings of the detailed elements as well the weights/importance of this elements. Thus, let R_j and W_j, where $j = 1, 2,..., n$, be the fuzzy rating and fuzzy weighting given to factor j, respectively. To know the general assessment, the consolidation of the fuzzy numbers is calculated as the fuzzy attractiveness ratio (FAR) as:

$$FAR = \frac{\sum_{j=1}^{n}\left(W_j \otimes R_j\right)}{\sum_{j=1}^{n} W_j} \tag{1}$$

The fuzzy attractiveness ratio FAR, consolidates fuzzy ratings and fuzzy weights of all the factors that will influence on some decision or general assessment. The highest the FAR value, the more promising the source of financing is. If two or more sources are comparing, the one with the highest FAR value is the most suitable for the company.

Once the FAR has been calculated, this value can be approximated by a similar close linguistic term (LT) from the fuzzy values predefined scale. Several methods for approximating the FAR with an appropriate corresponding linguistic term have been proposed (e.g. [41, 86]). The Euclidean distance will be used since it is the most intuitive from the human perception of approximation and the most commonly used method [63]. If the natural – language expression set LT is {very low, low, fair, high, very high}, then the distance between FAR and each fuzzy number member of LT can be calculated as follows:

$$D(FAR, LT_i) = \left\{\sum_{x=1}^{t}\left(f_{FAR}(x) - f_{LT_i}(x)\right)^2\right\}^{1/2} \tag{2}$$

5 Equity Crowdfunding vs Issuing Shares for Family Businesses

Due to the subjective nature of the evaluation criteria as well as the vague and imprecise nature of the available information, it is easier to express the values and the weights in the natural language terms rather than using crisp values. The linguistic terms could be evaluated through the use of fuzzy logic. There are proposed in the literature many scales to represent linguistic terms using fuzzy intervals. However, most of them use 5–9 intervals (see [18, 35, 47]). According to Lin and Chen [63], for this research, the author adopted the same linguistic terms and their corresponding values for the values and weights respectively. They are given in Table 1.

To consolidate the fuzzy values and weights of all important determinants of choosing the financing sources in family businesses into one fuzzy attractiveness ratio (FAR), the author follow the procedure of Lin and Chen [63].

Analysing the financial logic of family businesses described in the first part of this paper, we can find that maintaining the family control of the business is the top priority for all such companies. This fact we can see also in the research made by KPMG [57], where maintaining the control is the crucial determinant of the financing decisions (76%). Between the factors which might prevent family businesses from engaging in specific source of financing are possible loss of independence (67%), high technical/report requirements (48%), dilution of family traditions (48%), pressure to focus on short – term returns (37%). Another research [95] shows also: maintenance of the company's

Table 1. Fuzzy values for linguistic terms and their values [63]

Linguistic term		Generalized fuzzy numbers
Weights of criteria	Values of ratings	
Very low (VL)	Worst (W)	(0.0, 0.0, 0.2)
Low (L)	Very poor (VP)	(0.0, 0.2, 0.4)
Fairly low (FL)	Poor (P)	(0.2, 0.35, 0.5)
Fair (F)	Fair (F)	(0.3, 0.5, 0.7)
Fairly high (FH)	Good (G)	(0.5, 0.65, 0.8)
High (H)	Very good (VG)	(0.6, 0.8, 1.0)
Very high (VH)	Best (B)	(0.8, 1.0, 1.0)

existence in the long term (78.6%), maintenance of the company's independence from the third parties (58.2%), minimalizing the economic risk (43.5%) and the long term increase in value of the company (41.4%).

From the point of view of the topical analysis in this article, the above findings suggest that the factor named as "loss of control" is the most important to the family firms. Thus, it is given the rating "very high". The next determinant – "cost of capital" is the most important economic factor taken into account in financial decision process. Despite the fact that it is significant, it is not as important as the non-economic factors, especially the possibility of losing independence. We can see such findings in the previous research: [8, 26, 45, 98] and others. Therefore, the proper rating for it will be "high". The other determinants as "low requirements", "process duration" and "limitations" are seen by family firms as medium important for the financing decision process. We can see it for example in the research: [43, 57, 69, 91]. Especially in KPMG research we find that for 48% of surveyed firms the process and report requirements is an important factor. This is about 30% less than in the case of "loss of control". Therefore, the rating for them is "fair".

Hereby, for each factor there was determined the assessment of the validity (importance of factor) for the family firm's point of view. Afterwards, the sources of capital, e.g. equity crowdfunding and IPO/issuing the shares, were appraised, taking into account the value of each factor in the specific source in comparison with each other or other possibilities on the market.

The IPO or issuing the shares is the kind of source of capital, which is possible to use only for joint-stock companies and the capital companies in general. Thus, it is not dedicated to small and medium enterprises, what compared to the equity crowdfunding suggests that factor "limitations" has here lower value. Both of these sources exclude the possibilities of used by the companies without legal personality. However, the equity crowdfunding does not discriminate the small and medium entities. Therefore, the "limitations" value for the equity crowdfunding should be "fair" and for the IPO/issuing shares – "very poor".

The acquisition process is very complex in the case of issuing shares. There are many law restrictions, especially when the offer is public. These requirements are different in the preparation phase and after the acquisition. The first one is connected with preparing whole documentation needed for Financial Authorities (analysis, prospectus, valuation, etc.). The second one is connected with supervision and transparency. These requirements are much lower in the crowdfunding case. Thus, the value of "law requirements" factor for the issuing shares should be "worst" and for crowdfunding – "fair".

The process of raising funds using the issuing the shares or the crowdunding is very extended in time. On the beginning the company should prepare itself to be the public one. Then, prepare all needed documentation, find the partners, etc. Although, the time spent on this activities is almost the same in both cases (i.e. issuing the shares and the crowdfunding), it is longer comparing to alternatives. Thus, the value of "process duration" factor should be "poor" for issuing shares as well for crowdfunding.

The cost of using the capital from a share offer is divided into two parts: first - appropriate for preparing the offer, and second - appropriate for managing and quotation of the shares. The first part consists of cost of auditor (20%), prospectus (30%), promotion (15%), underwriter (15%) and other administrative costs (20%). All these costs summarize to 5-7% of the desired amount of funds [83]. Additionally, the company is charged by the administration costs (e.g. managing and quotation of the shares), which cannot exceed 106 500PLN (about 26000EUR). The shareholders can, additionally, decide to pay a dividend. The average rate of dividend paying in 2019 was 4.14% (https://strefainw estorow.pl/artykuly/dywidendy/20191216/dywidendy-podsumowa nie-2019). The cost of equity crowdfunding with regards to the research made by Motylska-Kuzma [74] is about 6% commission fee, what is comparable to the issuing shares. Nevertheless, the additional costs, like preparing the campaign, engage the influencers, etc., add another 5–10% of the raised funds. These costs, however, are disposable, whereas most of the additional costs in the case of issuing shares are regular. Summarizing, the costs of both sources are pretty high comparing to the alternative financing sources, especially these of debt financing. Thus, using the linguistic scale and taking into account the differences between our two cases, we can rate the crowdfunding as "poor" and the IPO/issuing shares – "very poor".

The last factor using in this analysis is the "loss of control". In the case of equity crowdfunding the impact on control is considerably small. Theoretically, every shareholder has the right to vote for strategic decisions. However, in practice, in the case of equity crowdfunding, the number of new shareholders is very high. It dilutes their voting power. Besides, already at the stage of acquiring funds, the applicant can prepare the campaign so that it will eliminate the possibility of buying the majority of shares by one investor, thus protecting the owner from losing control. The use of such restrictions is hindered by the traditional issue of shares. In consequence, we can rate the "loss of control" factor in the equity crowdfunding as "fair" while in the issuing shares – "very poor".

The results of analyses are summarized in Table 2.

Following the procedure of calculating the fuzzy attractiveness ratio (FAR), describing above, we obtain:

$$FAR(eq\_cr) = (0.2522; 0.4319; 0.6171)$$
$$FAR(IPO) = (0.0261; 0.1924; 0.3829)$$

Table 2. Fuzzy values and weights of main criteria of equity crowdfunding vs IPO

Factor	Weight	Equity crowdfunding (eq_cr)	IPO/issuing shares (IPO)
		Values of rating	Values of rating
Loss of control	Very high	Poor	Very poor
Cost of capital	High	Fair	Very poor
Process duration	Fair	Fair	worst
Law requirements	Fair	Poor	Poor
Limitations	Fair	Fair	Very poor

By using Eq. 2, the Eucliedean distance from FAR to each member in the set LT is calculated to be:

D(FAR(eq_cr),W) = 0.6511	D(FAR(IPO),W) = 0.2668
D(FAR(eq_cr),VP) = 0.4055	**D(FAR(IPO),VP) = 0.0321**
D(FAR(eq_cr),P) = 0.1521	D(FAR(IPO),P) = 0.2623
D(FAR(eq_cr),F) = 0.1175	D(FAR(IPO),F) = 0.5198
D(FAR(eq_cr),G) = 0.3775	D(FAR(IPO),G) = 0.7797
D(FAR(eq_cr),VG) = 0.6349	D(FAR(IPO),VG) = 1.0389
D(FAR(eq_cr),B) = 0.8772	D(FAR(IPO),B) = 1.2775

Matching the linguistic terms with minimum distance (D) the value corresponds to the linguistic term *fair* in the case of equity crowdfunding and *very poor* in the case of IPO/issuing shares. Thus we can see that equity crowdfunding is more suitable for family businesses than IPO/issuing shares.

6   Conclusions

Although the external equity funds are not very desired by the family firms, sometimes are very useful for future development and setting the position on the market. Nowadays such funds are much more expensive than their debt counterparts but their usage has a lot of advantages. First of all, they give to the company increase in creditworthiness and help in sustainable development not raising the liquidity risk. This finding is especially required by the family firms which are very sensible for long term view.

It should be noted that the market of alternative finance is no longer just a response to the crisis, but an increasingly rapidly growing segment of the modern financial market. And while this is still a market niche compared to European credit assets, the AF market has a huge potential for growth. The existing research of alternative financing try to exploring the questions: if, how and which entrepreneurs rely on this relatively new sources of financing, what the advantages and disadvantages of this financial model are compared to the more traditional sources, and how the entrepreneurial environment is going to be affected by the emergence of these new funding sources [11].

The article meets these needs in several dimensions. It compares the traditional sources of capital with the new phenomenon, i.e. equity crowdfunding, taking into account the most frequent factors influencing the financing decisions. Additionally, it analyses the possibility of using crowdfunding by the family businesses, contrasting the financial logic of such entities with the basic characteristics of crowdfunding.

Analysing two sources of equity financing, the IPO/issuing shares and its alternative counterpart – equity crowdfunding, we can see that from the family firm's point of view, the second one is much more suitable. The cost of raising funds is more or less the same on the beginning, nevertheless the equity crowdfunding has lower law requirement and low influence on the loss of control. Additionally, it does not exclude the small and medium companies, what is very important when we analyse the family businesses, because much of them belong to the SME sector.

Although the results are very clear, they require further research. First, the values and weights using in the analysis as well the choosing factors are subjective judgment of the author, made on the basis of definitions and previous research of the equity crowdfunding and the financial logic of family businesses. Thus, they should be check in practice and require the credible research.

Secondly, the future research could be addressing the question of how the socioemotional context influences the response of the crowd to projects branded by family businesses. Are people more likely to support such projects or rather afraid about the nepotism and so close social relations? Are there any differences between the family and non-family companies?

References

1. Ahlers, G.K., Cumming, D., Günther, C., Schweizer, D.: Signaling in equity crowdfunding. Entrep. Theory Pract. **39**(4), 955–980 (2015)
2. Allison, T.H., Davis, B.C., Short, J.C., Webb, J.W.: Crowdfunding in a prosocial microlending environment: examining the role of intrinsic versus extrinsic cues. Entrep. Theory Pract. **39**, 53–73 (2014)
3. Al-Mutairi, M.S., Hipel, K.W., Kamel, M.S.: Trust and cooperation from a fuzzy perspective. Math. Comput. Simul. **76**(5–6), 430–446 (2008)
4. Ampenberger, M., Schmid, T., Achleitner, A.-K., Kaserer, Ch.: Capital structure decisions in family firms – Empirical evidence from a bank – based economy. Center for Enterpreneurial and Financial Studies (CEFS), Working Paper 2009 – 5, EFA Bergen Meeting Paper (2011)
5. Anderson, A.R., Jack, S.L., Dodd, S.D.: The role of family members in entrepreneurial networks: beyond the boundaries of the family firm. Fam. Bus. Rev. **18**, 135–154 (2005)
6. Anderson, R., Reeb, D.M.: Founding family ownership and firm performance: evidence from the S&P500. J. Finan. **58**, 1301–1329 (2003)
7. Astrachan, J.H., Klein, S.B., Smirnyos, K.X.: The F-PEC scale of family influence: a proposal for solving a family business definition problem. Fam. Bus. Rev. **15**(1), 45–58 (2002)
8. Astrachan, J.H., Jaskiewicz, P.: Emotional returns and emotional costs in privately held family businesses: advancing traditional business valuation. Fam. Bus. Rev. **21**, 139–149 (2008)
9. Baeck, P., Collins, L.: Not disrupting, building—crowdfunding and P2P lending will be an integral part of new financial systems in developing economies, 15 July 2015. http://www.nesta.org.uk/blog/not-disrupting-building-crowdfunding-and-p2p-lending-will-be-integral-part-new-financial-systems-developing-economies. Accessed 12 June 2017

10. Baloi, D., Price, A.D.F.: Modeling global risk factors affecting construction cost performance. Int. J. Project Manag. **21**(4), 261–269 (2003)
11. Bellavitis, C., Filatotchev, I., Kamurivo, D.S., Vanacker, T.: Entrepreneurial finance: new frontiers of research and practice. Venture Cap. **19**(1–2), 1–16 (2017)
12. Bennedsen, M., Nielsen, K., Perez-Gonzalez, F., Wolfenzon, D.: Inside the family firms: the role of families in succession decisions and performance. Q. J. Econ. **122**(2), 647–691 (2007)
13. Bertoni, F., Colombo, M.G., Quas, A.: The patterns of venture capital investment in Europe. Small Bus. Econ. **45**(3), 543–560 (2015). https://doi.org/10.1007/s11187-015-9662-0
14. Bih, J.: Paradigm shift - an introduction to fuzzy logic. Potentials IEEE **25**, 6–21 (2006). https://doi.org/10.1109/mp.2006.1635021
15. Blanco-Mazagatos, V., Quevedo-Puente, D., Castrillo, L.A.: The trade-off between financial resources and agency costs in the family business: an exploratory study. Fam. Bus. Rev. **20**(3), 199–213 (2007)
16. Block, J., Sandner, P.: What is the effect of the financial crisis on venture capital financing? Empirical evidence from US internet start-ups. Venture Capital **11**(4), 295–309 (2009)
17. Blumentritt, T., Mathews, T., Marchisio, G.: Game theory and family business succession: an introduction. Fam. Bus. Rev. **26**(1), 51–67 (2013)
18. Bordogna, G., Fedrizzi, M., Passi, G.: A linguistic modeling of consensus in group decision making based on OWA operators. IEEE Trans. Syst. Man Cybern. **27**, 126–132 (1997)
19. Buckley, G.: Microfinance in Africa: is it either a problem or the solution? World Dev. **25**(7), 1081–1093 (1997)
20. Burtch, G., Ghose, A., Wattal, S.: An empirical examination of the antecedents and consequences of contribution patterns in crowd-funded markets. Inf. Syst. Res. **24**, 499–519 (2013)
21. Calessens, S., Djankov, J., Lang, L.: The separation of ownership and control in East Asian corporations. J. Finan. Econ. **58**(1–2), 81–112 (2000)
22. Cassar, G.: The financing of business start-ups. J. Bus. Ventur. **19**(2), 261–283 (2004)
23. Chen, T.-Y., Dasgupta, S., Yu, Y.: Transparency and financing choices of family firms. J. Finan. Quant. Anal. **49**(2), 387–408 (2014)
24. Cholakova, M., Clarysse, B.: Does the possibility to make equity investments in crowdfunding projects crowd out reward-based investments? Entrep. Theory Pract. **39**, 145–172 (2014)
25. Chrisman, J.J., Patel, P.C.: Variations in R&D investments of family and non-family firms: behavioral agency and myopic loss aversion perspectives. Acad. Manag. J. **55**, 976–997 (2012)
26. Chrisman, J.J., Chua, J.H., Litz, R.A.: A unified systems perspective of family firm performance: an extension and integration. J. Bus. Ventur. **18**(4), 467–472 (2003)
27. Coleman, S., Carsky, M.: Sources of capital for small family-owned businesses: evidence from the national survey of small business finances. Fam. Bus. Rev. **12**(1), 73–84 (1999)
28. Cosh, A., Cumming, D., Hughes, A.: Outside enterpreneurial capital. Econ. J. **119**(540), 1494–1533 (2009)
29. Cowling, M., Liu, W., Ledger, A.: Small business financing in the UK before and during the current financial crisis. Int. Small Bus. J. **30**(7), 778–800 (2012)
30. Craig, J.B., Dibrell, C., Davis, P.S.: Leveraging family-based brand identity to enhance firm competitiveness and performance in family businesses. J. Small Bus. Manag. **46**, 351–371 (2008)
31. Crespí, R., Martín-Oliver, A.: Do family firms have better access to external finance during crises? Corp. Gov. Int. Rev. **23**(3), 249–265 (2015)
32. Czubak, K.: Modele crowdfundingu (2014). http://akademiacrowdfundingu.pl/modele-cro wdfundingu/. Accessed 28 July 2017
33. De Buysere, K., Gajda, O., Kleverlaan, R., Marom D.: A framework for european crowdfunding (2012). http://www.crowdfundingframework.eu/. Accessed 1 July 2015

34. Debicki, B.J., Kellermanns, F.W., Chrisman, J.J., Pearson, A.W., Spencer, B.A.: Development of socioemotional importance (SEWi) scale for family firm research. J. Fam. Bus. Strategy **7**, 47–57 (2016)
35. Delgado, M., Herrera, F., Herrera-Viedma, E., Martinez, L.: Combining linguistic and numerical information in group decision making. Inf. Sci. **7**, 177–194 (1998)
36. Denison, D., Lief, C., Ward, J.L.: Culture in family-owned enterprises: Recognizing and leveraging unique strengths. Fam. Bus. Rev. **17**, 61–70 (2004)
37. Di Giuli, A., Caselli, S., Gatti, S.: Are small family firms financially sophisticated? J. Bank. Finan. **35**, 2931–2944 (2011)
38. Distelberg, B., Sorenson, R.L.: Updating system concepts in family businesses: a focus on values. Resour. Flows Adapt. Fam. Bus. Rev. **22**, 65–81 (2009)
39. Dubois, D., Prade, H.: Possibility theory, probability theory and multiple-valued logics: a clarification. Ann. Math. Artif. Intell. **32**, 35–66 (2001). https://doi.org/10.1023/A:101674 0830286
40. Dyer Jr., W.G.: Examining the "family effect" on firm performance. Fam. Bus. Rev. **19**(4), 253–273 (2006)
41. Eshragh, F., Mandani, E.H.: A general approach to linguistic approximation. Int. J. Man Mach. Stud. **11**, 501–519 (1979)
42. Faccio, M., Lang, L.: The ultimate ownership of western European corporation. J. Finan. Econ. **65**(3), 365–395 (2002)
43. Feltham, T.S., Feltham, G., Barnett, J.J.: The dependence of family businesses on a single decision-maker. J. Small Bus. Manag. **43**(1), 1–15 (2005)
44. Florin, J., Lubatkin, M., Schulze, W.: A social capital model of high-growth ventures. Acad. Manag. J. **46**(3), 374–384 (2003)
45. Gómez-Mejía, L.R., Haynes, K.T., Nunez-Nickel, M., Jacobson, K.J.L., Moyano-Fuentes, J.: Socioemotional wealth and business risks in family-controlled firms: evidence from Spanish olive oil mills. Adm. Sci. Q. **52**, 106–137 (2007)
46. Habbershon, T.G., Williams, M.L., MacMillan, I.C.: A unified systems perspective of family firm performance. J. Bus. Ventur. **18**(4), 451–465 (2003)
47. Herrera, F., Herrera-Viedma, E., Verdegay, J.L.: A model of consensus in group decision making under linguistic assessments. Fuzzy Sets Syst. **79**, 73–87 (1996)
48. Holt, G.D.: Which contractor selection methodology? Int. J. Proj. Manag. **16**(3), 153–164 (1998)
49. Karra, N., Tracey, P., Phillips, N.: Altruism and agency in the family firm: exploring the role of family, kinship, and ethnicity. Entrep.: Theory Pract. **30**, 861–887 (2006)
50. Keasey, K., Martinez, B., Pindado, J.: Young family firms: financing decisions and the willingness to dilute control. J. Corp. Finan. **34**, 47–63 (2015)
51. Khavul, S.: Microfinance: creating opportunities for the poor? Acad. Manag. Perspect. **24**, 58–72 (2010)
52. Khavul, S., Chavez, H., Bruton, G.D.: When institutional change outruns the change agent: the contested terrain of entrepreneurial microfinance for those in poverty. J. Bus. Ventur. **28**, 30–50 (2013)
53. King, M.R., Santor, E.: Family values: ownership structure, performance and capital structure of Canadian firms. J. Bank. Finan. **32**(11), 2423–2432 (2008)
54. Kirchmaier, T., Grant, J.: Corporate ownership structure and performance in Europe. Eur. Manag. J. **2**(3), 231–245 (2005)
55. Klein, S.B., Astrachan, J.H., Smirnyos, K.X.: The F-PEC scale of family influence: construction, validation, and further implication of theory. Entrep. Theory Pract. **29**(3), 321–338 (2005)
56. Kosko, B.: Fuzzy Thinking: The New Science of Fuzzy Logic. Hyperion, New York (1993)

57. KPMG: Family matters. Financing family Business growth through individual investors, Report (2014). https://home.kpmg.com/xx/en/home/insights/2014/08/financing-family-bus iness-growth-through-individual-investors.html. Accessed 14 June 2017
58. Kuppuswamy, V., Bayus, B.L.: Crowdfunding creative ideas: the dynamics of project backers in Kickstarter. SSRN Electron. J. (2014). https://doi.org/10.2139/ssrn.2234765
59. La Porta, R., Lopez de Silanes, F., Shleifer, A.: Corporate ownership around the world. J. Finan. 54(2), 471–517 (1999)
60. Le Breton-Miller, I., Miller, D.: Why do some family businesses out-compete? Governance, long-term orientations, and sustainable capability. Entrep. Theory Pract. 30, 731–746 (2006)
61. Lehner, O.M.: Crowdfunding social ventures: a model and research agenda. Venture Capital 15(4), 289–311 (2013)
62. Leu, S.S., Cheng, A.T., Yang, C.H.A.: GA-based fuzzy optimal for construction time-cost trade-off. Int. J. Proj. Manag. 19(1), 47–58 (2001)
63. Lin, C., Chen, Y.: Bid/no-bid decision-making—a fuzzy linguistic approach. Int. J. Proj. Manag. 22, 585–593 (2004)
64. López-Gracia, J., Sánchez-Andújar, S.: Financial structure of the family business: evidence from a group of small Spanish firms. Fam. Bus. Rev. 20(4), 269–287 (2007)
65. Margaritis, D., Psillaki, M.: Capital structure, equity ownership and firm performance. J. Bank. Finan. 34(3), 621–632 (2010)
66. Mazzi, Ch.: Family business and family performance: current state of knowledge and future research challenges. J. Fam. Bus. Strategy 2, 166–181 (2011)
67. McConaughy, D.L., Matthews, C.H., Fialko, A.S.: Founding family controlled firms: performance, risk, and value. J. Small Bus. Manag. 39(1), 31–49 (2001)
68. Mishra, C., Randoy, T., Jenssen, J.: The effect of founding family influence on firm value and corporate governance: a study of Norwegian firms. J. Int. Finan. Manag. Account. 12(3), 235–259 (2001)
69. Morresi, O., Naccarato, A.: Are family firms different in choosing and adjusting their capital structure? An empirical analysis through the lens of agency theory. Int. J. Econ. Finan. 8(7), 216–232 (2016)
70. Motylska-Kuźma, A.: Alternative finance and sustainable development. Cent. Eur. Rev. Econ. Manag. 2, 175–187 (2018)
71. Motylska-Kuźma, A.: Cost of crowdfunding as a source of capital for the small company. In: Proceedings of the 18th International Academic Conference, London, e-book, ISSN 2336-5617 (2015)
72. Motylska-Kuźma, A.: Crowdfunding and sustainable development. Sustainability 10(12), 4650 (2018). https://doi.org/10.3390/su10124650
73. Motylska-Kuźma, A.: Strategie finansowe firm rodzinnych – stan wiedzy, Przedsiębiorczość i Zarządzanie, Wydawnictwo SAN, Tom XVI, Zeszyt 7, cz.I, Łódź, pp. 217–230 (2015)
74. Motylska-Kuźma, A.: The cost of crowdfunding capital. In: Proceedings of the 3rd International Multidisciplinary Scientific Conference on Social Sciences and Arts SGEM (2016), Албена, Bulgaria, 22–31 August 2016, vol. III, pp. 601–612 (2016). https://doi.org/10.5593/sgemsocial2016b23
75. Motylska-Kuźma, A.: The financial decisions of family businesses. J. Fam. Bus. Manag. 7(3), 351–373 (2017)
76. Olson, P.D., Zuiker, V.S., Danes, S.M., Stafford, K., Heck, R.K.Z., Duncan, K.A.: The impact of the family and the business on family business sustainability. J. Bus. Ventur. 18, 639–666 (2003)
77. PARP: Raport końcowy "Badanie firm rodzinnych", Polska Agencja Rozwoju Przedsiębiorczości (PARP), Warszawa, December 2009
78. Peng, M.W., Jiang, Y.: Institutions behind family ownership and control in large firms. J. Manag. Stud. 47(2), 253–273 (2010)

79. Pindado, J., Requejo, I., La Torre, C.: Does family control shape corporate capital structure? Empir. Anal. Eurozone Firms J. Bus. Finan. Account. **42**(7–8), 965–1006 (2015)
80. Puri, M., Zarutskie, R.: On the life cycle dynamics of venture-capital-and non-venture-capital-financed firms. J. Finan. **67**(6), 2247–2293 (2012)
81. Ralcheva, A., Roosenboom, P.: On the road to success in equity crowdfunding. Available at SSRN 2727742 (2016)
82. Randoy, T., Goel, S.: Ownership structure, founder leadership, and performance in Norwegian SMEs: Implications for financing entrepreneurial opportunities. J. Bus. Ventur. **18**(5), 619–637 (2003)
83. Raport Kapitał z giełdy. https://seg.org.pl/sites/seg13.message-asp.com/files/kapital_z_gie ldy_2010.pdf. Accessed 20 Jan 2020
84. Romano, C.A., Tanewski, G.A., Smyrnios, K.X.: Capital structure decision making: a model for family business. J. Bus. Ventur. **16**(3), 285–310 (2001)
85. Sapienza, H.J., Korsgaard, M.A., Forbes, D.P.: The self-determination motive and entrepreneurs'choice of financing. In: Cognitive Approaches to Entrepreneurship Research. Emerald Group Publishing Limited (2003)
86. Schmucker, K.J.: Fuzzy Sets, Natural Language Computations, and Risk Analysis. Computer Science Press, USA (1985)
87. Setia-Atmaja, L., Tanewski, G., Skully, M.: The role of dividends, debt and board structure in the governance of family controlled firms. J. Bus. Finan. Account. **36**(7/8), 863–898 (2009)
88. Signori, A., Vismara, S.: Does success bring success? The post-offering lives of equity-crowdfunded firms. J. Corp. Finan. **50**, 575–591 (2018)
89. Tsao, S.-M., Lien, W.-H.: Family management and internationalization: the impact of firm performance and innovation. Manag. Int. Rev. **53**, 189–213 (2013). https://doi.org/10.1007/s11575-011-0125-9
90. Vanacker, T.R., Manigart, S.: Pecking order and debt capacity considerations for high-growth companies seeking financing. Small Bus. Econ. **35**(1), 53–69 (2010). https://doi.org/10.1007/s11187-008-9150-x
91. Vandemaele, S., Vancauteren, M.: Nonfinancial goals, governance, and dividend payout in private family firms. J. Small Bus. Manag. **53**(1), 166–182 (2015)
92. Villalonga, B., Admit, R.: How do family ownership, management, and control affect firm value? J. Finan. Econ. **80**(2), 385–417 (2006)
93. Vismara, S.: Equity retention and social network theory in equity crowdfunding. Small Bus. Econ. **46**(4), 579–590 (2016). https://doi.org/10.1007/s11187-016-9710-4
94. Walthoff-Borm, X., Schwienbacher, A., Vanacker, T.: Equity crowdfunding: first resort or last resort? J. Bus. Ventur. **33**(4), 513–533 (2018)
95. Weclawski, J.: Capital market financing of family enterprises. Bus. Econ. Horizons **10**(4), 272–280 (2014)
96. Young, M., Peng, M.W., Ahlstrom, D., Bruton, G., Jiang, Y.: Corporate governance in emerging economies: a review of the principal–principal perspective. J. Manag. Stud. **45**(1), 196–220 (2008)
97. Zadeh, L.A.: Fuzzy sets. Inf. Control **8**, 338–353 (1965)
98. Zellweger, T.M., Astrachan, J.H.: On the emotional value of owning a firm. Fam. Bus. Rev. **21**, 347–363 (2008)
99. Zellweger, T.M., Frey, U., Halter, F.A.: A behavioral perspective to financing decisions in family and nonfamily firms. University of St. Gallen, Center for Family Business, Switzerland, p. 253 (2005)

Some Propositions of Approaches for Measuring Indirect Control Power of Firms and Mutual Connections in Corporate Shareholding Structures

Izabella Stach[1]([⊠]) [iD], Jacek Mercik[2] [iD], and Cesarino Bertini[3] [iD]

[1] AGH University of Science and Technology, Al. Mickiewicza 30, 30-059 Krakow, Poland
istach@zarz.agh.edu.pl
[2] WSB University in Wroclaw, Fabryczna 29/31, 53-609 Wroclaw, Poland
jacek.mercik@wsb.wroclaw.pl
[3] Department of Management, Economics, and Quantitative Methods, University of Bergamo,
Via dei Caniana, 2, 24127 Bergamo, Italy
cesarino.bertini@unibg.it

Abstract. This paper discusses some game-theoretical methods that use power indices for measuring the indirect control power of firms and mutual connections in complex corporate shareholding networks. Only a few of the methods considered in the literature so far measure the control power of all firms involved in shareholding networks; meanwhile, none of them regard measuring the importance of linkages. The intention of this article is first to propose a modification of the Mercik-Łobos and Mercik-Stach methods using the Banzhaf index to measure the direct and indirect control of investors and stock companies. Second, having already estimated the control power of nodes (firms) in a network, we consider the relationship of this power to the power of the linkages that connect the companies in directed networks. Then, we present our own idea of how such link's power can be measured. We regard to the power of the link in relation to the firms as well as (more significantly) in relation to the entire corporate network.

Keywords: Cooperative game theory · Corporate shareholding structures · Indirect control · Power indices

1 Introduction

Many scholars have focused their attention on the measurement of the indirect control power of firms in complex corporate networks. It is not immediately obvious from the shareholding ownership data to understand whether a particular firm is in control of other companies in a complex network with many firms involved and the presence of circular cross-ownerships. Game theoretical models and, in particular, power indices provide a rigorous approach for getting around this problem. The first who indicated this area of application of power indices were Penrose in [1] and Shapley and Shubik in [2]. Next, only in the 1990s, Gambarelli and Owen [3] proposed the first method for measuring the

© Springer-Verlag GmbH Germany, part of Springer Nature 2020
N. T. Nguyen et al. (Eds.): TCCI XXXV, LNCS 12330, pp. 116–132, 2020.
https://doi.org/10.1007/978-3-662-62245-2_8

voting power of investors (i.e., firms without shareholdings) in shareholding networks without loops. Then, other interesting methods for modeling and measuring the indirect control of individual investors were proposed. It is not our intention here to present an in-depth analysis of the literature on the use of power indices to measure the power of companies in corporate networks; the reader can find it in such publications as [4–7], for example. Here, we limit ourselves to providing a list of papers that deal with such kinds of methods. Among these papers are [3–5, 8–15]. Only a few of the methods considered in the literature so far measure the control power of all firms involved in shareholding networks. In this paper, we concentrate only on those game-theoretical approaches that use power indices to estimate the direct and indirect control power of all firms (which means the investors and stock companies) involved in complex corporate shareholding structures. To our knowledge, the first approach that takes measuring the control power of all firms into consideration was the Karos and Peters method proposed in 2015 [5]. This method references the Shapley-Shubik index [2]. Then, in 2016, Mercik and Łobos [13] introduced a method that uses the Johnston power index [16]. The Mercik and Łobos approach was modified in 2018 by Mercik and Stach [7]. The Levy and Szafarz approach [14] uses the Banzhaf index [1, 17]. Some of the mentioned methods were compared in the following papers: [6, 7, 18, 19] as well as the forthcoming [15]. Moreover, some considerations about the reasonable properties for indirect control power index can be found in [7, 15]. Some methods proposed in the literature do not take corporate networks with the presence of loops into consideration; i.e., circular cross-ownerships. The complex real-world corporate shareholding networks feature multiple levels of ownership, cross-shareholdings, and even circular cross-ownerships (i.e., loops) that complicate the relation between ownership and control power, and thus the modeling of such networks by rigorous mathematical models. Some methods proposed in the literature are not well defined for the occurrence of cycles in the corporate networks. It means that some models fails in occurrence of the loops in corporate networks. The model proposed by Gambarelli and Owen [3] in occurrence of cycles does not always guarantee the uniqueness of the solution, for example. The methods proposed by Karos and Peters [5], Mercik and Łobos [13], and Mercik and Stach [7] estimate the indirect control of all firms in networks with the presence of loops.

Analogously to classical voting power measures, a measure of indirect control power should also be characterized by adequate properties. In [5, 20], Karos and Peters imposed a set of properties (null player, symmetry, constant-sum (which plays the role of the usual efficiency property), transfer (which is related to the Dubey's transfer property used to characterize the Shapley value [21, 22]), and the so-called controlled player) with a plausible interpretation in the area of a corporate network and arrived at the unique index. Our approach is different; we would like to improve only the existing measures so that they can have good properties. Namely, one aim of this paper is to present a new proposition of a measure of the indirect control power of firms in shareholding corporate networks as a variation of the Mercik and Łobos [13] and Mercik and Stach [7] approaches. Both of the mentioned approaches use the Johnston index. In particular, instead of referring to the Johnston index [16] in the evaluation of power, we propose substituting it with the Banzhaf index [1, 17]. Our motivations and argumentations for this change are as follows:

- The Banzhaf and Shapley-Shubik indices are the most important and most commonly used indices of voting power; see [23–26], for example.
- The Shapley-Shubik index [2] would be an alternative favored by some, but it has been argued by numerous writers (including Coleman [27], Felsenthal and Machover [23, 24], and Leech [11, 28]) that the properties of the Shapley-Shubik index are inferior to the Banzhaf as a general measure of voting power. The Banzhaf index is easier to use, being a simple probability measure (an absolute index).
- The Shapley-Shubik [2] index takes the order in which votes are cast in a voting process into account. According to Banzhaf [17], a power voting measure should depend on the number of combinations rather than the number of the permutations of the players. He claimed that the order in which the votes are cast is not significant (see also [25, p. 6]).
- Taking into account the formal definition of the Johnston and Banzhaf indices, we see that these indices are very similar. This is not a case, as the Johnston index was introduced as a modification of the Banzhaf index. However, Felsenthal and Machover have shown the limitations of the Johnston index [16] as a voting measure (of which they are highly critical; see [24]).

So, the more prominent tool seems to be the Banzhaf index [1, 17] rather than the Johnston index [16] for analyzing the control power of firms in corporate shareholding networks. For this reason, we propose a modification of the Mercik-Łobos and Mercik-Stach methods of applying the Banzhaf index.

The second aim of this paper is to assess the voting power of linkages in corporate shareholding networks; that is, the voting power of a particular link between two nodes (for example, when Company 5 owns, say, 25% of Company 2; see Fig. 1). This is a different problem from the more basic one of finding the voting power associated with a single node – in other words, a shareholder, whether it is an individual or a corporation. Then, once having estimated the power of firms in a network, the management of a firm can put forth the following questions: How important is a given link to us? If it disappears, will it affect the control power of our company? How? Does the control power of a company decrease/increase? For example, if Company 5 in Fig. 1 sells all shares in Company 2 to Investor 6, then the shareholding network will change. Namely, the link from Company 5 to Company 2 will disappear. So, will this change in linkages affect the indirect control power of Company 3, for example? How? If a linkage disappears, which company will suffer the most?

The rest of the paper is structured as follows. In Sect. 2, we provide a theoretical background; i.e., the preliminary definitions and notations of cooperative game theory and power indices. In Sect. 3, following the approaches of Mercik and Łobos [13] and Mercik and Stach [7], we introduce an approach to measure the power of all firms in corporate networks using the Banzhaf [17] index for this purpose. In Sect. 4, we present our idea to measure the power of linkages in corporate shareholding structures. Finally, Sect. 5 concludes with some parting remarks.

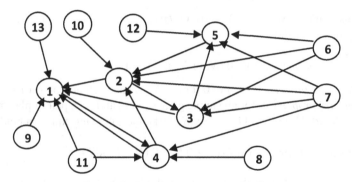

Fig. 1. Corporate shareholding network with 13 firms. Source: [19].

2 Cooperative Game Background: Definitions and Notations

A *cooperative n-person game* is a pair (N, v) where $N = \{1, 2, \ldots, n\}$ is a finite set of n players and v is a real-valued function, $v : 2^N \to R$ with $v(\emptyset) = 0$. 2^N denotes the set of all subsets of N. Each element $S \in 2^N$ is called a *coalition*, $\emptyset$ is called the *empty coalition*, and N is called the *grand coalition*. $v(S)$ stands for the *worth* of coalition S in game v, i.e., the maximal value that the players in coalition S can guarantee themselves by cooperating with each other. $|S|$ denotes the cardinality of S, so $|N| = n$. A cooperative game is *monotonic* if $v(S) \leq v(T)$ holds true whenever $S \subset T \subseteq N$. A *simple* game is monotonic cooperative game such that $v(S) \in \{0, 1\}$ for all $S \subseteq N$ and $v(N) = 1$. In simple games, we call coalitions with property $v(S) = 1$ *winning coalitions*, while those with $v(S) = 0$ are called *losing coalitions*. By W, we denote the set of all winning coalitions in cooperative game (N, v). Any simple game may be unequivocally described by its set of winning coalitions. A simple game is *proper* if the following condition holds: $\forall S \subseteq N$ if $v(S) = 1$, then $v(N \backslash S) = 0$. In this paper, we only analyze those proper simple games (for more on a proper simple game, see [29], for example) that are often used to model decision-making situations. A player is *critical* (or a *swinger,* or *decisive*) in a winning coalition if his/her removal from the coalition makes the coalition losing. For each player i in N, $C_i = \{S \subseteq N : i \in S \wedge v(S) = 1 \wedge v(S \backslash \{i\}) = 0\}$ denotes the collection of all coalitions in which i is critical. For each coalition $S \in 2^N$, $Cr(S)$ states for the number of players who are critical in S. If for a player $i \in N$ his/her marginal contribution to each coalition is zero [i.e., $v(S \cup \{i\}) = v(S)$ for all coalitions $S \subseteq N \backslash \{i\})$], then i is called a *null player*. If a coalition has at least one critical player [i.e., $Cr(S) > 0$], then it is called a *vulnerable* (or *sensitive*) coalition. VC denotes the set of all vulnerable coalitions. A winning coalition S is called a *minimal winning coalition* if each proper subset of S is a losing coalition. A simple game (N, v) is called a *weighted majority game* and represented by $[q; w_1, \ldots, w_n]$ if there exists a non-negative vector of the weights of players $(w_1, \ldots, w_n)$, $\sum_{i \in N} w_i = 1$, and a majority quota $q \sum_{i \in N} w_i \geq q > 0$ such that $v(S) = 1$ if and only if $\sum_{i \in S} w_i > q$. Weighted majority games are often used to model corporate shareholder voting in stock companies. There, the weights are the voting rights owned in a stock company. A *power index f* is a function that assigns a unique vector $f(v) = (f_1(v), f_2(v), \ldots, f_n(v))$ to each simple game (N, v). We say that f satisfies:

- the *efficiency property* if for all (N, v) $\sum_{i \in N} f_i(v) = 1$.
- the *null player property* if $f_i(v) = 0$ for all (N, v) and each null player $i \in N$.
- the *symmetry property* if, for all simple games (N, v) and each pair of players $i, j \in N$ such that $\forall S \in 2^{N \setminus \{i, j\}}$ $v(S \cup \{i\}) = v(S \cup \{j\})$, the following equation holds: $f_i(v) = f_j(v)$.
- the *non-negativity property* if $f_i(v) \geq 0$ for all (N, v) and $i \in N$.

In the definitions below, the three classical power indices considered in this paper are presented. The Shapley-Shubik index, σ, for simple game (N, v) and every $i \in N$ is given by

$$\sigma_i(v) = \sum_{S \in C_i} \frac{(|S| - 1)!(n - |S|)!}{n!}.$$

For more about of σ, see [2, 26, 30], for example.

Penrose (in [1]) and then Banzhaf (in [17]) proposed the same measure of voting power commonly known as the Banzhaf index. Given (N, v), the absolute Banzhaf index (briefly, β) is defined as follows:

$$\beta_i(v) = \frac{|C_i|}{2^{n-1}} \text{ for every } i \in N.$$

The relative Banzhaf index (β') is defined as

$$\beta'_i(v) = \frac{|C_i|}{\sum_{j \in N} |C_j|}.$$

For more on the Banzhaf indices, see [31], for example.

The Johnston power index (briefly, γ) was defined in [16] as follows. Given simple game (N, v),

$$\gamma_i(v) = \frac{J_i}{\sum_{j \in N} J_j} \text{ for every } i \in N,$$

where J_i (called the raw Johnston index or the Johnston score) is given as

$$J_i(v) = \begin{cases} 0 & \text{if } i \text{ is a null player;} \\ \sum_{S \in VC, \, i \in S} \frac{1}{Cr(S)} & \text{otherwise.} \end{cases}$$

For a comparison of these three indices, see [25, 32], for example.

In this paper, we will call an "investor" a firm without shareholdings and a "company" (or "stock company") a firm that is owned by shareholders. For example, in Fig. 1, Firms 1, 2, 3, 4, and 5 are companies and Firms 6, 7, 8, 9, 10, 11, 12, and 13 are investors.

In the definitions below, we define three indices introduced for measuring the indirect control power of all firms in shareholding networks. Karos and Peters (in [5, 20]) introduced the Φ index for each firm i in N (N is the set of all firms in a network) as follows:

$$\Phi_i(IMS) = \sum_{k \in N} \sigma_i(v_k^{IMS}) - v_i^{IMS}(N),$$

where σ is the Shapley-Shubik index, and IMS is a so-called invariant mutual structure; i.e., a vector of simple games where each simple game v_k^{IMS} indicates all coalitions of firms that control firm k ($v_k^{IMS}(S) = 1$ if k is controlled by S). Karos and Peters note: "In this index, each player accumulates his Shapley-Shubik power index assignments from controlling other players, diminished by the sum of the Shapley-Shubik power index assignments to other players controlling him" (see [20, p. 1]).

Mercik and Łobos [13] introduced the implicit index (π) in order to measure indirect control. This method uses the Johnston power index [16]. Let $N = N^C \cup N^I$ be the set of all firms in a network, where N^C is the set of all companies and N^I is the set of all investors; N_j^C is the set of companies that are shareholders of company j, whereas N_j^I is the set of investors of company j, $j \in N^C$. The v_j game is the weighted majority game in company j. For each investor $i \in N^I$ the π index is defined as follows

$$\pi_i = \frac{absolut\pi_i}{\sum_{r \in N^I} absolut\pi_r}, \text{ where } absolut\pi_i = \sum_{j \in N^C} \left(J_i(v_j) + \sum_{\substack{k \in N_j^C \\ i \in N_k}} \frac{J_k(v_j)}{|N_k|} \right).$$

For each company $j \in N^C$ the π index is defined as follows

$$\pi_j = \frac{absolut\pi_j}{\sum_{r \in N^C} absolut\pi_r}, \quad absolut\pi_j = \sum_{i \in N_j^I} J_i(v_j) + \sum_{k \in N_j^C} \sum_{i \in N_k} \frac{J_j(v_j)}{|N_k|}.$$

For the deep consideration, see [13]. Here below, we give also a three-step procedure to calculate this index.

Step 1. For each stock company j in a corporate shareholding network, we assign a weighted majority game $[q; w_1, \ldots, w_k]$ where q is a majority quota of the shares necessary to pass a bill in the assembly of j, k is the number of direct shareholders in j, and vector $(w_1, \ldots, w_k)$ presents the ownerships of each k shareholder. Then, having the set of sensitive coalitions in company j (VC_j), we calculate the absolute Johnston index (J_i) for each shareholder of j.
Step 2. Every value of the power index (J_i) assigned to stock company j in Step 1 is divided equally among all shareholders of j.
Step 3. For each investor and for each company in the whole network, we sum up the values assigned in Steps 1 and 2. In this way, we obtain the absolute implicit power index for each firm. Then, we appropriately standardized these absolute values for investors and stock companies separately. The goal of this is to produce the standardized implicit

index π_i for each firm i in a corporate network so that the index values of all investors add up to 1 (and those for all stock companies also add up to 1).

Mercik and Stach (in [7]) proposed index π' as a modification of the π index. The motivation for introducing π' was to obtain a measure of indirect control power similar to π but satisfying the null player property. The difference between π and π' lies only in Step 2 of the procedure for calculation π given above. In particular, the amount assigned to the stock company in Step 1 is distributed proportionally to the raw Johnston index distribution given in the first step instead of dividing this amount equally among their shareholders. The first and third steps are the same as for π.

3 Method for Measuring Firm Indirect Control Power

In this section, we introduce our proposition for a relative measure of the indirect control power in corporate shareholding networks with the presence of loops. We denote this index as π^β because it can be seen as a modification (or improvement) of the π or π' indices (see Sect. 2). Indices π and π' (introduced by Mercik and Łobos [13] and Mercik and Stach [7], respectively) use an adaptation of the Johnston index [16] to calculate indirect control power. Since the Johnston index fails some recognized properties of a good measure of voting power (see [23, 24], for example), we try to improve indices π and π' in order to obtain a measure of indirect control that has properties that are analogous to the power index used (so, the Banzhaf power index in this case). π^β is closer to π' than to π, as we would like to have a measure that satisfies the null player property. The main (and unique) difference between π^β and π' lies in the choice of the index used in Steps 1 and 2 of the algorithms of the calculation of these indices (see Sect. 2). The three-step algorithm to calculate the π^β index for investors and stock companies in a corporate network is as follows.

Step 1. For each company in a shareholding corporate network, the absolute value of the Banzhaf index is calculated by taking only direct ownership into account.
Step 2. For each shareholder company i, we distribute the amount assigned in the first Step 1 to i among its investors proportionally to the Banzhaf index distribution given in the first step.
Step 3. For each company, the absolute value of the π^β index is calculated by summing up the appropriate values in the whole corporate network. For each investor, the absolute value of the π^β index is calculated by summing up the appropriate values assigned to this investor across the entire system of companies. Then, these absolute values are appropriately standardized to obtain the π^β index of each shareholder and each company.

Among the standard postulates of the power indices in simple games are the symmetry, null player, efficiency, and non-negativity properties. Of course, all of these properties are fulfilled by the Banzhaf index. By the algorithm given above, we see that π^β satisfies the symmetry, null player, and negativity properties. Moreover, this index is also efficient for investors and companies separately.

Let us consider an illustrative example of a corporate network given by the matrix of direct ownerships in Table 1 and the graphical presentation in Fig. 1. In order to estimate the control power of all firms in this example, we consider a simple majority rule; i.e., a threshold of $q = 50\%$ that describes the necessary voting rights (in percentages) to make a bill pass.

Table 1. Direct ownership relationships in illustrative example. Source: [7]

Firm	Company 1	Company 2	Company 3	Company 4	Company 5
1				3%	
2	35%		30%		
3	20%				10%
4	30%	5%			
5		25%			
6		5%	30%		15%
7		30%	40%	90%	30%
8				5%	
9	5%				
10		35%			
11	5%			2%	
12					45%
13	5%				

In order to calculate π^β in the illustrative example, we must know the number of coalitions for each firm $i \in \{1, 2, \ldots, 13\}$ in which she/he is critical. Table 2 provides this information. To realize Step 1 of the procedure of calculating π^β, we need to calculate the absolute Banzhaf index of each company of the network (taking only direct ownership into account). So, for each company i ($i \in \{1, 2, 3, 4, 5\}$) and each shareholder j, we have to calculate C_j; i.e., the number of coalitions in which j is critical.

The results of calculating the π^β index in the illustrative example are given in Table 3.

Based on the calculation of π^β in Table 3, we see that Investor 7 is the most powerful in the sense of power control, whereas Investor 8 (being a null player) is the least powerful. The rankings of the investors is as follows: 7, 6, 12, 10, 9 = 11 = 13, 8. Meanwhile, the rankings of the companies from most to least powerful is 5, 2, 3, 1, 4. In [7], the authors analyzed the Karos and Peters as well as the Mercik and Łobos approaches, and they calculated the Φ and π indices for the same illustrative example. The π' index was calculated in [15] for the same example. Table 4 shows the rankings of all considered here indices in the illustrative example given by Table 1 and Fig. 1. Comparing the rankings obtained for π^β with the rankings of Φ, π, and π', we can make the following inferences.

Table 2. C_j and vulnerable coalitions in each company in example.

Company i	Vulnerable coalitions considering only direct control. All critical players are underscored	C_j
$i = 1$	$\{\underline{2}, \underline{3}\}$, $\{\underline{2}, \underline{4}\}$, $\{\underline{2}, 3, 4\}$, $\{\underline{2}, \underline{3}, 9\}$, $\{\underline{2}, \underline{3}, 11\}$, $\{\underline{2}, \underline{3}, 13\}$, $\{\underline{2}, \underline{4}, 9\}$, $\{\underline{2}, \underline{4}, 11\}$, $\{\underline{2}, \underline{4}, 13\}$, $\{\underline{3}, \underline{4}, \underline{9}\}$, $\{\underline{3}, \underline{4}, \underline{11}\}$, $\{\underline{3}, \underline{4}, \underline{13}\}$, $\{2, 3, 4, 9\}$, $\{2, 3, 4, 11\}$, $\{2, 3, 4, 13\}$, $\{\underline{2}, \underline{3}, 9, 11\}$, $\{\underline{2}, \underline{3}, 9, 13\}$, $\{\underline{2}, \underline{3}, 11, 13\}$, $\{\underline{2}, \underline{4}, 9, 11\}$, $\{\underline{2}, \underline{4}, 9, 13\}$, $\{\underline{2}, \underline{4}, 11, 13\}$, $\{\underline{3}, \underline{4}, 9, 11\}$, $\{\underline{3}, \underline{4}, 9, 13\}$, $\{\underline{3}, \underline{4}, 11, 13\}$, $\{\underline{2}, \underline{3}, 9, 11, 13\}$, $\{\underline{2}, \underline{4}, 9, 11, 13\}$, $\{\underline{3}, \underline{4}, 9, 11, 13\}$	$C_2 = 20$, $C_3 = 15$, $C_4 = 15$, $C_9 = C_{11} = C_{13} = 1$
$i = 2$	$\{\underline{5}, \underline{7}\}$, $\{\underline{5}, \underline{10}\}$, $\{\underline{7}, \underline{10}\}$, $\{4, \underline{5}, \underline{7}\}$, $\{4, \underline{5}, \underline{10}\}$, $\{4, \underline{7}, \underline{10}\}$, $\{\underline{5}, 6, \underline{7}\}$, $\{\underline{5}, 6, \underline{10}\}$, $\{6, \underline{7}, \underline{10}\}$, $\{4, \underline{5}, 6, \underline{7}\}$, $\{4, \underline{5}, 6, \underline{10}\}$, $\{4, 6, \underline{7}, \underline{10}\}$	$C_5 = C_7 = C_{10} = 8$, $C_4 = C_6 = 0$
$i = 3$	$\{\underline{2}, \underline{6}\}$, $\{\underline{2}, \underline{7}\}$, $\{\underline{6}, \underline{7}\}$	$C_2 = C_6 = C_7 = 2$
$i = 4$	$\{\underline{7}\}$, $\{1, \underline{7}\}$, $\{\underline{7}, 8\}$, $\{\underline{7}, 11\}$, $\{1, \underline{7}, 8\}$, $\{1, \underline{7}, 11\}$, $\{\underline{7}, 8, 11\}$, $\{1, \underline{7}, 8, 11\}$	$C_7 = 8$, $C_1 = C_8 = C_{11} = 0$
$i = 5$	$\{\underline{3}, \underline{12}\}$, $\{\underline{6}, \underline{12}\}$, $\{\underline{7}, \underline{12}\}$, $\{\underline{3}, \underline{6}, \underline{7}\}$, $\{3, \underline{6}, \underline{12}\}$, $\{3, 7, \underline{12}\}$, $\{6, 7, \underline{12}\}$. $\{3, 6, 7, \underline{12}\}$	$C_3 = C_7 = 2$, $C_6 = 3$, $C_{12} = 7$

- For investors, π^{β} results in the same rankings as Φ. The ranking of π differs, standing as 7, 6, 10, 12, 11, 8, 9 = 13. Surprisingly, Firm 8 (which does not take part of any vulnerable coalition) is ranked higher than Firms 9 and 13. The rankings of inverstors by π' is 7, 10, 12, 6, 9 = 11 = 13, 8. The π' index (satisfying the null player property) ranks Firm 8 properly (i.e., as the least powerful). However, π' results in less power for Firm 6 than the other indices do. Given the fact that Firm 6 is critical in the vulnerable coalitions of two companies (3 and 5) whereas Firms 10 and 12 are critical in the vulnerable coalitions of only one firm (i.e., Firm 10 in Company 2 and Firm 12 in Company 5), then we should expect a greater indirect power control in Firm 6 than the respective indirect power control of Firms 10 and 12 in the entire network (see Table 2). Thus, the π^{β} index satisfies our expectations.
- For companies, π^{β} gives different rankings than the Φ, π, and π' indices. The Karos and Peters index ranks the companies in the following order: 2, 5, 3, 4, 1. However, π results in totally different rankings for the companies (1, 2, 4 = 5, 3). By the way, if we take the number of shareholders of a company into account, we obtain the same rankings as those produced by π. Meanwhile, π' orders the companies as follows: 1, 4, 5, 2, 3. Taking the indirect control power of companies into account, we should expect that the company that does not directly control any firm is the least powerful in a network. In the considered example, Company 1 does not directly control any firm. According to Φ, Company 1 receives null power. The indices that consider

Table 3. Absolute and standardized values of π^β in illustrative example.

Investor	Company					Absolute index of investor	π^β of investor
	1	2	3	4	5		
6	0.15625	0.10714	0.50000	0	0.45833	1.22173	0.18180
7	0.83333	0.57143	0.66667	1.00000	0.33333	3.40476	0.50664
8	0	0	0	0	0	0	0
9	0.03125	0	0	0	0	0.03125	0.00465
10	0.20833	0.50000	0.16667	0	0	0.87500	0.13020
11	0.03125	0	0	0	0	0.03125	0.00465
12	0	0.25000	0	0	0.87500	1.12500	0.16740
13	0.03125	0	0	0	0	0.03125	0.00465
Absolute index of company	1.29167	1.42857	1.33333	1.00000	1.66667	6.72024	
π^β of company	0.19220	0.21258	0.19841	0.14880	0.24801		1

the Johnston index (i.e., π and π') rank Company 1 as the most powerful in the entire network. The π^β index places Company 1 in second-to-last place (i.e., ahead of Company 4). The indices from the π group also consider the position of a company ("position-power") in an entire shareholding corporate network. This means that these indices take a company's shareholders into account when calculating the power of companies; if a shareholder is a stock company, these indices consider this fact. So, the "fractions" of control power assigned to the investors of a company's shareholders increase the power of a company in the process of estimating a company's power in the entire network. For indices π and π' (i.e., the indices that use the Johnston index), the fraction of the "position-power" exceeds the fraction of the "control-power" assigned to the companies. For this reason, the rankings of π and π' differ significantly from those of indices Φ and π^β. Therefore, π^β seems to be better than its "colleagues" from the π group. Then, let us attempt to justify a worse position of Company 4 as compared to Company 1 in the rankings given by π^β. If we take the "decisiveness" of the companies into consideration (see Table 2 and C_i), we can order the companies as follows: 2, 3, 4, 5, 1. However, if we take indirect control into consideration, we can see that Company 5 can control Companies 1, 2, and 3, while Company 4 can only control Company 1. So, Company 5 is more indirectly powerful than 4. Next, Company 4 has a worse "power-position" than Company 1 in the network. This is because the shareholders of Company 4 are three investors along with Company 1. Company 1 is not decisive in any winning coalitions, but its "position-power" is strong. Company 1 has three investors and three strong companies as shareholders in the network.

Table 4. Ranking of firms according to Φ, π, π', and π^β indices

Position of firm in ranking		Ranking of firms in accordance with			
		Φ	π	π'	π^β
Companies	1	2	1	1	5
	2	5	2	4	2
	3	3	4, 5	5	3
	4	4	3	2	1
	5	1		3	4
Investors	1	7	7	7	7
	2	6	6	10	6
	3	12	10	12	12
	4	10	12	6	10
	5	9, 11, 13	11	9, 11, 13	9, 11, 13
	6	8	8	8	8
	7		9, 13		
	8				

4 Measurement of Importance of Mutual Connections in Corporate Networks

Once the control power of all firms in a corporate shareholding network is evaluated, we can ask about the importance of the mutual linkages. How is a linkage important for a particular firm in a network? If a link disappears due to the resale of shares or as a result of a takeover (for example), how will this affect the control power of the firms presented in the network? The disappearance of the link can significantly change the graph in various ways and thus affect the change in the distribution of the control power in the corporate network. In this paper, we do not focus on detailed consideration of all possible scenarios, although this issue is very interesting and requires in-depth study. For instance the shares may be sold to another agent, as is mentioned in Sect. 1, where Company 5 (in Fig. 1) sells all shares in Company 2 to Investor 6, for example. In this case, the network described by Table 1 remains complete (it means, the sum of shares owned by the shareholders of each company i that appear in the network is equal to 100%). Of course, the distribution of the ownership change and so direct and indirect control of some firms could change significantly. Another scenario may be that the shares are sold to the "ocean" of small investors, so they may be viewed as disappearing. Then, the float (it means, the set of unidentified small shareholders of the company) can be model in different way. So, the situation (distribution of control power) may be very different in the different scenarios.

In [15], an idea of how to estimate the importance of a linkage was proposed. In this method, a corporate network is modeled by a directed graph where loops and isolated nodes are possible. Generally speaking, according to this idea, the power of a linkage connecting Firm i with Firm j—link (i, j)—is equal to the difference between the power values calculated for Firm i before and after removing this link from the network. In this paper, we use this idea; however, we propose a method for measuring the following:

– the power (importance) of a link for any firm in a network;
– the power (importance) of a link in an entire network.

Let M^L stand for a corporate shareholding network with the set of linkages L and set N of all firms. Note that, in network M^L, circular cross-ownerships can be present. Next, let f be a power index that estimates the power of all of the firms in M^L. So, $f_i(M^L)$ denotes the power control of Firm i in M^L. Now, we can define the measure of power of link $l \in L$ for Firm i (briefly, $\Delta_l^i(M)$) as

$$\Delta_l^i(M^L) = f_i(M^L) - f_i(M^{L \setminus \{l\}})$$

and the measure of power of link $l \in L$ in the entire M^L (briefly, $\Delta_l(M^L)$) as

$$\Delta_l(M^L) = \max_{i \in N} \left[f_i(M^L) - f_i(M^{L \setminus \{l\}}) \right].$$

Now, we can state some propositions about the measures defined above. Let f be a power index that estimates the power of all of the firms in a corporate network (M^L).

Proposition 1. If f satisfies the null player property, then $\Delta_{(i,j)}^i(M^L) = \Delta_{(i,j)}(M^L) = 0$ for all $j \in N$ for each null Firm i.

Proof. Let $i \in N$ be a null firm in network M^L. So, $f_i(M^L) = 0$. Consider all linkages $l = (i, j) \in L, j \in N$. Then $f_k(M^L) = f_k(M^{L \setminus \{(i,j)\}})$ for all $j, k \in N$ since the elimination of a linkage that starts in the null player (here, i) does not change the power of Firm i nor the power of the other firms in the network. Hence, $\Delta_{l=(i,j)}^i(M^L) = f_i(M^L) - f_i(M^{L \setminus \{l\}})$ $= 0$ and $\Delta_{(i,j)}(M^L) = \max_{k \in N} \left[f_k(M^L) - f_k(M^{L \setminus \{(i,j)\}}) \right] = 0$ for every $j \in N$ such that $l = (i, j) \in L$. QED.

Now, we can introduce the definition of a null link. A link in network M^L is called a *null link* if $\Delta_l(M^L) = 0$.

Proposition 2. If f is the efficient power index for every network M^L, then $\sum_{i \in N} \Delta_l^i(M^L) = 0$ for every $l \in L$.

Proof. The demonstration is immediate. If f is efficient, then $\sum_{i \in N} f_i(M) = 1$ for each M^L.
Given network M^L, let $l \in L$. By definition, $\sum_{i \in N} \Delta_l^i(M) = \sum_{i \in N} \left[f_i(M^L) - f_i(M^{L \setminus \{l\}}) \right] =$
$\sum_{i \in N} f_i(M^L) - \sum_{i \in N} f_i(M^{L \setminus \{l\}}) = 0$. QED.

The range of $\Delta_l^i(M)$ (and so, also $\Delta_l(M)$) depends on the index f applied.

Proposition 3. If f is not non-negative and an efficient power index for every network M^L, then $\Delta_l^i(M^L) \leq 1$ and $\Delta_l(M^L) \leq 1$ for every $l \in L$.

Proof. If f is non-negative and efficient, then $0 \leq f_i(M) \leq 1$. Hence, we immediately have $\Delta_l^i(M^L) = f_i(M^L) - f_i(M^{L\setminus\{l\}}) \leq 1$ and, as a consequence, $\Delta_l(M) = \max_{i \in N} \Delta_l^i(M^L) \leq 1$. QED.

Of course, the values of $\Delta_l^i(M^L)$ and $\Delta_l(M^L)$ can be negative (but not lower than -1). In both cases, when $\Delta_l^i(M^L) > 0$ or $\Delta_l^i(M^L) < 0$, link l is important for Firm i. If $\Delta_l^i(M^L) > 0$ (i.e., $f_i(M^L) > f_i(M^{L\setminus\{l\}})$), then the elimination of link l decreases the control power of Firm i. While, $\Delta_l^i(M^L) < 0$, the elimination of link l increases the control power of Firm i.

Let us regard the illustrative example considered in Sect. 3 (see also Fig. 1 and Table 1). Then, let us estimate the power of linkage $(7, 4)$ using the method proposed in this section as well as the π^β index proposed in Sect. 3. Firm 7 has 90% of the voting rights in Company 4; therefore, we expect that the value of $\Delta_{(7,4)}^7$ will be positive and respectively high. In order to find the $\Delta_{(7,4)}^i$ for each $i \in N$, we must calculate π^β for the network without link $(7, 4)$. If we eliminate this link, we observe that all of the vulnerable coalitions in Company 4 become losing along with $C_i = 0$ for each shareholder $i = 1, 7, 8, 11$ of Company 4. Conversely, there are no changes in the set of vulnerable coalitions for the other companies. Thus, it is not difficult to calculate the power distribution of the firms in the network without link $(7, 4)$. For this propose, we can use the results given in Table 3. Precisely, we must decrease the "Absolute index of investor" by 1 for Firm 7. Then, we need to change the "Absolute index of company" to 0 for Company 4. Next, the values of the absolute index for the investors and companies must be stanadrized. In Table 5 (the column titled "Network without link $(7, 4)$"), we provide the values of index π^β for all firms in network $M^{L\setminus\{7,4\}}$ (i.e., in the network M^L without link $(7, 4)$) where M^L denotes the network defined in Table 1.

Based on the results in Table 5, the power of linkage $(7, 4)$ in the whole network is

$$\Delta_{(7,4)} = \Delta_{(7,4)}^4 = 0.14880.$$

This means that link $(7, 4)$ is the most important for Firm 4; meanwhile, the importance of link $(7, 4)$ for Firm 7 is lower (and is equal to $\Delta_{(7,4)}^7 = 0.08624$). Only Firms 4 and 7 "suffer" from the disappearance of link $(7, 4)$. The other firms increase their relative power with the disappearance of this link; meanwhile, the absolute values of the power of these firms remain unchanged.

Since Firm 8 is a null player in Company 4, the power of linkage $(8, 4)$ is null according to our approach and π^β.

Table 5. Calculation of power of linkage (7, 4) for each firm

Firm	Power distribution of firms in accordance with π^β		Power of link (7,4) for Firm i
	Network with link (7, 4)	Network without link (7, 4)	
1	0.19220	0.22581	−0.03361
2	0.21258	0.24974	−0.03716
3	0.19841	0.23309	−0.03468
4	0.14880	0.00000	0.14880
5	0.24801	0.29136	−0.04335
6	0.18180	0.21358	−0.03178
7	0.50664	0.42040	0.08624
8	0.00000	0.00000	0.00000
9	0.00465	0.00546	−0.00081
10	0.13020	0.15297	−0.02277
11	0.00465	0.00546	−0.00081
12	0.16740	0.19667	−0.02927
13	0.00465	0.00546	−0.00081

5 Conclusions and Further Developments

This paper deals with a notable question that potentially has many real-world applications. Many corporate networks can be difficult to understand in terms of control and voting power; however, understanding them is vital to learning whether any particular corporation or individual shareholder is in control of other companies in the network. This is not immediately obvious from the shareholding ownership data on an organizational chart. Berle and Means [33] were likely the first to investigate the relationships between the concentration of share ownership, shareholder voting power, and a company's control power in detail (see [11], for example). After this, other authors began to address this topic. Among the different methods proposed for measuring the indirect control of firms in a shareholding network, the game theoretical approaches that used the so-called power indices are quite prominent. Power indices provide a rigorous approach for getting around this problem; however, applying them is complicated.

One of the novel contributions of this paper is the proposition of a measure of the firms in corporate networks as a modification of the Mercik and Łobos [13] and Mercik and Stach [7] methods as well as applying the Banzhaf index [1, 17] for this purpose (see Sect. 3).

The second novel contribution of the paper is to address the problem of finding the voting power implications of an edge in a corporate shareholding network. In Sect. 4, a method to measure linkage power in corporate shareholding structures was proposed.

One further development may be the consideration of the "geographical aspects" of corporate shareholding networks. Up until now, we have considered the analysis of a graph represented on a white sheet, but a corporate shareholding network is a graph that could be "drawn on a map." In one sense, a link from one company to another should be "weighed" by possible geographical implications; this assumes a particular importance when "tax havens" are involved. If one or (worse still) more links in a graph have a connection with an offshore company located in a tax haven, it is especially difficult to estimate the situation. This uncertain situation should at least be considered by analyzing various scenarios. Under these circumstances, the following may be helpful: a consideration of the power indices with a priori unions; a sub-coalitional approach (see [34], for example); the measure of the power as a confidence interval rather than one-point measure; and a fuzzy logic approach (as proposed in [35]). The seminal paper of Myerson [36] as well as the paper of Peters, Timmer, van Den Brink [37] and Forlicz, Mercik, Ramsey, Stach [38] related to the multigraph (for example) could provide a good development orientation. After these, the paper of van den Brink [39] on the Apex power measure for directed networks might provide a new path forward. Last but not least, the use of the power indices that take abstention in consideration (as introduced by Freixas and Zwicker in [40]) could be helpful in further developments in this area.

Acknowledgements. This research is financed by the following funds: "Subsidy for maintenance and development of research potential" (No. 16.16.200.396) of AGH University of Science and Technology, MUR, research grants from the University of Bergamo, and research funds from WSB University in Wroclaw.

References

1. Penrose, L.S.: The elementary statistics of majority voting. J. R. Stat. Soc. **109**(1), 53–57 (1946). https://doi.org/10.2307/2981392
2. Shapley, L.S., Shubik, M.: A method for evaluating the distributions of power in a committee system. Am. Polit. Sci. Rev. **48**(3), 787–792 (1954). https://doi.org/10.2307/1951053
3. Gambarelli, G., Owen, G.: Indirect control of corporations. Int. J. Game Theory **23**, 287–302 (1994)
4. Crama, Y., Leruth, L.: Power indices and the measurement of control in corporate structures. Int. Game Theory Rev. **15**(3), 1–15 (2013). https://doi.org/10.1142/S0219198913400173
5. Karos, D., Peters, H.: Indirect control and power in mutual control structures. Games Econ. Behav. **92**, 150–165 (2015). https://doi.org/10.1016/j.geb.2015.06.003
6. Bertini, C., Mercik, J., Stach, I.: Indirect control and power. Oper. Res. Decis. **26**(2), 7–30 (2016). https://doi.org/10.5277/ord160202
7. Mercik, J., Stach, I.: On measurement of control in corporate structures. In: Nguyen, N.T., Kowalczyk, R., Mercik, J., Motylska-Kuźma, A. (eds.) Transactions on Computational Collective Intelligence XXXI. LNCS, vol. 11290, pp. 64–79. Springer, Heidelberg (2018). https://doi.org/10.1007/978-3-662-58464-4_7
8. Turnovec, F.: Privatization, ownership structure and transparency: how to measure the true involvement of the state. Eur. J. Polit. Econ. **15**, 605–618 (1999)
9. Hu, X., Shapley, L.S.: On authority distributions in organizations: equilibrium. Games Econ. Behav. **45**, 132–152 (2003)
10. Hu, X., Shapley, L.S.: On authority distributions in organizations: controls. Games Econ. Behav. **45**, 153–170 (2003)
11. Leech, D.: Shareholder voting power and ownership control of companies. Homo Oeconomicus **19**, 345–371 (2002). Republished in: Holler, M.J., Nurmi, H. (eds.) Power, Voting, and Voting Power: 30 Years After, pp. 475–498. Springer, Heidelberg (2013)

12. Crama, Y., Leruth, L.: Control and voting power in corporate networks: concepts and computational aspects. Eur. J. Oper. Res. **178**, 879–893 (2007). https://doi.org/10.1016/j.ejor.2006.02.020
13. Mercik, J., Łobos, K.: Index of implicit power as a measure of reciprocal ownership. In: Nguyen, N.T., Kowalczyk, R., Mercik, J. (eds.) Transactions on Computational Collective Intelligence XXIII. LNCS, vol. 9760, pp. 128–140. Springer, Heidelberg (2016). https://doi.org/10.1007/978-3-662-52886-0_8
14. Levy, M., Szafarz, A.: Cross-ownership: a device for management entrenchment? Rev. Finance **21**(4), 1675–1699 (2017). https://doi.org/10.1093/rof/rfw009
15. Stach, I., Mercik, J.: Measurement of control power in corporate networks. Central Eur. J. Oper. Res. (2020, forthcoming)
16. Johnston, R.J.: On the measurement of power. Some reactions to Laver. Environ. Plan. A **10**(8), 907–914 (1978). https://doi.org/10.1068/a100907
17. Banzhaf, J.F.: Weighted voting doesn't work: a mathematical analysis. Rutgers Law Rev. **19**(2), 317–343 (1965)
18. Kołodziej, M., Stach, I.: Control sharing analysis and simulation. In: Sawik, T. (ed.) Conference Proceedings ICIL 2016. 13th International Conference on Industrial Logistics, Zakopane, Poland, pp. 101–108. AGH University of Science and Technology, Krakow (2016)
19. Stach, I.: Indirect control of corporations: analysis and simulations. Decis. Mak. Manuf. Serv. **11**(1–2), 31–51 (2017). https://doi.org/10.7494/dmms.2017.11.1-2.31
20. Karos, D., Peters, H.: Indirect control and power in mutual control structures. GSBE Research Memorandum 13/048, Maastricht (2013)
21. Dubey, P.: On the uniqueness of the Shapley value. Int. J. Game Theory **4**, 131–139 (1975)
22. Shapley, L.S.: A value for n-person games. In: Kuhn, H.W., Tucker, A.W. (eds.) Contributions to The Theory of Games II, pp. 307–317. Princeton University Press, Princeton (1953)
23. Felsenthal, D., Machover, M.: Postulates and paradoxes of relative voting power – a critical reappraisal. Theor. Decis. **38**, 195–229 (1995)
24. Felsenthal, D.S., Machover, M.: The Measurement of Voting Power: Theory and Practice, Problems and Paradoxes. Edward Elgar Publishers, London (1998)
25. Laruelle, A.: On the choice of a power index. Working Papers AD 1999-20, Instituto Valenciano de Investigaciones Económicas (Ivie) (1999)
26. Bertini, C., Gambarelli, G., Stach, I., Zola, M.: On some applications of the Shapley-Shubik index for finance and politics. In: Algaba, E., Fragnelli, V., Sánchez-Soriano, J. (eds.) Handbook of the Shapley Value, pp. 393–417. Chapman and Hall/CRC Press, Taylor & Francis Group, New York (2020). https://doi.org/10.1201/9781351241410
27. Coleman, J.S.: Control of collectivities and the power of collectivity to act. In: Liberman, B. (ed.) Social Choice, pp. 269–300. Gordon and Breach, New York (1971)
28. Leech, D.: An empirical comparison of the performance of classical power indices. Polit. Stud. **50**, 1–22 (2002)
29. Stach, I.: Proper simple game. In: Dowding, K. (ed.) Encyclopedia of Power, pp. 537–539. SAGE Publications, Los Angeles (2011)
30. Stach, I.: Shapley-Shubik index. In: Dowding, K. (ed.) Encyclopedia of Power, pp. 603–606. SAGE Publications, Los Angeles (2011)
31. Bertini, C., Stach, I.: Banzhaf voting power measure. In: Dowding, K. (ed.) Encyclopedia of Power, pp. 54–55. SAGE Publications, Los Angeles (2011)
32. Bertini, C., Freixas, J., Gambarelli, G., Stach, I.: Comparing power indices. Int. Game Theory Rev. **15**(2), 1340004-1–1340004-19 (2013)
33. Berle, A., Means, G.: The Modern Corporation and Private Property. Commerce Clearing House, New York (1932)

34. Stach, I.: Sub-coalitional approach to values. In: Nguyen, N.T., Kowalczyk, R., Mercik, J. (eds.) Transactions on Computational Collective Intelligence XXVII. LNCS, vol. 10480, pp. 75–87. Springer, Cham (2017). https://doi.org/10.1007/978-3-319-70647-4

35. Gładysz, B., Mercik, J., Stach, I.: Fuzzy Shapley value-based solution for communication network. In: Nguyen, N.T., Chbeir, R., Exposito, E., Aniorté, P., Trawiński, B. (eds.) ICCCI 2019. LNCS (LNAI), vol. 11683, pp. 535–544. Springer, Cham (2019). https://doi.org/10.1007/978-3-030-28377-3_44

36. Myerson, R.: Graphs and cooperation in games. Math. Oper. Res. **2**(3), 225–229 (1977)

37. Peters, H., Timmer, J., van Den Brink, R.: Power on digraphs. Oper. Res. Decis. **26**(2), 107–125 (2016). https://doi.org/10.5277/ord160207

38. Forlicz, S., Mercik, J., Stach, I., Ramsey, D.: The Shapley value for multigraphs. In: Nguyen, N.T., Pimenidis, E., Khan, Z., Trawiński, B. (eds.) ICCCI 2018. LNCS (LNAI), vol. 11056, pp. 213–221. Springer, Cham (2018). https://doi.org/10.1007/978-3-319-98446-9_20

39. van den Brink, R.: The Apex power measure for directed networks. Soc. Choice Welf. **19**(4), 845–867 (2002). https://doi.org/10.1007/s003550200162

40. Freixas, J., Zwicker, W.: Weighted voting, abstention, and multiple levels of approval. Soc. Choice Welf. **21**, 399–431 (2003). https://doi.org/10.1007/s00355-003-0212-3

Some Strategic Decision Problems in Networks

Manfred J. Holler[1] and Florian Rupp[2(✉)]

[1] University of Hamburg, Hamburg, Germany
`manfred.holler@uni-hamburg.de`
[2] Center of Conflict Resolution, Munich, Germany
`florian.rupp@ccr-munich.de`
`http://www.ccr-munich.de/`

Abstract. The following analysis demonstrates that network efficiency is a very delicate matter. Neither the restriction to suitable core-subnets, nor intelligent enlargements guarantee efficient results in any case. For instance, the numerical example in Myerson (1977) contains a *prisoners' dilemma* situation for some agents in the network. Of course, the outcome is inefficient from the perspective of these players – but not for the unrestricted network. Breass' paradox shows that the enlargement of a network can lead to an inefficient outcome in the *Nash equilibrium* even if all players are taken into consideration. Restricting the network can create a Pareto efficient outcome. A third model discusses the strategic problem of a cyber network attack in the form of an *inspection game*. From the defender's point of view, the question arises which nodes of the network are essential attack targets and thus need special security attention. In principle two types of nodes are critical: important ones and unimportant ones. Important nodes, as they connect to many other essential nodes and are therefore suitable multipliers for network malware and information capture, and unimportant nodes, from the attacker's point of view, which are, in general, not in the focus of security attention, such that infiltration via them may be undetected for a long time.

Keywords: Network · Game form · Nash equilibrium · Braess paradox · BloodHound · Inspection game · Mixed-strategy equilibrium · Prisoners' dilemma

JEL Codes: C70 · C72 · D72 · D85 · L14 · Z13

1 Strategic Inefficiency in Networks

Networks may be seen as social or physical relations or as virtual entities. In a socio-economic environment networks typically connect nodes and nodes may represent decision-makers often with quite opposing interests resulting in competing decisions concerning the network's outcome. In a standard environment, the network produces a joint product and the question arises what share a member of the network will receive and what share of the costs – contributions to the network – the member has to cover. This standard economic argument carries over into the domain of cyber networks where the benefits of belonging to a network are swift global connectivity, worldwide access to experts, and in general the quality of speed and volume of information exchange.

Typically, in small enough social and economic networks members will issue their claims on the benefits of the network and their contributions to the network depending on the other members' claims and contributions. Given the dimensions of todays cyber-social platforms and the globally interlinked networks, the set of alternatives enlargenes drastically. If the claims and contributions are not specified, decision-makers have to form expectations and thereby, given the interdependence of the decisions, will put themselves into the shoes of the other "players" deriving an estimate of their choices which are a constraint to their own decisions. If the agents follow this line of reasoning, then the decisions on claims in (and contributions to) networks are strategic problems and game theory is likely to be an adequate instrument to analyze them. That is, here we focus on a non-cooperative approach.[1] The network itself can be interpreted as a representation of the game form. The preferences of the nodes have to be specified to make it a game.

In this paper, we analyze three cases of strategic inefficiency in networks. The first case, in Sect. 2, is characterized by a prisoners' dilemma situation that results from additional links created by the agents – i.e., extending a network endogenously. The second case, in Sect. 3, discusses the strategic aspects of the Braess paradox (which seems to be well known to mathematicians). In this case, the network is enlarged exogenously inducing an inefficient Nash equilibrium. In Sect. 4, we analyze the case of a cyber network that is under attack by hostile hackers. The defender has to decide which nodes of the network are essential attack targets and thus need special security attention. There are important nodes and unimportant ones. Important nodes are connected to many other essential nodes and are therefore suitable multipliers for network malware and information capture. Unimportant nodes can be considered, from the attacker's point of view, as not really in the focus of security attention, such that infiltration via them may be undetected for a long time. Thus, there is a strategic relationship. An inspection game is an adequate model to study this relationship.

At first glance, the selection of these three cases looks somewhat arbitrary, but they represent strategic decision problems, to analyze with game-theoretical instruments, that are fundamental when dealing with networks. Of course, there are many other strategic decision situations that we come across when dealing with real or cyber networks, but the following analysis demonstrates a way of how to approach them. Although formulated in a concrete context these decision problems should be seen as decision situations in other network situations as well. For instance, Braess' problem, discussed below, is of vital importance for routing in cyber-physical networks and provides interesting implications for social interaction networks when discussing the diffusion of ideas or fake news.

---

[1] For a power index analysis of networks, i.e., based on cooperative game theory, see Holler and Rupp (2019).

2 The Prisoners' Dilemma of Enlarging a Network

In his seminal paper, Myerson (1977) gives an example of a social network that demonstrates that making use of all the links in a network can be "inefficient for some agents" since they can gain larger benefits if they can cut some links.

Myerson's example assumes a characteristic function game (v, N) such that $N = \{1, 2, 3\}$ and $v(\{1\}) = v(\{2\}) = v(\{3\}) = 0$, $v(\{1, 3\}) = v(\{2, 3\}) = 6$, $v(\{1, 2\}) = v(\{1, 2, 3\}) = 12$. Here N is the set of players; $v(.)$ is the characteristic function that allocates values to coalitions, i.e., subsets of N. The allocation of these values to the individual members of the coalitions follows from the equal-gains principle which says

$$\text{(EG)} \qquad \forall g \in GR, \ \forall i{:}j \in g, \quad Y_i(g) - Y_i(g \setminus i{:}j) = Y_j(g) - Y_j(g \setminus i{:}j)$$

In (EG) g is a graph, representing a network structure; GR is set of all graphs g on the set of players N; $i{:}j$ is an unordered pair of players connected by a link such that $i{:}j = j{:}i$; $Y_i(g) =$ and $Y_j(g)$ are the payoffs of the players i and j in the case of graph g.

The equal-gains principle (EG) implies that the net gains of the players are identical when they are linked and join an existing graph in the form of a pair: net dividends are divided equally. This principle follows, for instance, if we apply the Nash bargaining solution and utilities are transferable, i.e., if the utility frontier is linear.

Let the vector $Y = (Y_1, \ldots, Y_n)$ summarize the allocation of payoffs for the n players that are elements of N and apply (EG), then we get the following imputations for the game (v, N) given as an example above:[2]

$Y(\emptyset) = (0, 0, 0)$	$Y(\{1{:}2, 1{:}3\}) = (7, 4, 1)$
$Y(\{1{:}2\}) = (6, 6, 0)$	$Y(\{1{:}2, 2{:}3\}) = (4, 7, 1)$
$Y(\{1{:}3\}) = (3, 0, 3)$	$Y(\{1{:}3, 2{:}3\}) = (3, 3, 6)$
$Y(\{2{:}3\}) = (0, 3, 3)$	$Y(\{1{:}2, 1{:}3, 2{:}3\}) = (5, 5, 2)$

The members of coalition $\{1{:}2\}$ could achieve larger payoffs if they could cut their links with player 3. However, if, for example, player 1 cuts his link with player 3, but player 2 does not so, then player 2 can get an even larger payoff as $Y(\{1{:}2, 2{:}3\}) = (4, 7, 1)$. As the corresponding result applies to player 1, neither player 1 nor player 2 will cut the links with player 3 and $Y(\{1{:}2, 1{:}3, 2{:}3\}) = (5, 5, 2)$ is the equilibrium outcome. "Not cutting the links" is the strictly dominating strategy for players 1 and 2 and the outcome is inefficient if we just consider these two players. Clearly, the underlying decision situation represents a prisoners' dilemma situation for the two players. Of course, the outcome is efficient, if we take player 3 into consideration.[3]

---

[2] Take, for instance, $Y(\{1{:}2, 1{:}3, 2{:}3\}) = (5, 5, 2) = (x, y, z)$. According to 1:2: $x - 3 = y - 3$. According to 1:3: $x - 6 = z - 3$. According to 2:3: $y - 6 = z - 3$. These equations determine $(5, 5, 2)$.

[3] In the original story of the prisoners' dilemma (see, e.g., Luce and Raiffa 1957: 93), if we take the district attorney's preferences into consideration then the outcome is no longer inefficient – however, then the game is no longer a prisoners' dilemma. See Holler and Klose-Ullmann (2020: 49ff) for a discussion.

To illustrate the issue, think about two companies doing joint business, or one being the seller and the other being the buyer, who have access to a law firm that promises some advantages if hired by one of the firms or by both to supervise the cooperation. If only one firm hires the law firm, then the law firm's competence can be used to outsmart the other.

The example demonstrates that reducing a network can be profitable for the remaining nodes. We can think about an exogenous mechanism that substitutes the player 3, i.e., "the law firm," at a price of zero, – e.g., a lucid legal system with "very low" enforcement costs – or refer to the folk theorem and the many endogenous mechanisms that allow for efficient outcomes in prisoners' dilemma situations – like, e.g., repeated games.[4] The Braess paradox which we discuss in the next section also demonstrates this effect. However, it is not based on a prisoners' dilemma game.

3   Coordination Problems and Inefficient Network Extension

The Braess paradox shows that, in equilibrium, agents do not make full use of the potential of the network and some links remain unemployed – and thereby the equilibrium implies an inefficient outcome.[5] In his summary Braess (1968: 258) observes that "whether a street is preferable to another one depends not only upon the quality of the road but also upon the density of the flow. If every driver takes that path that looks most favorable to him, the resultant running times need not be minimal. Furthermore, it is indicated by an example that an extension of the road network may cause a redistribution of the traffic which results in longer individual running times." It is assumed that the costs of traveling are a result of the traveling time. Drivers will minimize travel time. An immediate consequence of this is that, in equilibrium, *travel time will be the same for each path* used if there are no capacity constraints – and there are no capacity constraints in Braess' model. At first glance, Braess paradox may look like a hypothetical curiosity though evidence is growing that it represents indeed a real-world phenomenon in large networks (see Valiant and Roughgarden 2010; Amaral and Aghezzaf 2014).

3.1   The Toy Model

The starting point of Braess' analysis is a traffic system as described in Fig. 1. Drivers want to get from A to D as quickly as possible. A driver can choose to travel via node B or C. In the case of choosing B the route is ABD. The corresponding traveling costs result from summing up the costs of traveling AB and of traveling BD. It is assumed that the costs of traveling BD are $c_{BD}(x) = 1$ where x is the share of drivers going from B to D, i.e., $x \in [0, 1]$. Thus $c_{BD}(x) = 1$ implies that the costs of traveling on road BD are maximal and independent of the intensity of traffic on this road.[6] The corresponding

---

[4] Of course. if the interaction of players 1 and 2 is with "unforeseeable end" (and the discounting of future payoffs is moderate) then we have no longer a prisoners' dilemma situation.

[5] The following discussion of the Braess paradox is based on Stefan Napel's elaboration of the paradox in Holler et al. (2019) – also to simplify the notation and the calculations.

[6] This assumption is to simplify the analysis. In Braess (1968) all costs vary with the intensity of traffic.

assumption holds for traveling from A to C: $c_{AC}(x) = 1$. The costs of traveling on AB and CD, however, depend on the number of cars that take this road: $c_{AB}(x) = x$ and $c_{CD}(x) = x$, respectively. Because of $x \in [0, 1]$, this implies that $c_{AB}(1) = 1$, if every driver takes the route AB, and $c_{AB}(0) = 0$ if only one driver is on this route. In fact, we should assume $c_{AB}(x) = 0$ for small quantities of x, measured in terms of the capacity of the road, which excludes congestions. We could interpret x as the probability of congestions. For larger numbers of cars, this probability equals 1 if all cars take the same route. Moreover, it is assumed that "each driver induces the same delay for the other drivers as the other one does for him" (Braess et al. 2005: 450). Note, in the basic model the total flow, i.e., "travel demand," is assumed to be fixed: cars do not stay in the garage when drivers learn about possible congestions.

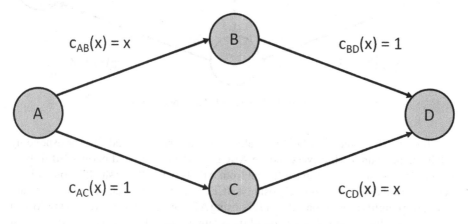

Fig. 1. The original network

Given the assumptions of the model, it is immediate that, in equilibrium, half of the total flow will travel via B and the other half will travel via C with a total travel time of 1.5 units for each driver. A distribution of cars that satisfies this condition is a Nash equilibrium since no driver can travel faster, given the choice of the others. The problem is how to coordinate the decisions of the drivers such that an equilibrium result evolves.[7] This we will discuss in the subsection that follows below.

Next, following Braess (1968), we assume that nodes B and C get connected with a (one way) high-speed road (see Fig. 2 for illustration). In fact, it is assumed that cars can now travel from B to C at the speed of light irrespective of how many cars are choosing this route, i.e., $c_{BC}(x) = 0$. It looks very advantageous to use this route. There is an equilibrium that characterized by all drivers using the route ABCD and the total traveling time of each driver will be 2.0 time units. If a driver i deviates from this path, for instance, by traveling ACD, i's total traveling time will still be 2.0 units, so i will not improve, given the other drivers stay on the route ABCD. In fact, drivers traveling

---

[7] Note for an equilibrium we have to specify the strategies (i.e., the path) that individual drivers will choose. In the minimum case of only four cars there are already six equilibria that are consistent with the (½, ½) on AB and AC, alternatively.

ABCD will have a marginal advantage if i chooses the route ACD as the travel time on AB will decrease. These drivers will be even less inclined to join the deviating i on his or her path ACD.

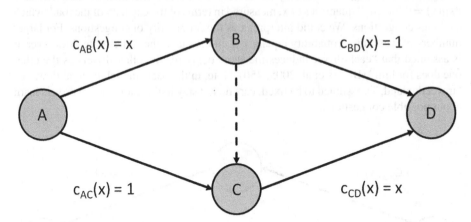

Fig. 2. The extended network

Choosing the route ABCD is a weakly dominant strategy and the corresponding ABCD-equilibrium ("all drivers choose ABCD) is trembling-hand perfect.[8] If driver i expects drivers j to choose paths different from ABCD with a "very small" probability ε, then it is profitable to stay with choosing ABCD. In principle, ε can be infinitely small. There are n equilibria with some driver i choosing ACD and n − 1 drivers choosing ABCD and total traveling time for these equilibria is smaller than for the ABCD-equilibrium but they do not satisfy trembling-hand perfectness.

3.2 Expectations and Efficiency

Obviously, in the ABCD-equilibrium, adding the super-fast track from B to C induces an increase of travel time from 1.5 to 2.0 time units and thereby to an augmentation of travel costs – it creates an inefficient outcome. Braess emphasized this conflict between individual rational behavior and collective inefficiency – i.e., in his terms, critical flows and optimal flows.[9] The result is that an extension of the network leads to an increase in total costs, but also to an increase in individual costs. This result has come to be known as the Braess paradox.

The decision situation in the extended network looks like a prisoners' dilemma: individual rational behavior leads to an inefficient outcome. However, as already pointed out, taking the ABCD route is only a weakly dominant strategy. An individual driver i can choose the route ACD without losing or gaining time compared to taking the ABCD route, given that the other drivers take the ABCD path. But if driver j chooses ACD as

---

[8] This concept was introduced in Selten (1975).

[9] Nagurney and Boyce (2005: 443) introduce user optimization and system optimization in this context.

well, then it pays for i to choose ABCD. Thus, whether ABCD is a preferable strategy depends on what other drivers are doing.[10] Observing or forming expectations on what the other drivers are doing is essential for a "rational choice."

An obvious cure to this problem of inefficiency is not to build the high-speed road BC. Alternatively, an authority could increase the price of making use of BC such that $c_{BC}(x) > \frac{1}{2}$ so that drivers will ignore the net extension BC. Once there is such an authority, there are alternative arrangements available. For instance, it could authorize every second car taking the road AB to use BC. To start with, let us assume that half of the cars will choose AB and the other half AC, then ¾ will use CD if ¼ is authorized to make use of BC. As a consequence, ¼ of the cars will have a travel time of 1.25, ¼ will have 1.5, and ½ will have 1,75 travel time. Therefore, the average travel time will be 6.5/4 which is lower than the 2 time units that resulted in the equilibrium of the extended network in Fig. 2, but larger than the 1.5 units in the equilibrium of the original network in Fig. 1. Yet, there is ¼ of drivers doing better when the authority reserves access to BC for them. Is there an allocation of cars on the routes ABD, ABCD, and ACD that minimizes average travel costs, given that the authority can allocate the cars? (Of course, such a problem should be relevant in the discussion of autonomous driving).

Needless to say that (¼, ¼, ½) on the routes ABD, ABCD, and ACD is not an equilibrium. Drivers who are expected to use AC will steer their cars to node A to profit from the shorter traveling time that results from the authority's cap on the use of BC. This will increase $c_{AB}(x)$ and decrease $c_{CD}(x)$? Is there an equilibrium? If there is an equilibrium, then it will depend on the authority's cap on the use of BC.

Nagurney and Boyce (2005: 445) commented that in Braess (1968) "game theoretic concepts were invoked that…utilized a min-max construct" while Braess himself argued that his "approach differs significantly from the approach in a game-theoretic consideration" (Braess et al. 2005: 449). His assumption that "each driver attempts to find for himself the most favorable path" concurs with a game theoretical approach but then he also assumes that drivers obtain "the information that is necessary for determining the route" (Braess et al. 2005: 449). The second assumption is rather heroic. It seems to be acceptable for the case of the extended network in Fig. 2 since following the path ABCD is a weakly dominant strategy for the individual driver. However, it seems questionable for the original network in Fig. 1. The (½, ½) allocation only describes the numerical condition of a Nash equilibrium – half of the cars will take the route ABD the other half the route ACB. First of all, a driver has to do some thinking to find out about this equilibrium condition and, secondly, knowing this equilibrium condition does not help him very much: it does not help him to form expectations that help him minimize his travel time. If n, the number of cars, is large the number of equilibria is immense – too large for a driver to specify the set of equilibria. In any case, such a specification would not help him to pick an equilibrium and choose the route for his car in accordance with it, i.e., whether to travel AB or AC. Behind this veil of ignorance, it does not matter whether he chooses AB or AC. He is ignorant as long as he lacks observation being reduced to thinking. Observation can be helpful; however, as we all experienced, observing the

---

[10] A prisoners' dilemma is characterized by strictly dominant strategies: players choose dominant strategy, irrespective of the choices they observe or they expected of the other players.

density of traffic from the point of view of a single car can be rather misleading. Interestingly, taking such local information is the cornerstone of machine learning approaches to overcome Braess paradox (see Tumer and Wolpert 2000).

There is a serious coordination problem in the original network. The (½, ½) allocation equilibrium implies a strategic indifference, very similar to the mixed strategy equilibrium in the inspection game that we discuss in the next section. At least the driver can say to himself that he has done nothing wrong when he has chosen AB and AB turns out to be overly crowded. Most likely he does not even know that AC was overly crowded as well.

Besides Braess paradox that shows that additional connections may reduce the overall performance of a network, there are several, quite similarly paradoxical results described in the network literature. The Downs-Thomson paradox (see Amaral and Aghezzaf 2014) discusses the situation of road and railway networks, where the frequency of train operations is determined by the demand of users. In this setting, it can happen that although the capacity of roads increases the equilibrium travel time for all users increases as well. Amaral and Aghezzaf (2014) give a generalization of this situation in terms of cars and buses being the transport media. There are lanes shared by cars and buses and there are lanes dedicated specifically to cars and, alternatively, to buses. Again, an increase in the capacity of the car lanes may lead to an increase in the equilibrium travel time. Another paradox is presented in Smith (1978): it shows that in certain network situations the increase in local travel costs at congestions may decrease total travel costs.

Although we formulated and discussed the Braess paradox in terms of traffic networks, it is also highly important for modern cyber networks and the transfer of packages through them; see, e.g., Kelly (2000). "…it was the Braess paradox that provided one of the main linkages between transportation science and computer science" (Boyce et al. 2005: 97).

4   Issue of Protection: BloodHound and Inspection Game

State of the art pen-testing tools, like BloodHound,[11] nearly effortlessly allow a comprehensive view on the topology of cyber-physical networks and thus enable friendly pen-testers or hostile hackers to catch essentials of the network. Hence, we can indeed assume that under attack the underlying graph of the cyber network (its topology) is known. From the defender's point of view, the question arises which nodes of the network are essential attack targets and thus need special security attention. In principle two types of nodes are critical: important ones and unimportant ones. Important nodes (IM), on the one hand, as they connect to many other essential nodes and are therefore suitable multipliers for network malware and information capture. On the other hand, unimportant nodes (UN) can be considered, from the attacker's point of view, as not

---

[11] BloodHound uses graph theory to reveal the hidden and often unintended relationships within an Active Directory environment. Attacks can use BloodHound to easily identify highly complex attack paths that would otherwise be impossible to quickly identify. Defenders can use BloodHound to identify and eliminate those same attack paths. Both blue and red teams can use BloodHound to easily gain a deeper understanding of privilege relationships in an Active Directory environment, see https://github.com/BloodHoundAD/Bloodhound/wiki.

really in the focus of security attention, such that infiltration via them may be undetected for a long time.

4.1 The Game Model

In order to illustrate the strategic problem here involved assume that there are only two agents: the Attacker 1 and the Defender 2. They are the players in a game in which 1 can choose between attacking IM or UN and 2 can choose between defending IM or UN. They can choose either alternative with degree p and q, respectively. We specify p by assuming that it implies that player 1 chooses attacking IM with probability p and UN with probability $1 - p$. Correspondingly, q expresses that player 2 chooses to defend IM and UN with probabilities q and $1 - q$, respectively. In game theoretical terms, these assumptions define S_1 and S_2, i.e., the strategy spaces of the two players. Next, we specify the payoffs that players 1 and 2 assign to the alternative outcomes. For instance, we have to answer how players 1 and 2 evaluate an outcome that results from player 1 attacking UN and player 2 defending IMP. This is not very favorable to player 2 because he or she defends a node which is not attacked while player 1 is successfully attacking the undefended node UN. This is the best player 1 can get if player 2 defends node IM. Of course, we have to assume that the payoff of player 1 is larger if he attacks IM while player 2 defends UN.

Since we are looking for generalizing this strategic decision problem, we specify the payoffs as in Fig. 3 by assuming

(PR1) $b > a$, $b > d$, $c > a$, $c > d$ and $\alpha > \beta$, $\alpha > \gamma$, $\delta > \beta$, $\delta > \gamma$

Note the following analysis and its results also apply if we assume

(PR2) $a > c$, $a > b$, $d > b$, $d > c$ and $\beta > \alpha$, $\beta > \delta$, $\gamma > \alpha$, $\gamma > \delta$.

However, the assumption implied by (PR2) does not concur with what we expect for the preferences of the two players.

We argued that it is quite plausible that $b > c$, but this has no immediate implication for the described strategic problem as we will see below although it will have an impact on the equilibrium choice of player 2 (and, perhaps surprisingly at the first glance, not of player 1).

Note that choices are assumed to be made simultaneously: player 1 does not know the strategy choice of player 2 when choosing to attack either IM or UN while player 2 does not know the choice of player 1 when choosing to defend either IM or UN. Simultaneity is a strategic quality determined by the information – and not depending on the time measured by the clock. The information in this game is *not perfect*.

Which strategies will be chosen? If the agents understand the strategic problem, then the answer to this question depends on their expectations and how they form the latter. In what follows we will discuss the Nash equilibrium and the maximin solution to this end.

Player 1 (Attacker) 2 (Defender)	IM_2	UN_2
IM_1	(a, α)	(b, β)
UN_1	(c, γ)	(d, δ)

Fig. 3. Inspection game

4.2 The Nash Equilibrium

The *inspection game* in Fig. 1 does not have a Nash equilibrium in pure strategies. Choose any pair of pure strategies and you will see that one player will always be better off by choosing an alternative strategy, *given the strategy of the other player*. According to Nash's proof, this game must have an equilibrium.[12] As there is none in pure strategies, there must be one in mixed strategies. For the game in Fig. 1 such an equilibrium implies that player 1 chooses IM_1 with probability p^* and UN_1 with probability $1 - p^*$. Correspondingly for player 2, we can define that he plays strategy IM_1 with probability q^*.[13] Thus the equilibrium in mixed strategies for a game of this type may be expressed by the pair (p^*, q^*).

The equilibrium conditions for (p^*, q^*) are fulfilled if player 1 chooses p^* such that player 2, being indifferent regarding his pure strategies IM_2 and UN_2, chooses q^* which makes player 1 indifferent with regard to his pure strategies IM_1 and UN_1. Then neither player 1 nor player 2 can achieve a higher payoff by deviating from p^* and q^*, respectively. Note, if a player is indifferent towards two pure strategies x and y, he is, of course, also indifferent towards all linear combinations of x and y according to: If $ui(x) = ui(y)$ holds, also $ui(x) = pui(x) + (1 - p)ui(y)$ is valid. Therefore, given (p^*, q^*) the two players are indifferent between any strategy they can choose, irrespective of whether pure or mixed.

Applying this reasoning to the game in Fig. 1, p^* must be chosen such that the following indifference condition holds for player 2:

$$\alpha p^* + \gamma(1 - p^*) = \beta p^* + \delta(1 - p^*) \tag{1a}$$

---

[12] Nash's proof holds for finite games: a game is finite if each player has only a finite number of pure strategies.

[13] It follows immediately that a pure strategy may be considered a special form of a mixed strategy to be played with probability 1.

The left side of the equation reflects the expected utility (the payoff) if player 2 chooses strategy IM_2, and the right side if UN_2 is chosen. Solving the indifference condition for p^*, we get:

$$p^* = \frac{\delta - \gamma}{\alpha - \beta - \gamma + \delta} \tag{1}$$

On the other hand, the indifference condition of player 1 is fulfilled for q^* if

$$aq^* + b(1 - q^*) = cq^* + d(1 - q^*) \tag{2a}$$

holds, with

$$q^* = \frac{d - b}{a - b - c + d} \tag{2}$$

following therefrom. Thus, the equilibrium strategies p^* and q^* are defined. Inserting p^* and q^* into the corresponding indifference conditions, we receive the payoffs of player 1 and 2:

$$u_1(p, q^*) = \frac{ad - bc}{a - b - c + d} = u_1^* \tag{3}$$

$$u_2(p^*, q) = \frac{\alpha\delta - \beta\gamma}{\alpha - \beta - \gamma + \delta} = u_2^* \tag{4}$$

The equilibrium conditions (1) and (2) reveal a somewhat surprising result: p^*, the equilibrium strategy of player 1, depends solely on the payoffs of player 2, and vice versa q^*, the equilibrium strategy of player 2, solely on the payoffs of player 1. If, for instance, the payoff b of player 1, the attacker, increases, indicating larger benefits for choosing IM_1 when player 2 chooses UN_2, this has no impact on player 1's willingness to select IM_1 in equilibrium: p^* will be unchanged. However, the defender's inclination to choose IM_2, protecting the important node, will increase (i.e., q^* will increase) thereby balancing the attacker's larger gain b from the outcome that results from the choices (IM_1, UN_2).

Cheng and Zhu (1995) demonstrated that the peculiar result, namely, e.g., p^* not depending on the payoffs of player 1, is due to the linear relationship between probabilities and utilities in the expected utility hypothesis implied by the indifference condition (1a) and thereby incorporated in (1). If you write down the expected value of the game in Fig. 1, and, knowing nothing about game theory, you try to maximize this value from the point of view of player 1. In order to get the first-order condition for a maximum, you calculate the first derivative of the expected value with respect to p, i.e., player 1's action parameter – then you will see that this first derivative does not give you an answer to how to choose p as the variable p drops out; it is not an element of the first derivative. This is indeed not surprising because the expected value of player 1 is linear in p.[14]

---

[14] For further details, see Holler (1990).

4.3 The Maximin Solution

This result applies to the equilibria of all games described by Fig. 3 satisfying conditions (PR1) or (PR2) which is a rather substantial, but little known, set of 2-by-2 games. Because of the paradoxical results regarding the equilibrium we might try to find a more convincing solution. Concepts like trembling-hand-perfectness or subgame-perfectness as a refinement of the Nash equilibrium do not help since the games of this class have only one Nash equilibrium with selection procedures for the equilibrium not being relevant. Therefore, it makes sense to look for solutions differing from the Nash equilibrium, e.g., the maximin solution.

We will see that given preferences fulfill (PR1) or (PR2), the maximin solutions are mixed. The corresponding probabilities p° and q° guarantee a certain payoff to a player regardless of the strategy the other player will choose. They guarantee a payoff level such that this payoff level is maximized. With regard to the game in Fig. 3, the payoff that player 1 can secure for himself is determined by a mixed strategy p°. Player 1 mixes his pure strategies such that he receives value u_1°, regardless of player 2's strategy choice. If player 1 chooses his strategy IM_1 with probability p° and UN_1 with probability $1 - p^{\circ}$, p° guarantees the *security level* u_1°, if p° satisfies

$$ap^{\circ} + c\left(1 - p^{\circ}\right) = bp^{\circ} + d\left(1 - p^{\circ}\right) \tag{5a}$$

The left side of the equation is the expected utility of player 1 if player 2 chooses strategy IM2, the right side reflects the expected utility of 1 if player 2 chooses strategy UN2. From (5a) follows

$$p^{\circ} = \frac{d - c}{a - b - c + d} \tag{5}$$

If player 1 mixes his pure strategies according to probability p°, he receives the same payoff regardless of whether player 2 chooses his strategies s_{21} or s_{22} or a mixture thereof.

For player 2 the following condition applies for his maximin strategy q°:

$$\alpha q^{\circ} + \beta(1 - q^{\circ}) = \gamma q^{\circ} + \delta(1 - q^{\circ}), \tag{6a}$$

Solving for q° gives us

$$q^{\circ} = \frac{\delta - \beta}{\alpha - \beta - \gamma + \delta} \tag{6}$$

Equations (5) and (6) specify the maximin solution (p°, q°) for the game in Fig. 1. Inserting (5) and (6) in (5a) and (6a) we get the related payoff values

$$u_1\left(p^{\circ}, q\right) = \frac{ad - bc}{a - b - c + d} = u_1^{\circ} \tag{7}$$

$$u_2\left(p, q^{\circ}\right) \frac{\alpha\delta - \beta\gamma}{\alpha - \beta - \gamma + \delta} = u_2^{\circ} \tag{8}$$

Comparing these results with (3) and (4) we get

$$u_1\left(p, q^*\right) = u_1\left(p^\circ, q\right) \text{ or } u_1^* = u_1^\circ$$

and

$$u_2\left(p^*, q\right) = u_2\left(p, q^\circ\right) \text{ or } u_2^* = u_2^\circ$$

We see that, by choosing his maximin strategy, player 1 can secure a payoff u_1° which is identical to the payoff u_1^* that he receives from the Nash equilibrium. The latter, however, presupposes that the opponent player 2 chooses his equilibrium strategy q^*. Why should player 1 rely on the equilibrium strategy of player 2? Note that the payoffs are identical for Nash equilibrium and maximin solution, but the strategies p^* and p° or q^* and q° usually differ. Which behavior is to be expected in such a decision situation and how should you decide if you are one of the two players?

From (5) and (6) follows that the maximin strategy of player i is solely determined by his own payoffs. There seem to be no incentive problems involved. If, however, α increases, the defender's probability of protecting the important node, q°, decreases. This seems paradoxical at first glance. However, to balance the payoffs of protecting the important and the unimportant node it seems quite plausible to focus more on the protection of unimportant one.

4.4 Maximin Solution or Nash Equilibrium

The result $u_1(p, q^*) = u_1(p^\circ, q) = u_1^*$ and $u_2(p^*, q) = u_2(p, q^\circ) = u_2^*$ demonstrates that the Nash equilibrium (p^*, q^*) is not (Pareto) efficient. Since the maximin solution (p°, q°) is not a Nash equilibrium, player 1 can, for example, choose a p' different from p° and thereby increase his payoff while player 2 can guarantee himself the security level $u_2(p, q^\circ) = u_2(p^*, q) = u_2^*$ by choosing q°. Therefore, a payoff pair $(u_1(p', q^\circ), u_2^*)$ with $u_1(p', q^\circ) > u_1(p, q^*) = u_1^*$ is feasible. Of course, (p', q°) is not a Nash equilibrium as q° is not a "best reply" to p'.

Harsanyi (1977: 104–107) suggested to realize the maximin solution or use it as guiding rule for decision making if utility values in the Nash equilibrium are identical to the security levels of the players. This applies to the game that we just analyzed. Following Harsanyi's recommendation, we should concentrate on the maximin solution when analyzing, not to speak of playing, such a game.

There is a number of articles that discuss the paradoxical incentive problem that characterizes the Nash equilibrium strategies p^* and q^* in accordance with (1) and (2).[15] There are publications that focus on the problem of equal payoffs for maximin solution and Nash equilibrium as, e,g., Frey and Holler (1997, 1998), Holler (1990), and Holler and Klose-Ullmann (2019, 2020). There is a pioneering paper by Aumann and Maschler (1972) that covers both aspects. Despite its very lucid presentation, this paper has been almost forgotten – and hardly ever quoted in the context of the Inspection Game.

---

[15] See, e.g., Andreozzi (2002, 2004), Avenhaus et al. (1996), Holler (1993), Tsebelis (1990), and Wittman (1985).

The strategic decision problems we have discussed so far are either based on manipulations of the underlying network or on specifics of this network. In that sense, they discuss essential core questions regarding networks. Of course, there are more complex economic transactions in networks (see, e.g., Simon and Apt 2012; Simon and Apt 2015). Apt et al. (2015: 663) show "that more services or products may have adverse consequences for all members of the network and conversely that restricting the number of choices may be beneficial for every member of the network." We did not discuss product variety, but Braess paradox could be interpreted accordingly. Indeed, at least some of the fundamental problems of strategic interactions in networks we have captured in this paper.

References

Amaral, R.R., Aghezzaf, E.-L.: The downs-thomson paradox in multimodal networks. In: Proceedings of the 2nd International Conference on Traffic and Transport Engineering (ICTTE), pp. 76–85 (2014)

Andreozzi, L.: Oscillations in the enforcement of law: an evolutionary analysis. Homo Oeconomicus **18**, 403–428 (2002)

Andreozzi, L.: Rewarding policemen increases crime: another surprising result from the inspection game. Public Choice **121**, 69–82 (2004). https://doi.org/10.1007/s11127-004-6166-x

Apt, K.R., Markakis, E., Simon, S.: Paradoxes in social networks with multiple products. Synthese **193**(3), 663–687 (2015). https://doi.org/10.1007/s11229-015-0864-4

Aumann, R.J., Maschler, M.: Some thoughts on the minimax principle. Manag. Sci. **18**, 54–63 (1972)

Avenhaus, R., Canty, M., Kilgour, M., von Stengel, B., Zamir, S.: Inspection games in arms control and disarmament, invited review. Eur. J. Oper. Res. **90**, 383–394 (1996)

Boyce, D.E., Mahmassani, H.S., Nagurney, A.: A retrospective on Beckmann, McGuire and Winsten's studies in the economics of transportation. Pap. Reg. Sci. **84**, 85–103 (2005)

Braess, D.: Über ein Paradoxon aus der Verkehrsplanung. Unternehmensforschung **12**, 258–268 (1968). https://doi.org/10.1007/BF01918335

Braess, D., Nagurney, A., Wakolbinger, T.: On a paradox of traffic planning. Transp. Sci. **39**, 446–450 (2005). Translation of Braess (1968)

Cheng, L.K., Zhu, M.: Mixed strategy Nash equilibrium based upon expected utility and quadratic utility. Games Econ. Behav. **9**, 139–150 (1995)

Frey, B.S., Holler, M.J.: Moral and immoral views on paying taxes. In: Hellsten, S., Kopperi, M., Loukola, O. (eds.) Taking the Liberal Change Seriously. Ashgate, Aldershot (1997)

Frey, B.S., Holler, M.J.: Tax compliance policy reconsidered. Homo Oeconomicus **15**, 27–44 (1998)

Harsanyi, J.C.: Rational Behavior and Bargaining in Games and Social Situations. Cambridge University Press, Cambridge (1977)

Holler, M.J.: The unprofitability of mixed-strategy equilibria in two-person games: a second folk-theorem. Econ. Lett. **32**, 319–323 (1990)

Holler, M.J.: Fighting pollution when decisions are strategic. Public Choice **76**, 347–356 (1993). https://doi.org/10.1007/BF01053304

Holler, M.J., Illing, G., Napel, S.: Einführung in die Spieltheorie. Springer, Heidelberg (2019). https://doi.org/10.1007/978-3-642-31963-1

Holler, M.J., Klose-Ullmann, B.: Machiavelli's conspiracy games revisited. Munich Soc. Sci. Rev. New Ser. **2**, 33–58 (2019)

Holler, M.J., Klose-Ullmann, B.: Scissors and Rock: Game Theory for Those Who Manage. Springer, Heidelberg (2020). https://doi.org/10.1007/978-3-030-44823-3

Holler, M.J., Rupp, F.: Power in networks: a PGI analysis of Krackhardt's kite network. In: Nguyen, N.T., Kowalczyk, R., Mercik, J., Motylska-Kuźma, A. (eds.) Transactions on Computational Collective Intelligence XXXIV. LNCS, vol. 11890, pp. 21–34. Springer, Heidelberg (2019). https://doi.org/10.1007/978-3-662-60555-4_2

Kelly, F.P.: Mathematical modelling of the internet. In: Engquist, B., Schmid, W. (eds.) Mathematics Unlimited – 2001 and Beyond, pp. 685–702. Springer, Berlin (2000). https://doi.org/10.1007/978-3-642-56478-9_35

Luce, D.R., Raiffa, H.: Games and Decisions. Wiley, New York (1957)

Myerson, R.B.: Graphs and cooperation in games. Math. Oper. Res. **2**, 225–229 (1977)

Nagurney, A., Boyce, D.: Preface to 'on a paradox of traffic planning'. Transp. Sci. **39**, 443–445 (2005)

Selten, R.: Reexamination of the perfectness concept for equilibrium points in extensive games. Int. J. Game Theory **4**, 25–55 (1975)

Simon, S., Apt, K.R.: Choosing products in social networks. In: Goldberg, P.W. (ed.) WINE 2012. LNCS, vol. 7695, pp. 100–113. Springer, Heidelberg (2012). https://doi.org/10.1007/978-3-642-35311-6_8

Simon, S., Apt, K.R.: Social network games. J. Log. Comput. **1**, 207–242 (2015)

Smith, M.J.: In a road network – increasing delay locally can reduce delay globally. Transp. Res. **12**, 419–422 (1978)

Tsebelis, G.: Penalty has no impact on crime: a game theoretic analysis. Ration. Soc. **2**, 255–286 (1990)

Tumer, K., Wolpert, D.H.: Collective intelligence and Braess' paradox. In: Proceedings of the 7th National Conference on Artificial Intelligence and 12th Conference on Innovative Applications of Artificial Intelligence, pp. 104–109 (2000)

Vailaint, G., Roughgarden, T.: Braess's Paradox in large random graphs. Random Struct. Algorithms **37**, 495–515 (2010)

Wittman, D.: Counter-intuitive results in game theory. Eur. J. Polit. Econ. **1**, 77–89 (1985)

An IoT Virtual eLearning Space

Emil Doychev$^{(\boxtimes)}$, Asya Stoyanova-Doycheva, Stanimir Stoyanov,
Todorka Glushkova, and Vanya Ivanova

University of Plovdiv, Plovdiv, Bulgaria
{e.doychev,astoyanova,stani}@uni-plovdiv.net,
{glushkova,vantod}@uni-plovdiv.bg

Abstract. This paper presents the Virtual eLearning Space implemented as an Internet of Things ecosystem. The components of the space inhabit three layers – a sensing layer, an operative and analytical layer, and a cognitive layer, which are described in more detail. One of the advantages of the space is that integrating the virtual world with the physical world of the university campus provides effective support to disabled students. This new opportunity is demonstrated by an example scenario. At the same time, VeLS is enhanced to be a reference architecture that can be adapted for new IoT applications. In the reference architecture, virtualization of "things" is supported by three formal tools – AmbiNet, TNet, and ENet. Future directions are also briefly discussed.

Keywords: eLearning · IoT · Virtual eLearning Space · Intelligent agents · Ambient-oriented modeling

1 Introduction

In recent years, a Distributed eLearning Centre (DeLC) project has been implemented in the Faculty of Mathematics and Informatics at the University of Plovdiv aiming at the development of an eLearning environment [1]. DeLC is implemented as a network infrastructure, which consists of separate nodes, called eLearning Nodes. Each eLearning Node represents a real education unit (laboratories, departments, faculties, colleges, and universities), which offers a complete or partial education cycle. Each eLearning Node is an autonomous host of a set of electronic services.

DeLC suffers from the shortcomings of the widely used eLearning systems that ignore the physical world, which they operate in. Taking into account the temporal and spatial characteristics of the physical world and the events that take place in it is particularly important to support disabled users (in our case disabled learners). The effective support of the learning process is many-sided and dependent on actions and events occurring in different places and at different times, e.g. attending lectures and seminars, self-studies, examinations, consultations. However, an analysis of the results of the learning process has to take into account all the various aspects and it can make a connection between them. Adapting approaches from closely related concepts of CPSS [2] and IoT, we endeavored to transform DeLC into a new infrastructure, known as the Virtual

© Springer-Verlag GmbH Germany, part of Springer Nature 2020
N. T. Nguyen et al. (Eds.): TCCI XXXV, LNCS 12330, pp. 148–169, 2020.
https://doi.org/10.1007/978-3-662-62245-2_10

eLearning Space (VeLS), where users, time, location, autonomy, and context-awareness are first-class citizens, and which enables a uniform treatment and interpretation of information coming from both the virtual environment and the physical world [3]. With this transformation, we pursue the following three objectives:

- To support disabled learners by integrating the virtual environment of DeLC with the physical world of the university campus.
- The new system to be the basis of a subsequent reference infrastructure that can be adapted to develop IoT applications in various domains.
- To provide users with a smarter interface of the system in the form of personal assistants.

The rest of the paper is organized as follows: Sect. 2 provides an overview of the virtual space, Sect. 3 presents the assistants of the space, and Sect. 4 presents the DeLC 2.0 portal as a special entry point of the space.

2   Related Works

The broad usage of the Internet and its steady transformation into a network of objects [4], as well as the globalization of cyberspace, are a foundation for the rapid development of cyber-physical social systems, which will lead to essential technological, economical and sociological consequences in the following years. The IoT paradigm began to be used in the field of education. In [5], a project is presented, which aims to combine both the virtual and the physical environments, providing a better learning experience to the students. Learners with increasing social skills are supported by a specific technical framework of a ubiquitous learning environment based on the Internet of Things (IoT). The environment integrates three layers: a perception layer, a network layer, and an application layer [6]. In this way, IoT-based learning can occur at any place, any time, with any people, and any content. The current situation of M-learning under the Internet of Things is discussed in [7]. In [8], a combination of IoT architecture and techniques of learning analytics is considered, which can be used to record and conduct an analysis of the students' learning process and further enable learners and schools to obtain the feedback that they need and establish an effective lifelong learning environment. The paper in [9] presents a Tempus project aimed at collaborating distant virtual laboratories of different European universities using IoT interoperability. In [10] the concept of the Internet of Things is described and its role in the evolution of a SCORM-based eLearning application is demonstrated. In this case, the Content Aggregation Model of SCORM specifies a general framework that can be used in the learning process supported by the IoT standard.

Generated at the end of 20th century, the idea of using intelligent agents for assisting people in their daily business and personal activities has developed as an area of ever increasing scientific and practical interest. Artificial intelligence techniques have opened opportunities for constructing intelligent systems that can autonomously execute tasks on behalf of the users, and in their benefit. Intelligent assistants can support both the operative daily management and the long-term strategic management, execution and control of various types of tasks. Nowadays, these assistants are usually located on mobile devices; they can use social networks as a resource, and they can self-learn. One of the developing trends is the use of robots as intelligent assistants.

In the United States, *PAL (Personalized Assistant that Learns)* [11] is one of the first multipurpose research programs in the area of cognitive systems. The program aims at the radical improvement of the way computers interact with people. In Europe, in the frames of the Horizon 2020 programme, the project for development of the intelligent assistants *COMPANIONS* [12] aims to change the traditionally perceived way people and computers interact. A virtual *"Companion"* is an agent that shares long periods of time with the user, while 'creating' a friendly relation and 'exploring' the person's preferences and desires. Corporate developments of personal assistants for supporting people in their daily routine are, for instance, *Siri* [13] (which is currently being migrated from a mobile application to a standalone device/gadget), *Microsoft Cortana* [14], *Google Now* [15], and many others.

In recent years, significant efforts have been made for the development of intelligent assistants to support disadvantaged people. Realizing the need for multimedia technologies for people with disabilities, the *Center for Cognitive Ubiquitous Computing (CUbiC)* at the University of Arizona has concentrated their efforts to meet this challenge. A sample project of the Center is dedicated to the design and implementation of a social interaction assistant for improving the interaction opportunities of people with visual impairments [16]. In [17], the aim was to present an intelligent agent that provides personalized care for elderly patients, which is implemented as an integrated service and comprises a range of intelligent sub-services. The general architecture of the service contains three main components – *Virtual Nurse, Virtual Care Personalizer (VCP)*, and *Care Template*. For the effective provision of the integrated service, the *VCP* controls and generates the necessary personalization of the activities in a special "cloud" (*Care Cloud*). The occurrence of intelligent personal agents is an example of a supply of new types of services, using electronic devices with a huge potential, and exhibiting the achievements of Artificial Intelligence.

In the projects for intelligent assistant development, there is a growing trend of combining results from the research in the area of Internet of Things (IoT), robotics, and machine learning. Blending the concept of intelligent assistants with the paradigm of IoT offers new opportunities for providing context-aware services to the end-users. In [18], a healthcare assistance scenario is offered where a mobile gateway has been integrated into an intelligent assistant. The project *PAL (Personal Assistant for healthy Lifestyle)* [19] envisages development of a *NAO*-based social robot, its mobile avatar and a scalable set of mobile applications in the area of healthcare, which use a shared knowledge base and an inference method. *PAL* can serve as an assistant and a teacher of children, too.

3   VeLS in a Nutshell

A number of publications describe in detail the general characteristics and architecture of VeLS. In some more recent texts the space is presented as an IoT ecosystem. The current state of the project will be given here briefly.

3.1 VeLS Features

Initially, certain requirements to the new system were specified to support the successful transformation of DeLC. The basic features of VeLS can be summarized as follows:

- *Modularity and Autonomy* – the transformation of a distributed and well-structured environment, such as DeLC, into an IoT space requires a new type of components. Basically, autonomous components can react appropriately to changes in the dynamic environment, take initiative and provide appropriate mechanisms for activating functional modules. An agent-oriented approach is extremely appropriate for this purpose.
- *Intelligence* – besides autonomous, reactive and proactive, we need intelligent components to build VeLS. An intelligent space [20] can control what happens in it, interact with the components included, infer, make decisions, and act in accordance with these decisions.
- *Context-awareness* – the context is all the information, which can be used to characterize the situation of an identity where an identity can be a human, a place or an object, which are viewed as significant for the interaction between a user and the system. According to the definition of a context, a system is context-aware if it uses contexts to deliver essential information or services important for the user's tasks [21]. In our case, context-awareness means the ability of a system to find, identify and interpret changes in its environment and, depending on their nature, to undertake appropriate actions such as, for example, personalization or adaptation. Personalization is the system's ability to adapt to individual features, desires, intentions, and goals of the users. Adaptation is the system's ability to adapt to the remaining context features such as areas of knowledge, school subjects, and types of devices used by the end-users.
- *Scenario-orientation* – from a user's point of view, the Virtual Education Space is an environment delivering separate e-learning services or completed educational scenarios accessible through both the DeLC 2.0 portal and the personal assistants. Scenarios are implemented by corresponding workflows rendering an account of the environment's state where it is possible to take into account various temporal attitudes of the education process (e.g. duration, repetition, frequency, start, end) or events (planned or accidental), which can impede or alter the running of the current educational scenario. To deal with possible emergencies (such as an earthquake, flood or fire) emergency scenarios are defined to be executed with the highest priority.
- *Controlled access* – the virtual education space is a controlled ecosystem, which means that access to the resources of the space is only possible through the specialized supporting modules known as "entry points". The personal assistants operate as typical entry points while the DeLC 2.0 portal is a special entry point. A user has to be in possession of a personal assistant or use the portal to be able to work in the space.

3.2 VeLS Architecture

The architecture of VeLS contains different types of components (Fig. 1). In the next section will be considered assistants implemented as rational BDI-agents, which play an important role in the space.

The basic functionality delivered by the space is deployed in both subspaces (D- and A-) that interact intensively during the execution of educational scenarios. The D-Subspace is designed for direct support of the education process providing the following three engines:

- *SCORM Engine (SEng)* – this engine delivers teaching content in the form of SCORM 2004 electronic packages to support the students' self-study. The SCORM Engine integrates three separate modules (SCORM Player, SCORM Manager, and SCORM Statistics) implemented according to the ADL's SCORM 2004 R4 specification [22]. The electronic packages are stored in a digital library that can be accessed by the students during their self-study. The SCORM Engine traces the progress of the students actually working with the teaching material and the collected information (metadata) can be used by the TNB (Teacher's Note Book) for analysis and evaluation of the students' performance.

- *Test Engine (TEng)* – it provides all its functionalities in agreement with the QTI 2.1 standard [23] as a result of the communication between two base modules – a User Interaction Provisioning (UIP) and an Assessment Provisioning (AP) module. The UIP provides the sensing means of the system to the users' environment, and the AP is responsible for the analysis of the data received from all the eTesting system's sensors – not only the sensors targeting the user's environment (UIP) but also the ones referring to the inner VES space changes concerning the personalized learning state of the user (extracted from the SCORM engine).

- *Event Engine (EEng)* – shared by both subspaces, it implements the event model specified for the whole space. The events are used to create more complex structures such as plans, schedules, and personal calendars. The interface also provides an event editor.

Furthermore, a digital library is managed in the D-Subspace where the teaching content is prepared mainly in accordance with the SCORM and QTI standards (other formats are also possible, e.g. .pdf, .ppt, .doc, etc.). In addition, the digital library provides a flexible security mechanism allowing the definition of cascading access rules per user, roles and/or role groups. There are three different access rights: to view, download, and manage, each of which with several access levels.

The A-Subspace secures all activities related to the organization, control and documentation of the education process. In the administrated database all the necessary information is stored, which is used for planning, organizing, protocoling, and documenting the education process.

4   VeLS as an IoT Ecosystem

The IoT paradigm will make it possible for virtually anything around us to exchange information and work in synergy with each other [24], bringing the communication on a higher, semantically enriched level. It is no longer just a transportation method for meaningless messages; rather, it becomes an act of knowledge exchange and accumulation. The main features of VeLS define it as a socially designated information space that integrates heterogeneous ICT technologies and pedagogical approaches [25]. Thus, the space, in terms of IoT, can be defined as an IoT ecosystem, in which everything (processes, content, and participants) is interconnected throughout the ecosystem in a seamless manner, capable of adjusting its own behaviour based on sensing, analyzing, accumulating knowledge, and reasoning about decisions in an intelligent way.

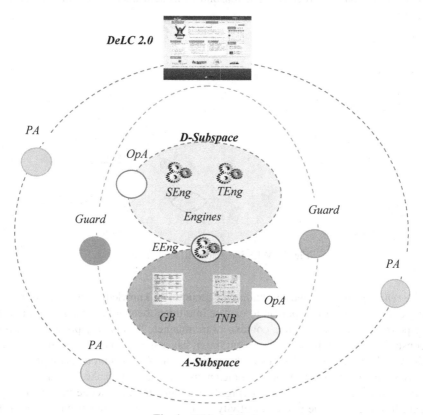

Fig. 1. VES architecture

An IoT ecosystem is a system that consists of networks of sensors, actuators and smart objects, whose purpose is to interconnect "all" *things*, including everyday and industrial objects, in such a way as to make them intelligent, programmable and more capable of interacting with humans and each other [26]. The *things* are the base units in an IoT ecosystem and implement the connection between the real physical world of objects and the digital world of the Internet. To operate as an interconnected unit in an IoT ecosystem, a *thing* must have monitoring, sensing, actuating, computing, and processing capabilities that define it as an autonomous, proactive entity that can share gained knowledge with all the other ecosystem entities so that it can enhance the decisions making, planning, and reaching of shared or personal goals. All these specific characteristics are defined and classified by the IoT stack consisting of the following four layers: a sensing layer, a data integration layer, an analytical and operative layer, and a cognitive layer. Seamless *connectivity and communication* between the *things* is another major aspect of the IoT paradigm and the emphasis is placed on the social aspect of communication based on an appropriate infrastructure that enhances it.

To define VeLS as an IoT eLearning ecosystem, it must fulfil the features and functionalities of each layer in the IoT Stack and ensure the seamless flow of knowledge, cognitive-based perceptions and reasoning mechanisms between these layers [27] (Fig. 2):

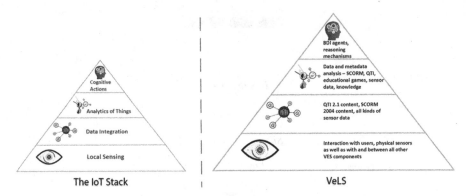

Fig. 2. VeLS integration in the IoT stack

- The *sensing layer* is used to obtain and accumulate knowledge from the surrounding environment. A component to expose intelligent behavior, it needs to be able to responsibly act and react in a context-aware manner. This is only possible if it is in constant contact with the environment, i.e. it has a stable time and location connectivity and awareness of changes in the environment. As a result, this component can retrieve and share information from the environment to help make it aware.

- The *data integrity layer* is for sharing the accumulated knowledge into the ecosystem. It implements the interconnectivity of things, which is the basic concept of the Internet of Things paradigm. The data integration layer of VeLS is enhanced by adopting several specifications (SCORM 2004, QTI 2.1.) providing unified digital models for learning content along with fine-grained and easily processed meta information integrated in the content representation. Implementing a specification-compliant content ensures the expandability of the system and its seamless data exchange with any other specification-compliant source manager in a unified way regardless of its implementation.

- The *analytical and operative layer* defines knowledge processing to support decisions making, planning, and co-operation. The proactivity and autonomy of the components is based on the analytical results of a study of states and events occurring in the ecosystem.

- The *cognitive layer* is the most complex but also the most important in the context of IoT. It integrates cognitive processes and actions that are needed to make decisions, react, act, make plans, and set up goals that would be proactively completed based on accumulated knowledge, analytical data and conclusions prepared in the lower layers. This layer provides the intelligent behavior of the IoT ecosystem.

4.1 Sensing Layer

The main function of the sensing layer is to collect, register, transform, and transfer various data essential to the operation and management of the space. Generally, two types of sensors – virtual and physical, are supported in the space.

Virtual sensors are abstractions, usually presented as data structures. Typical sources of virtual sensor data in the space are the three engines:

- SCORM 2004 Engine – it provides sensor information about the students' self-study;
- QTI 2.1. Engine – it gives sensor information about the students' examinations;
- Event Engine – it reveals sensor information about space events.

In addition, various user interactive components such as personal assistants and the web application directly accessible to the users (DeLC 2.0) can provide virtual sensor data.

Usually, physical sensor information is obtained in the space through the guards. As far as the space is concerned, the physical world is a set of physical sensors accessible to the guards. The guards collect raw (primary) data from single or group physical sensors. This data can be initially processed, transformed and transported to the other space components.

At the same time, the guards can also be sources of virtual sensor data operating in the virtual space. For example, they can deliver virtual sensor information monitoring the access to space information resources or detecting and controlling unauthorized access to the space.

The guards are implemented as special assistants, which are responsible for the safety and efficient execution of the educational scenarios in the space. They can be located anywhere in the space. Those of them operating in the virtual part of the space are implemented by means of the usual agent-oriented development tools.

Another type of guards acts as a specialized interface between both – the virtual and the physical – worlds in the space. In addition, these guards are responsible for activating emergency scenarios and are usually intelligent devices that react to various physical quantities in the environment such as smoke, temperature, and humidity. The software support of these guards has a more complex multi-layer architecture. Their sensors are implemented as OSGi modules placed on single-chip or single-board computers (for example Raspberry). The sensor's (or agent's) task is to collect data from one or a group of physical sensors located in the real world, and transfer it to the guard's core. The guard's core is usually in the virtual part of VES located on a server and implemented in JADE (Jadex). Communication between the guard's core and its sensor is realized through the JADE-OSGi interface.

4.2 Operative and Analytical Layer

This layer is of extreme importance for the level of space intelligence because all the sensor information is presented here. This allows for the conducting of decision-making models supporting the operation and management of the space. In the current version two interacting models are being developed, provisionally called Teacher's Notebook and Student's Book. The idea of the Teacher's Notebook [28] is to develop and continually update profiles of student achievements in individual academic subjects. The analyses performed to create such profiles use the following sensor information:

- Detailed information about the results from the electronic testing on the subject including the topic, type, and level of difficulty of each test question. The main source of this sensor data is the QTI 2.1. Engine.
- Information about the students' participation in lectures and seminars and their homework and project task achievements. Other relevant considerations are the relations between theory and practice, new material and repetitions, and the types of homework tasks and project assignments.

The Teacher's Notebook also tries to assist the teacher in order to improve the efficiency and refine the teaching methodology by identifying difficult topics for the majority of students, looking for correlations between the main points in lectures and seminars and the students' examination results.

For its part, by interacting with the Teacher's Notebook and the personal assistant, the Student's Book aims to create an individual profile of the student's learning behavior. The Student's Book makes use of the analyses of the Teacher's Notebook and receives additional sensor information about:

- The learner's work on the course material during self-study (the main source is the SCORM 2004 Engine).
- Information about the student's activity during lectures and seminars, coping with assignments, and the quality of submitted project tasks.

In addition, the Student's Book helps the student's personal assistant to look for opportunities to improve this profile and enhance the student's achievements.

Due to the inherent complexity, both models are implemented as the so called *operative assistants*. The operative assistants are active components exhibiting a more complex architecture. Usually, an operative assistant is implemented as a multi-agent system or an agent with integrated services. An agent in itself is not a suitable software component for delivering business functionality. A service is a good decision for the functionality but it is static and cannot operate as a separate component in the space. For that reason, corresponding service interfaces are implemented for the operative assistants. Since all functionalities that the VeLS components can use and expose while inhabiting the eLearning ecosystem are provided as services, the space is open for new components, which can provide their capabilities as services as well, regardless of the technologies used for their implementation.

Usually located on the server nodes of the space, the operative assistants support the execution of educational scenarios; therefore, they implement suitable interfaces to the available electronic services and data repositories. Operatives serve both subspaces – the A-Subspace and the D-Subspace.

For example, the Teacher's Notebook includes the following five agents:

- Agent One – Its main task is to analyze each test separately and in tests with unsatisfactory results it sets the flag for further analysis of the test. As an output, the agent calculates the average grade of the exam;
- Agent Two – It analyzes the sections of the marked tests for further analysis and provides summary results for specific sections of the exam tests. Finally, the agent sorts sections in an ascending order – from the section with the lowest results to the section with the highest ones. The agent also sets an additional flag if there is a need to analyze the individual questions in a particular section;
- Agent Three – It analyzes various questions in the marked sections for each test and provides summary results of the examination. The agent presents a list of questions that students most often answer incorrectly;
- Agent Four – It summarizes information received from the SCORM player – A4 checks the information about the activity of certain students in order to determine whether the learners have read through the material and have done the tests in the SCORM player;
- Agent Five – This agent systematizes the information obtained from the analyses, summarizes the results and provides them to the student's personal assistant in an appropriate form.

4.3 Cognitive Layer

Currently, the cognitive layer consists of two types of components, namely personal assistants and the educational portal DeLC 2.0.

4.3.1 Personal Assistants

The main purpose of a personal assistant (PA) is to assist users (students and teachers in this case) in their work in the space. VeLS is implemented as a CPSS-like application where the user is at the center of attention. From an architectural point of view this means that the PA is a central component primarily responsible for activating, providing and completing effective user's support. The personal assistant also takes decisions on how to personally assist the user in various situations.

Furthermore, access to the information resources and space services is accomplished mainly through PAs. In this case, they act as personalized entry points in the space. Students are provided with their own PA upon initial registration in the space. For this purpose, a genetic PA is maintained, which generates a user-specific PA by interacting with the educational portal and the registration module. The PAs are developed as BDI rational agents.

PAs have to perform two main functions providing the needed "entry points" of the space. Firstly, they operate as an interface between their owners and the space, and if necessary, carry out activities related to the personalization and adaptation. Secondly, they interact with other assistants in the space in order to start and control the execution of educational scenarios. The personal assistants will usually be deployed over the users' mobile devices.

In the current version of the space a type of a personal assistant is being developed to help students. This PA is known as LISSA (Learning Intelligent System for Student Assistance) and it is able to perform the following tasks [29]:

- It monitors the student's subsequent curriculum and reminds him/her of upcoming exams, lectures, seminars, etc. The time for reminders of upcoming events depends on the type of event, the time needed for preparation, and the student's current location thus taking into account the length of time needed to reach the location where the event will be taking place. In order to choose a specification in case of a conflict between two or more events, priorities are set, which can be used during the deliberation process. After solving a conflict, the agent warns the student that it has taken a certain decision and consults with them to check whether they agree with it.
- LISSA recommends useful bibliography to the student – upon a warning for an upcoming event it will suggest learning materials that the student can use to study.
- It automatically registers the student in the different events and, according to the student's location, it can determine whether they are present at a certain event (a lecture, seminar, exam, etc.) and will mark them as present.
- Voice commands – besides the normal interaction with the agent through the touch screen, LISSA will also allow voice commands. The voice commands are optimized so that there is no need for internet access to a server for their recognition, thus preserving battery life.

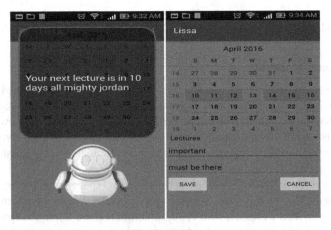

Fig. 3. LISSA

The early prototype of LISSA, implemented as a BDI agent, has a simplified design with an avatar on the main screen (Fig. 3). The mental attitudes of LISSA are events.

Activities implemented as a personal calendar are a container event including various domain-dependent events, which are under LISSA's control. Depending on the current assumptions (for date, time, and location), the current intention is determined from the personal calendar. In accordance with the type of the intention (event) a suitable plan can be activated. For example, when the agent wants to warn the student about an upcoming activity, it pronounces the message and synchronously displays it on the screen. The message is presented simultaneously visually and vocally so that the agent can be useful to visually impaired and hearing impaired students. The voice recognition allows calibration to easily recognize different voice types and accents. All announcement functionalities can be switched on and off. A simplified interface is integrated in LISSA with the ability to understand and generate phrases in a natural language (English).

4.3.2 The DeLC 2.0 Portal

The DeLC 2.0 portal acts as an entry point in VeLS, which provides access to the resources of the space without using personal assistants. The architecture of the portal (Fig. 4) consists of an educational portal with a user interface and a server side. These units communicate with each other by HTTP, RESTful services and Web Sockets. The browser side application is built with HTML 5 and CSS 3 together with JQuery and Bootstrap, which delivers the responsive nature of the user interface.

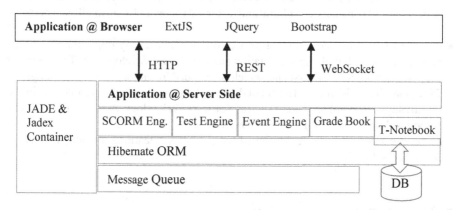

Fig. 4. DeLC 2.0 architecture

DeLC 2.0 provides the needed set of functionality for a modern web application: management of the static web content, security services, a control panel for management of all services, plugins and so on. As additional services the portal provides a Message Queue (MQ) and an ORM layer. The MQ acts as a transport environment for asynchronous communication between the plugins and the rest of the components. The ORM layer is a built-in mechanism for transforming the database relational data into objects.

The portal implements interfaces to the D- and A-Subspaces by using plugins. Some of the implemented plugins are the SCORM Engine, Grade Book, Event Engine, Test Engine, and Teacher Notebook. Interaction with the operative assistants of the space is ensured by integration of the JADE [30] and Jadex [31] containers within the portal's server side. These containers are intended to provide an environment for running software agents, which can communicate seamlessly with the operative assistants.

The current version of the educational portal supports two forms of electronic education – blended learning and lifelong learning. As regards blended learning, electronic lecture courses are offered on academic subjects, which are included in the curriculum. Students are examined through an electronic testing system available via the portal.

As to lifelong learning, materials are currently being developed in the following areas:

- *Cognitive robotics* – it is developed on the basis of a university course in line with the characteristics of lifelong learning. It is primarily intended for young people who are interested in the problems of robotics.
- *Cultural and historical heritage* – it includes development of electronic content and means for displaying the rich cultural and historical heritage of Bulgaria. Exploring the possibilities of semantic modelling (ontologies) for intelligent search and delivery of learning content in the space represents certain scientific interest to us. Two forms of presenting the electronic content are considered – as dynamically generated context-dependent and personalized cultural and historical routes and as an intelligent personal guide;
- *(English) Language learning* – a project offering interesting opportunities, which is in a process of initial experimentation and conceptual development. Two forms of support are regarded. The first one, which is designed for children, combines language with game-based learning. The second one is language teaching, specialized in the terminology of a number of areas such as Software Technology, Artificial Intelligence, Robotics, Internet of Things, and Mechatronics.
- *Language games* – these are developed for game-based learning intended mainly for secondary schools.

5   To an IoT Reference Architecture

As stated in the introduction, one of our goals is that VeLC should be an intermediate architecture that can subsequently be developed and perfected in an IoT reference architecture. The target reference architecture can be adapted to build IoP applications for various domains, for example a smart city, smart agriculture, and smart medicine. It is essential to create the desired reference architecture to maintain the virtualization of "things", possibly with formal and/or semi-formal means. By virtualization we mean an appropriate representation of physical objects in the virtual world including their intrinsic attributes, their temporal and spatial characteristics, as well as events associated with them.

The first step towards such an architecture is to develop and integrate formal virtualization tools into the analytical and operational layer. In this layer we include the following four new components that will be briefly presented below:

- AmbiNet – to present the spatial aspects of "things";
- TNet – to demonstrate the temporal aspects of "things";
- ENet – to display events;
- OntoNet – a network of ontologies presenting basic concepts and the links between them for the domain of interest.

AmbiNet. In this network, the objects of interest (in addition to physical they can also be abstract) are presented as ambients. An ambient is an identity that can be characterized by boundary, occupancy and mobility, and it is possible to create hierarchies or networks of ambients [32]. For modelling purposes, an ambient could be represented as a structure with the following elements: an identifier (name), a corresponding set of local agents, and a set of adjacent sub-ambients. Thus, there is the possibility of recursively building various more complex structures of ambients. AmbiNet is built on top of CCA (Calculus of Context-aware Ambients) [33] – a formal system providing appropriate mathematical notation and means of modelling mobile and context-aware ambients. A detailed context-aware model of DeLC, the predecessor of VeLS, is given in [34]. AmbiNet is supported by the following run-time and development tools: AmbiNet ccaPL Interpreter (a run-time interpreter of the formal modeling language ccaPL based on the CCA), AmbiNet Route Generator, AmbiNet Route Optimizer, AmbiNet Editor (a visual modeling editor), and AmbiNet Visualizer (to present the results as virtual reality).

TNet. This network is created based on an interpreting mechanism for Interval Temporal Logic (ITL). ITL [35] is a kind of temporal logic for describing time-dependent processes. The interpreter [36] is an executable subset of ITL, which uses the ITL syntax to identify time as a finite consequence of states. This environment is used as an instrument for verification of time-dependent processes using the ITL mechanisms. The verification is based on special assertion points in the code, which the environment checks for consistency with criteria for time and security that are presented with ITL notations. During the execution of a given program, those code points generate a sequence of values for certain variables, which are matched with pre-defined ITL statements to prove their validity. The existing version of Tempura was created in the C language [36] and repeatedly amended and expanded with new functionalities. Since VeLS is built of separate intelligent autonomous components where the electronic services are equipped with their own operational agents, we created a new agent-oriented version of the interpreter [37], which can be easily integrated in VeLS while maintaining the space's homogeneity.

ENet. In the current version of the space a suitable model of events is being developed, the purpose of which is to define, present and classify events as well as methods of working with them so that they can be used for proper and effective operation of the space components and their interaction. In general, an event is presented as the triple *(event_id, event_type, and event_attributes)* where *event_arguments* may also be events. Three basic types of events are distinguished in the model:

- Atomic events – these events define the location of things in time and space. Generally, they are used to present Beliefs to agents in the space or as attributes of other events. Typical atomic events are the date, hour, and location.
- System events – these events represent happenings connected with the operation of the software tools and the software architecture of the space. For example, depending on various conditions, the space architecture can dynamically generate new agents or remove existing ones. This process is identified through the events *generation/removing assistants*. Sending and receiving messages between agents is established via the events *sending/receiving messages*.
- Domain-dependent events – they present happenings connected with the specific area of application. In our case these are events related to the education process; e.g. lectures, tutorials, exams, self-study, and consultations.

Furthermore, the events can have different attributes regardless of their type, for example:

- Repeatability – events can happen only once (unique) or repeat with a certain frequency (periodic).
- Durability – events can happen instantly (discrete) or have a fixed duration (continuous).
- Purpose – events can have different purposes for example to be a holder of other events (container).

Proactive Management of Events

Instead of making every agent check for new events, the event engine reverses the process by making new events inform the interested parties about their existence. When the new event occurs, it is represented by its own agent, which announces its existence to the other agents in the system.

A small example demonstrates the use of CCA to provide effective services for disabled people. IoT and pervasive computing are closely connected with the concept of mobility and context-awareness. Within a system, some objects (students, devices, etc.) can be mobile. The system has to be able to sense the context and to use this information to adapt to the current situation. The Calculus of Context-aware Ambients (CCA) is a process calculus based on the notion of ambients. An ambient is an entity describing any object or component. It has a name, a boundary, and is connected with some ambient hierarchy. An ambient can be mobile and it has the ability to communicate with other ambients. CCA is used to model ambients in terms of process, location, and capability. To represent the properties of CCA processes a programming language ccaPL is available. Contextual expressions can be used to ensure fulfillment of a certain opportunity only under certain conditions of the environment, i.e. in a certain context.

The reference architecture provides an environment for operating of a variety of assistants. The role of the personal IoT assistant PA has been incredibly increasing for students with motor difficulties who attend lectures with their wheelchairs. When the student physically enters the university campus, an automatic identification process is started. His/her PA establishes contact with the relevant specialist assistants (SAs) and receives information about the next event, for example an exam on Software Engineering in 446 computer lab in 20 min' time. The PA starts bidirectional communication with the SAs for searching an appropriate route for a wheelchair. The Guard Assistant (GA) obtains information from the physical world and sends a list with active important zones for access by a wheelchair user (ramps, doors, elevators, etc.) to the SAs to generate a route from the current location of the student to his/her destination. Then the PA sends a message to the student who activates the movement on the generated route. We will look at the CCA modeling of this scenario and will present the CCA-processes of a different type of assistants. To verify this model, we will present a ccaPL prototype.

The ambients that will be presented are: a PA of the Student (PA), a specialist assistant of Analytical Subspace (SA_AS), a specialist assistant for route generation in AmbiNet SA_ANet, and a Guard Assistant – GA. The processes of the described ambients are presented below:

$$P_{PA} \Leftrightarrow \begin{pmatrix} !SA\_AS ::< stu\_id, location > .0 \mid \\ SA\_AS :: (ListServices, event\_examSE, place\_446\_lab, time\_to\_exam\_20). \\ SA\_AS ::< location, PAi, get\_route > .0 \mid \\ SA\_AS :: (ListRoutes).0 \end{pmatrix}$$

$$P_{SA\_AS} \Leftrightarrow \begin{pmatrix} !PA :: (stu\_id, location). \\ PA ::< ListServices, event\_examSE, place\_446\_lab, time\_to\_exam\_20 > .0 \mid \\ !PA :: (location, PAi, get\_route).GA ::< PAi, get\_IZ > .0 \mid \\ GA :: (PAi, ListIZ).SA\_ANet \downarrow < PAi, location, place\_446\_lab, ListIZ > .0 \mid \\ !SA\_ANet \downarrow (PAi, ListRoutes).PA ::< ListRoutes > .0 \end{pmatrix}$$

$$P_{SA\_ANet} \Leftrightarrow \begin{pmatrix} !SA\_AS \uparrow (PAi, location, place\_446\_lab, ListIZ). \\ !SA\_AS \uparrow< PAi, ListRoutes > .0 \end{pmatrix}$$

$$P_{GA} \Leftrightarrow \begin{pmatrix} !SA\_AS :: (PAi, getIZ). \\ !SA\_AS :: (PAi.ListIZ > .0 \end{pmatrix}$$

To create prototypes of the CCA models a special programming language ccaPL has been developed. The ccaPL realization of the example is presented below:

PA123
[!::send(stuID,location).0|SA_AS::recv(ListServices,event_examSE,place_446_lab,ti
me_to_exam_20).SA_AS::send(location,get_route).0|SA_AS::recv(ListRoutes).0] |
SA_AS
[PA123::recv(stuID,location).
    PA123::send(ListServices,event_examSE,place_446_lab,time_to_exam_20).0 |
    PA123::recv(location,get_route).GA::send(PA123,get_IZ).0 |
    GA::recv(PA123,ListIZ).SA_ANet#send(PA123,location,place_446_lab,ListIZ).0 |
    SA_ANet#recv(PA123,ListRoutes).PA123::send(ListRoutes).0 |
SA_ANet
    [SA_AS@recv(PA123,location,place_446_lab,ListIZ).SA_AS@send(PA123,ListR
outes).0]] |
    GA[SA_AS::recv(PA123,get_IZ).SA_AS::send(PA123,ListIZ).0]

The interpreter of ccaPL has been developed as a Java application. Based on the main version, we have developed a simulator for verification of the scenario described above. The notation " A === (X) ===> B" means that Ambient "A" sends an "X" message to Ambient "B". The notations "Child to parent", "Parent to child", and "Sibling to sibling" provide information on the relationship between the sender "A" and the receiver "B" in terms of the hierarchy of ambients. To facilitate reading, an animator to the ccaPL environment has been developed. The animator's goal is to present graphically the ambients and their processes. Transitions between processes are visualized as well as how and when every opportunity of an ambient is fulfilled, and how ambients move in the surrounding environment (Fig. 5).

6 Some Remarks to the Implementation of VeLS

Just like hardware and software, the space is a system with a high level of complexity where different types of hardware and software components are used. To assist effective development, a unified integrated technology is needed to provide:

- Homogeneity – if possible, a unified program base and a run-time environment;
- Connectivity – capabilities to use appropriate interfaces, protocols, and standards to ensure interoperability of different types of software and hardware components.

The integrated technology provides opportunities and means for effective interaction between the various types of components used in the space and located in the different architectural levels. The main components of the space are the assistants realized as intelligent agents that are autonomous and with a relatively complex internal architecture. An agent is a software component, which operates by rendering an account of the environmental dynamics and is inappropriate for delivery of business functionality. Services are a good solution to realize functionality but they are static and non-proactive so they cannot be independent components in the space. For this reason, agents include appropriate interfaces to services in their internal architecture. Thus the space operates as an ecosystem, which is open to expansion with new services. In addition, agents have to be able to communicate with the physical world, and the guards have to provide a uniform interface.

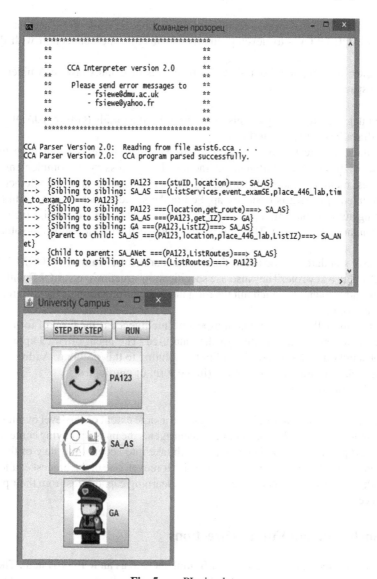

Fig. 5. ccaPL simulator

The basis of the integrated technology for realizing the space are the following Java-based standard technologies:

- Grails, Groovy – to implement the educational portal;
- Jadex, JADE, LADE-LEAP – to develop agents in the space;
- Android Studio, HTML5, JavaScript – to develop educational games and for the user interface of personal agents;
- WS-*, RESTful Services – the agents' service interfaces;

- Protégé, OWL 2 – to develop ontologies supporting the work of the agents;
- OSGi, JADE-OSGi – to develop guards establishing the connection with the real world;
- ITL (Interval Temporal Logics), CCA (Calculus of Context-aware Ambients) – to model space.

The integrated technology is also supported by the Grails (Groovy)-JADE and the HTML5/JavaScript-JADE interfaces.

The integrated technology ensures interoperability in VeLS but it is insufficient to create conditions for intelligent interaction. It is necessary to complement it with approaches, methods, and tools supporting the semantic aspects of the interaction. An agent-oriented approach is basically applied in the space, which is a powerful tool for developing autonomous intelligent software components with a mentality including an interaction language (ACL). This approach is enhanced with the following solutions:

- Wherever standards are possible, the two standards for e-learning SCORM 2004 and QTI 2.1 play a key role. They also use specification structures (e.g. LOM) with unique syntax and semantics, which allows for a unified interpretation of the different types of space components.
- Semantic modelling – an essential aspect of intelligence is the level of formalization and an automated interpretation of the data used. The agent-oriented approach and use of standards offer a partial and limited solution to this problem. Additionally, we use semantic information modelling (in the form of ontologies);
- A single unified space model of events.

The level of intelligence of VeLS depends to a large extent on the level of intelligence of the individual agents. We consider intelligent agents the ones displaying context-aware reactive and proactive social behaviour, which take into account the state of the virtual space and what is happening in the real world. Moreover, one of the biggest challenges is to provide the existing agents in the space with learning capabilities from their practical experience.

7   Conclusion and Future Directions

This paper provides an overview of VeLS implemented as an IoT ecosystem. The space is being implemented as a successor of an eLearning environment known as DeLC. In line with our practice, ignoring the realities in the surrounding physical environment is an essential deficiency, particularly unfavorable for a group of users, namely disabled learners. At the same time, the rapid enforcement of the concepts of CPSS and IoT, supporting the integration of virtual and physical spaces, reveals new opportunities to overcome this disadvantage. As a result, in this article we present a new architecture of an IoT ecosystem that can effectively assist people with disabilities in their movement. This new opportunity is demonstrated by an example scenario.

VeLS is progressively extended and experimented on in a real education process. In the last few years more than 3500 students have been educated using VES on more than 40 topics.

Our future intentions are mainly connected to completing the reference architecture to be adapted for two new domains – smart agriculture and a smart city. To achieve this goal, the main challenge is to provide synergies between AmbiNet, TNet, and ENet. Our idea is to specify an appropriate interaction protocol based on ACL. When performing a scenario, the necessary dialogue between the three systems is presented as an interaction graph. Fundamentally, ENet and TNet are implemented as multi-agent systems but AmbiNet is object-oriented. In this case, it is necessary to develop a suitable "wrapper" in order for AmbiNet to be able to participate in the implementation of the respective interaction graph.

Acknowledgment. The authors wish to acknowledge the partial support of the National Program "Young Scientists and Postdoctoral Students" of the Ministry of Education and Science in Bulgaria, 2018–2019.

References

1. Stoyanov, S., et al.: Intelligent distributed eLearning architecture. In: Koleshko, V.M. (ed.) Intelligent Systems, InTech, pp. 185–218, March 2012. 978-953-51-0054-6, Hard cover, 366 pages
2. Wang, F.-Y.: The emergence of intelligent enterprises: from CPS to CPSS. IEEE Intell. Syst. **25**(4), 85–88 (2010)
3. Valkanov, V., Stoyanov, S., Valkanova, V.: Building a virtual education space. In: The 19th World Multi-Conference on Systematics, Cybernetics and Informatics, Orlando, Florida, USA, 12–15 July 2015, pp. 322–326 (2015)
4. Kevin, A.: That "Internet of Things", in the real world things matter than ideas. RFID J. **22**, 97–114 (2009)
5. Domingo, M.G., Forner, J.M.: Expanding the learning environment: combining physicality and virtuality. The Internet of Things for eLearning. In: 10th IEEE International Conference on Advanced Learning Technologies, Tunisia, pp. 730–731 (2010)
6. Xue, R., Wang, L., Chen, J.: Using the IOT to construct ubiquitous learning environment. In: Proceedings of the Second International Conference on Mechanic Automation and Control Engineering (MACE), Inner Mongolia, China, pp. 7878–7880. (2011). ISBN 978-1-4244-9436-1
7. Yang, B., Nie, X., Shi, H., Gan, W.: M-learning mode research based on Internet of Things. In: Artificial Intelligence, Management Science and Electronic Commerce (AIMSEC), Zhenzhou, China, pp. 5623–5627 (2011). ISBN 978-1-4577-0535-9
8. Cheng, H.-C., Liao, W.-W.: Establishing an lifelong learning environment using IoT and learning analytics. In: The 14th International Conference on Advanced Communication Technology (ICACT2012), Phoenix Park, Pyeong Chang, Korea (South), pp. 1178–1183 (2012). ISBN 978-89-5519-163-9
9. Lamri, M., Akrouf, S., Boubetra, A., Merabet, A., Selmani, L., Boubetra, D.: From local teaching to distant teaching through IoT interoperability. In: International Conference on Interactive Mobile Communication Technologies and Learning (IMCL), Thessaloniki, Greece, pp. 107–110 (2014). https://doi.org/10.1109/imctl.2014.7011115
10. Pau, V.C., Mihailescu, M.I.: Internet of Things and its role in biometrics technologies and eLearning applications. In: 13th International Conference on Engineering and Modern Electric Systems (EMES), Oradea, Romania, pp. 177–180 (2015). ISBN 978-1-4799-7651-5

11. PAL: The PAL Framework. https://pal.sri.com/
12. Companions-project. http://www.companions-project.org/
13. Siri web page. http://www.apple.com/ios/siri/
14. Microsoft Cortana web page. https://www.microsoft.com/en-us/cloud-platform/cortana-int elligence-suite
15. Google Now web page. http://www.digitaltrends.com/mobile/how-to-use-google-now/
16. Panchanathan, S., Chakraborty, S., McDaniel, T.: Social interaction assistant: a person-centered, approach to enrich social interactions for individuals with visual impairments. IEEE J. Sel. Top. Signal Process. **10**(5), 942–951 (2016)
17. Tokunaga, S., Horiuchi, H., Tamamizu, K., Saiki, S., Nakamura, M., Yasuda, K.: Deploying service integration agent for personalized smart elderly care. In: 15th IEEE/ACIS International Conference on Computer and Information Science (ICIS 2016), Okayama, Japan, 26–29 June 2016, pp. 897–902 (2016)
18. Santos, J., Silva, B., Rodrigues, J., Casal, J., Saleem, K.: Internet of Things mobile gateway services for intelligent personal assistants. In: 17th International Conference on E-health Networking, Application & Services (HealthCom), Boston, MA, USA, 14–17 October 2015, pp. 311–316 (2015)
19. PAL: Personal Assistant for a Healthy Lifestyle. http://www.pal4u.eu/
20. Liu, B., et al.: Intelligent spaces: an overview. In: IEEE International Conference on Vehicular Electronics and Safety, Beijing, 13–15 December 2007 (2007). 978-1-4244-1266-2
21. Dey, A.K.: Understanding and using context. Pers. Ubiquitous Comput. J. **5**(1), 4–7 (2001)
22. SCORM 2004 Specification. http://adlnet.gov/adl-research/scorm/scorm-2004-4th-edition/
23. IMS Question & Test Interoperability Specification. https://www.imsglobal.org/question/index.html
24. Chilamkurti, N., Zeadally, S., Chaouchi, H.: Next-Generation Wireless Technologies: 4G and Beyond, pp. 190–192. Springer, London (2013). https://doi.org/10.1007/978-1-4471-5164-7
25. Dillenbourg, P., Schneider, D.K.: Virtual learning environments. In: Dimitracopoulou, A. (ed.) Proceedings of the 3rd Hellenic Conference Information & Communication Technologies in Education, Greece, 2002, pp. 3–18. Kastaniotis Editions, Greece (2002)
26. IEE Standards Association: Internet of Things (IoT) Ecosystem Study. Executive Summary, January 2015. https://standards.ieee.org/innovate/iot/iot_ecosystem_exec_summary.pdf
27. Gramatova, K., Stoyanov, S., Doychev, E., Valkanov, V.: Integration of eTesting in an IoT eLearning ecosystem - virtual eLearning Space. In: BCI 2015, Craiova, Romania. ACM (2015). Art. 14. ISBN 978-1-4503-3335-1/15/09
28. Kehayova, I., Valkanov, V., Malinov, P., Doychev, E.: Architecture of a module for analyzing electronic test results. In: 2016 IEEE 8th International Conference on Intelligent Systems, Sofia, 4–6 September, pp. 779–784 (2016)
29. Todorov, J., Daskalov, B., Stoyanov, S., Popchev, I., Valkanov, V.: Learning intelligent system for student assistance – LISSA. In: 2016 IEEE 8th International Conference on Intelligent Systems, Sofia, 4–6 September, pp. 748–753 (2016)
30. Bellifemine, F., Caire, G., Greenwood, D.: Developing Multi-Agent Systems with JADE. Wiley, Hoboken (2007)
31. Jadex Active Components. https://www.activecomponents.org/bin/view/About/New+Home
32. Cardelli, L., Gordon, A.D.: Mobile ambients. Theor. Comput. Sci. **240**, 177–213 (2000)
33. Siewe, F., Zedan, H., Cau, A.: The calculus of context-aware ambients. J. Comput. Syst. Sci. **77**, 597–620 (2011)
34. Al-Sammarraie, M.H.: Policy-based approach for context-aware systems, Ph.D. thesis, Software Technology Research Laboratory De Montfort University, Leicester, United Kingdom, July 2011
35. Moszkowski, B.: Executing Temporal Logic Programs. Cambridge University Press, Cambridge (1986)

36. Hale, R.W.S.: Programming in temporal logic. Ph.D. thesis, Computer Laboratory, Cambridge University, Cambridge, England, October 1988
37. Valkanov, V., Stoyanova-Doycheva, A., Doychev, E., Stoyanov, S., Popchev, I., Radeva, I.: AjTempura – first software prototype of C3A model. In: Angelov, P., et al. (eds.) Intelligent Systems'2014. AISC, vol. 322, pp. 427–435. Springer, Cham (2015). https://doi.org/10.1007/978-3-319-11313-5_38. ISBN 978-3-319-11313-5

Author Index

Bertini, Cesarino   116

Czarnecki, Adam   85

De Micheli, Chiara   1
Doychev, Emil   148

Fragnelli, Vito   1

Glushkova, Todorka   148

Holler, Manfred J.   133

Ivanova, Vanya   148

Malawski, Marcin   76
Mercik, Jacek   116
Motylska-Kuźma, Anna   99

Nurmi, Hannu   38

Orłowski, Cezary   85

Ramsey, David M.   52
Ramsza, Michał   21
Rupp, Florian   133

Sitek, Tomasz   85
Sosnowska, Honorata   21
Stach, Izabella   116
Stoyanov, Stanimir   148
Stoyanova-Doycheva, Asya   148

Ziółkowski, Artur   85

Printed in the United States
by Baker & Taylor Publisher Services